ᵀᴴᴱ DIALECTIC OF SEX

W9-BCK-809

THE DIALECTIC OF SEX

The Case for Feminist Revolution

Shulamith Firestone

QUILL

WILLIAM MORROW

NEW YORK

It is the policy of William Morrow and Company, Inc., and its imprints and affiliates, recognizing the importance of preserving what has been written, to print the books we publish on acid-free paper, and we exert our best efforts to that end.

Library of Congress Cataloging-in-Publication Data

Firestone, Shulamith.
    The dialectic of sex : the case for feminist revolution / by Shulamith Firestone.
        p.   cm.
    ISBN 0-688-12359-7
    1. Feminist theory.   2. Feminism—United States.   I. Title.
HQ1190.F57   1993
305.42'01—dc20   92-24384
                                                      CIP

Printed in the United States of America

1   2   3   4   5   6   7   8   9   10

for
Simone de Beauvoir
who endured

Contents

When we consider and reflect upon Nature at large or the history of mankind or our own intellectual activity at first we see the picture of an endless entanglement of relations and reactions, permutations and combinations, in which nothing remains what, where, and as it was, but everything moves, changes, comes into being and passes away. We see therefore at first the picture as a whole with its individual parts still more or less kept in the background; we observe the movements, transitions, connections, rather than the things that move, combine, and are connected. This primitive, naive, but intrinsically correct conception of the world is that of ancient Greek philosophy, and was first clearly formulated by Heraclitus: everything is and is not, for everything is fluid, is constantly changing, constantly coming into being and passing away.

FRIEDRICH ENGELS

Key to Abbreviations

AFL	American Federation of Labour
DAR	Daughters of the American Revolution
NAACP	National Association for the Advancement of Coloured People
NAWSA	National American Woman Suffrage Association
NOW	National Organization of Women
SDS	Students for a Democratic Society
VISTA	Volunteers in Service to America
WRM	Woman's Rights Movement

1   The Dialectic of Sex

Sex class is so deep as to be invisible. Or it may appear as a superficial inequality, one that can be solved by merely a few reforms, or perhaps by the full integration of women into the labour force. But the reaction of the common man, woman, and child – '*That? *Why you can't change *that!* You must be out of your mind!' – is the closest to the truth. We are talking about something every bit as deep as that. This gut reaction – the assumption that, even when they don't know it, feminists are talking about changing a fundamental biological condition – is an honest one. That so profound a change cannot be easily fitted into traditional categories of thought, e.g., 'political', is not because these categories do not apply but because they are not big enough: radical feminism bursts through them. If there were another word more all-embracing than *revolution* we would use it.

Until a certain level of evolution had been reached and technology had achieved its present sophistication, to question fundamental biological conditions was insanity. Why should a woman give up her precious seat in the cattle car for a bloody struggle she could not hope to win? But, for the first time in some countries, the preconditions for feminist revolution exist – indeed, the situation is beginning to *demand* such a revolution.

The first women are fleeing the massacre, and, shaking and tottering, are beginning to find each other. Their first move is a careful joint observation, to resensitize a fractured consciousness. This is painful: no matter how many levels of consciousness one reaches, the problem always goes deeper. It is everywhere. The division yin and yang pervades all culture, history, economics, nature itself; modern Western versions of sex discrimination are only the most recent layer. To so heighten one's sensitivity to sexism presents problems far worse than the black militant's new awareness of racism: feminists have to question, not just all of *Western* culture, but the organization of culture itself, and further, even the very organization of nature. Many women give up in despair: if *that's* how deep it goes they don't want to know. Others continue strengthening and enlarging the movement, their painful sensitivity to female oppression existing for a purpose: eventually to eliminate it.

Before we can act to change a situation, however, we must know how it has arisen and evolved, and through what institutions it now operates. Engels's '[We must] examine the historic succession of events from which the antagonism has sprung in order to discover in the conditions thus created the means of ending the conflict.' For feminist revolution we shall need an analysis of the dynamics of sex war as comprehensive as the Marx–Engels analysis of class antagonism was for the economic revolution. More comprehensive. For we are dealing with a larger problem, with an oppression that goes back beyond recorded history to the animal kingdom itself.

In creating such an analysis we can learn a lot from Marx and Engels: not their literal opinions about women – about the condition of women as an oppressed class they know next to nothing, recognizing it only where it overlaps with economics – but rather their analytic *method*.

Marx and Engels outdid their socialist forerunners in that they developed a method of analysis which was both *dialectical* and *materialist*. The first in centuries to view history dialectically, they saw the world as process, a natural flux of action and reaction, of opposites yet inseparable and interpenetrating. Because they were able to perceive history as movie rather than as snapshot, they attempted to avoid falling into the stagnant 'metaphysical' view that had trapped so many other great minds. (This sort of analysis itself may be a product of the sex division, as discussed in Chapter 9.) They combined this view of the dynamic interplay of historical forces with a materialist one, that is, they attempted for the first time to put historical and cultural change on a real basis, to trace the development of economic classes to organic causes. By understanding thoroughly the mechanics of history, they hoped to show men how to master it.

Socialist thinkers prior to Marx and Engels, such as Fourier, Owen, and Bebel, had been able to do no more than moralize about existing social inequalities, positing an ideal world where class privilege and exploitation should not exist – in the same way that early feminist thinkers posited a world where male privilege and exploitation ought not exist – by mere virtue of good will. In both cases, because the early thinkers did not really understand how the social injustice had evolved, maintained itself, or could be eliminated, their ideas existed in a cultural vacuum, utopian. Marx and Engels, on the other hand, attempted a scientific approach to history. They traced the class conflict to its real economic origins, projecting an economic solution based on objective economic preconditions already present: the seizure by the proletariat of the means of production would lead to a communism in which government had withered away, no longer needed to repress the lower class for the sake of the higher. In the classless society the interests of every individual would be synonymous with those of the larger society.

But the doctrine of historical materialism, much as it was a brilliant advance over previous historical analysis, was not the complete answer, as later events bore out. For though Marx and Engels grounded their theory in reality, it was only a *partial* reality. Here is Engels's strictly economic definition of historical materialism from *Socialism: Utopian or Scientific*:

Historical materialism is that view of the course of history which seeks the *ultimate* cause and the great moving power of all historical events in the economic development of society, in the changes of the modes of production and exchange, in the consequent division of society into distinct classes, and in the struggles of these classes against one another. (Italics mine)

Further, he claims:

. . . that all past history with the exception of the primitive stages was the history of class struggles; that these warring classes of society are always the products of the modes of production and exchange – in a word, of the economic conditions of their time; that the *economic* structure of society always furnishes the real basis, starting from which we can alone work out the *ultimate* explanation of the whole superstructure of juridical and political institutions as well as of the religious, philosophical, and other ideas of a given historical period. (Italics mine)

It would be a mistake to attempt to explain the oppression of women according to this strictly economic interpretation. The class analysis is a beautiful piece of work, but limited: although correct in a linear sense, it does not go deep enough. There is a whole sexual substratum of the historical dialectic that Engels at times dimly perceives, but because he can see sexuality only through an economic filter, reducing everything to that, he is unable to evaluate in its own right.

Engels did observe that the original division of labour was between man and woman for the purposes of child-breeding; that within the family the husband was the owner, the wife the means of production, the children the labour; and that reproduction of the human species was an important economic system distinct from the means of production.[1]

1. His correlation of the interdevelopment of these two systems in *Origin of the Family, Private Property and the State* on a time scale might read as follows:

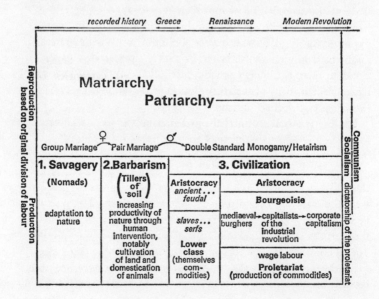

14

But Engels has been given too much credit for these scattered recognitions of the oppression of women as a class. In fact he acknowledged the sexual class system only where it overlapped and illuminated his economic construct. Engels didn't do so well even in this respect. But Marx was worse: there is a growing recognition of Marx's bias against women (a cultural bias shared by Freud as well as all men of culture), dangerous if one attempts to squeeze feminism into an orthodox Marxist framework – freezing what were only incidental insights of Marx and Engels about sex class into dogma. Instead, we must enlarge historical materialism to *include* the strictly Marxian, in the same way that the physics of relativity did not invalidate Newtonian physics so much as it drew a circle around it, limiting its application – but only through comparison – to a smaller sphere. For an economic diagnosis traced to ownership of the means of production, even of the means of *re*production, does not explain everything. There is a level of reality that does not stem directly from economics.

The assumption that, beneath economics, reality is psychosexual is often rejected as ahistorical by those who accept a dialectical materialist view of history because it seems to land us back where Marx began: groping through a fog of utopian hypotheses, philosophical systems that might be right, that might be wrong (there is no way to tell), systems that explain concrete historical developments by *a priori* categories of thought; historical materialism, however, attempted to explain 'knowing' by 'being' and not vice versa.

But there is still an untried third alternative: we can attempt to develop a materialist view of history based on sex itself.

The early feminist theorists were to a materialist view of sex what Fourier, Bebel, and Owen were to a materialist view of class. By and large, feminist theory has been as inadequate as were the early feminist attempts to correct sexism. This was to be expected. The problem is so immense that, at first try, only the surface could be skimmed, the most blatant inequalities described. Simone de Beauvoir was the only one who came close to – who perhaps has done – the definitive analysis. Her profound work *The Second Sex* – which appeared as recently as the early fifties to a world convinced that feminism was dead – for the first time attempted to ground feminism in its historical base. Of all feminist theorists De Beauvoir is the most comprehensive and far-reaching, relating feminism to the best ideas in our culture.

It may be this virtue is also her one failing: she is almost too sophisticated, too knowledgeable. Where this becomes a weakness – and this is still certainly debatable – is in her rigidly existentialist interpretation of feminism (one wonders how much Sartre had to do with this). This, in view of the fact that all cultural systems, including existentialism, are themselves determined by the sex dualism. She says:

Man never thinks of himself without thinking of the Other; he views the world under the sign of duality *which is not in the first place sexual in character*. But being different from man, who sets himself up as the Same, it is naturally to the category of the Other that woman is consigned; the Other includes woman. (Italics mine.)

Perhaps she has overshot her mark: Why postulate a fundamental Hegelian concept of Otherness as the final explanation – and then carefully document the biological and historical circumstances that have pushed the class 'women' into such a category – when one has never seriously considered the much simpler and more likely possibility that this fundamental dualism sprang from the sexual division itself? To posit *a priori* categories of thought and existence – 'Otherness', 'Transcendence', 'Immanence' – into which history then falls may not be necessary. Marx and Engels had discovered that these philosophical categories themselves grew out of history.

Before assuming such categories, let us first try to develop an analysis in which biology itself – procreation – is at the origin of the dualism. The immediate assumption of the layman that the unequal division of the sexes is 'natural' may be well-founded. We need not immediately look beyond this. Unlike economic class, sex class sprang directly from a biological reality: men and women were created different, and not equal. Although, as De Beauvoir points out, this difference of itself did not necessitate the development of a class system – the domination of one group by another – the reproductive *functions* of these

16

differences did. The biological family is an inherently unequal power distribution. The need for power leading to the development of classes arises from the psychosexual formation of each individual according to this basic imbalance, rather than, as Freud, Norman O. Brown, and others have, once again overshooting their mark, postulated, some irreducible conflict of Life against Death, Eros vs. Thanatos.

The *biological family* – the basic reproductive unit of male/female/infant, in whatever form of social organization – is characterized by these fundamental – if not immutable – facts:

(1) That women throughout history before the advent of birth control were at the continual mercy of their biology – menstruation, menopause, and 'female ills', constant painful childbirth, wetnursing and care of infants, all of which made them dependent on males (whether brother, father, husband, lover, or clan, government, community-at-large) for physical survival.

(2) That human infants take an even longer time to grow up than animals, and thus are helpless and, for some short period at least, dependent on adults for physical survival.

(3) That a basic mother/child interdependency has existed in some form in every society, past or present, and thus has shaped the psychology of every mature female and every infant.

(4) That the natural reproductive difference between the sexes led directly to the first division of labour at the origins of class, as well as furnishing the paradigm of caste (discrimination based on biological characteristics).

These biological contingencies of the human family cannot be covered over with anthropological sophistries. Anyone observing animals mating, reproducing, and caring for their young will have a hard time accepting the 'cultural relativity' line. For no matter how many tribes in Oceania you can find where the connection of the father to fertility is not known, no matter how many matrilineages, no matter how many cases of sex-role reversal, male housewifery, or even empathic labour pains, these facts prove only one thing: the amazing *flexibility* of human nature. But human nature is adaptable *to* something, it is, yes, determined by its environmental conditions. And the biological family that we have described has existed everywhere

17

throughout time. Even in matriarchies where woman's fertility is worshipped, and the father's role is unknown or unimportant, if perhaps not on the genetic father, there is still some dependence of the female and the infant on the male. And though it is true that the nuclear family is only a recent development, one which, as I shall attempt to show, only intensifies the psychological penalties of the biological family, though it is true that throughout history there have been many variations on this biological family, the contingencies I have described existed in all of them, causing specific psychosexual distortions in the human personality.

But to grant that the sexual imbalance of power is biologically based is not to lose our case. We are no longer just animals. And the kingdom of nature does not reign absolute. As Simone de Beauvoir herself admits:

The theory of historical materialism has brought to light some important truths. Humanity is not an animal species, it is a historical reality. Human society is an antiphysis – in a sense it is against nature; it does not passively submit to the presence of nature but rather takes over the control of nature on its own behalf. This arrogation is not an inward, subjective operation; it is accomplished objectively in practical action.

Thus the 'natural' is not necessarily a 'human' value. Humanity has begun to transcend Nature: we can no longer justify the maintenance of a discriminatory sex class system on grounds of its origins in nature. Indeed, for pragmatic reasons alone it is beginning to look as if we *must* get rid of it (see Chapter 10).

The problem becomes political, demanding more than a comprehensive historical analysis, when one realizes that, though man is increasingly capable of freeing himself from the biological conditions that created his tyranny over women and children, he has little reason to want to give this tyranny up. As Engels said, in the context of economic revolution:

It is the law of division of labour that lies at the basis of the division into classes. [Note that this division itself grew out of a fundamental biological division.] But this does not prevent the ruling class, once having the upper hand, from consolidating its power at the expense of the working class, from turning its social leadership into an intensified exploitation of the masses.

Though the sex class system may have originated in fundamental biological conditions, this does not guarantee once the biological basis of their oppression has been swept away that women and children will be freed. On the contrary, the new technology, especially fertility control, may be used against them to reinforce the entrenched system of exploitation.

So that just as to assure elimination of economic classes requires the revolt of the underclass (the proletariat) and, in a temporary dictatorship, their seizure of the means of *production*, so to assure the elimination of sexual classes requires the revolt of the underclass (women) and the seizure of control of *reproduction*: not only the full restoration to women of ownership of their own bodies, but also their (temporary) seizure of control of human fertility – the new population biology as well as all the social institutions of child-bearing and child-rearing. And just as the end goal of socialist revolution was not only the elimination of the economic class *privilege* but of the economic class *distinction* itself, so the end goal of feminist revolution must be, unlike that of the first feminist movement, not just the elimination of male *privilege* but of the sex *distinction* itself: genital differences between human beings would no longer matter culturally. (A reversion to an unobstructed *pansexuality* – Freud's 'polymorphous perversity' – would probably supersede hetero/homo/bi-sexuality.) The reproduction of the species by one sex for the benefit of both would be replaced by (at least the option of) artificial reproduction: children would be born to both sexes equally, or independently of either, however one chooses to look at it; the dependence of the child on the mother (and vice versa) would give way to a greatly shortened dependence on a small group of others in general, and any remaining inferiority to adults in physical strength would be compensated for culturally. The division of labour would be ended by the elimination of labour altogether (through cybernetics). The tyranny of the biological family would be broken.

And with it the psychology of power. As Engels claimed for strictly socialist revolution: 'The existence of not simply this or that ruling class but of any ruling class at all [will have] become an obsolete anachronism.' That socialism has never come near achieving this predicated goal is not only the result of unfulfilled or misfired economic preconditions, but also because the Marxian analysis itself was insufficient: it did not dig deep enough to the psychosexual roots of class. Marx was on to something more profound than he knew when he observed that the family contained within itself in embryo all the antagonisms that later develop on a wide scale within the society and the state. For unless revolution uproots the basic social organization, the biological family – the vinculum through which the psychology of power can always be smuggled – the tapeworm of exploitation will never be annihilated. We shall need a sexual revolution much larger than – inclusive of – a socialist one to truly eradicate all class systems.

*

I have attempted to take the class analysis one step further to its roots in the biological division of the sexes. We have not thrown out the insights of the socialists; on the contrary, radical feminism can enlarge their analysis, granting it an even deeper basis in objective conditions and thereby explaining many of its insolubles. As a first step in this direction, and as the groundwork for our own analysis we shall expand Engels's definition of historical materialism. Here is the same definition quoted above now rephrased to include the biological division of the sexes for the purpose of reproduction, which lies at the origins of class:

Historical materialism is that view of the course of history which seeks the ultimate cause and the great moving power of all historic events in the dialectic of sex: the division of society into two distinct biological classes for procreative reproduction, and the struggles of these classes with one another; in the changes in the modes of marriage, reproduction and child care created by these struggles; in the connected development of other physically-differentiated classes [castes]; and in the first division of labour based on sex which developed into the [economic-cultural] class system.

And here is the cultural superstructure, as well as the economic one, traced not just back to economic class, but all the way back to sex:

All past history [note that we can now eliminate 'with the exception of primitive stages'] was the history of class struggle. These warring classes of society are always the product of the modes of organization of the biological family unit for reproduction of the species, as well as of the strictly economic modes of production and exchange of goods and services. The sexual-reproductive organization of society always furnishes the real basis, starting from which we can alone work out the ultimate explanation of the whole superstructure of economic, juridical and political institutions as well as of the religious, philosophical and other ideas of a given historical period.

And now Engels's projection of the results of a materialist approach to history is more realistic:

The whole sphere of the conditions of life which environ man and have hitherto ruled him now comes under the dominion and control of man who for the first time becomes the real conscious Lord of Nature, master of his own social organization.

*

In the following chapters we shall assume this definition of historical materialism, examining the cultural institutions that maintain and reinforce the biological family (especially its present manifestation, the nuclear family) and its result, the psychology of power, an aggressive chauvinism now developed enough to destroy us. We shall integrate this with a feminist analysis of Freudianism: for Freud's cultural bias, like that of Marx and Engels, does not invalidate his perception entirely. In fact, Freud had insights of even greater value than those of the socialist theorists for the building of a new dialectical materialism based on sex. We shall attempt, then, to correlate the best of Engels and Marx (the historical materialist approach) with the best of Freud (the understanding of the inner man and woman and what shapes them) to arrive at a solution both political and personal yet grounded in real conditions. We shall see that Freud observed the dynamics of psychology correctly in its immediate social context, but because the fundamental structure of that social context was basic to all humanity – to different degrees – it appeared to be nothing less than an absolute existential condition which it would be insane to question – forcing Freud and many of his followers to postulate *a priori* constructs like the Death Wish to explain the origins of these universal psychological drives. This in turn made the sicknesses of humanity irreducible and incurable – which is why his proposed solution (psychoanalytic therapy), a contradiction in terms, was so weak compared to the rest of his work, and such a resounding failure in practice – causing those of social/political sensibility to reject not only his therapeutic solution, but his most profound discoveries as well.

2 On American Feminism

In the radical feminist view, the new feminism is not just the revival of a serious political movement for social equality. It is the second wave of the most important revolution in history. Its aim: overthrow of the oldest, most rigid class/caste system in existence, the class system based on sex – a system consolidated over thousands of years, lending the archetypal male and female roles an undeserved legitimacy and seeming permanence. In this perspective, the pioneer Western feminist movement was only the first onslaught, the fifty-year ridicule that followed it only a first counter-offensive – the dawn of a long struggle to break free from the oppressive power structures set up by nature and reinforced by man. In this light, let's take a look at American feminism.

I
THE WOMAN'S RIGHTS MOVEMENT IN AMERICA

Though there have always been women rebels in history,[1] the conditions have never before existed that would enable women effectively to overthrow their oppressive roles. Women's capacity for reproduction was urgently needed by the society – and even if it hadn't been, effective birth control methods were not available. So until the Industrial Revolution feminist rebellion was bound to remain only a personal one.

The coming feminist revolution of the age of technology was foreshadowed by the thought and writing of individual women, members of the intellectual élites of their day: in England Mary

1. For example, witches must be seen as women in independent political revolt: within two centuries eight million women were burned at the stake by the Church – for religion was the politics of that period.

Wollstonecraft and Mary Shelley, in America Margaret Fuller, in France the Bluestockings. But these women were ahead of their time. They had a hard time getting their ideas accepted even in their own advanced circles, let alone by the masses of men and women of their day, who had barely absorbed the first shock of the Industrial Revolution.

By the middle of the nineteenth century, however, with industrialization in full swing, a full-fledged feminist movement got underway. Always strong in the US – itself founded shortly before the Industrial Revolution, and thus having comparatively little history or tradition – feminism was spurred on by the Abolitionist struggle and the smouldering ideals of the American Revolution itself. (The Declaration passed at the first national Woman's Rights convention at Seneca Falls in 1848 was modelled on the Declaration of Independence.)

The early American Woman's Rights Movement[2] was radical. In the nineteenth century, for women to attack the Family, the Church (see Elizabeth Cady Stanton's *Woman's Bible*), and the State (law) was for them to attack the very cornerstones of the Victorian society in which they lived – equivalent to attacking sex distinctions themselves in our own time. The theoretical foundations of the early WRM grew out of the most radical ideas of the day, notably those of abolitionists like William Lloyd Garrison and such communalists as R. D. Owen and Fanny Wright. Few people today are aware that the early feminism was a true grass-roots movement: they haven't heard of the tortuous journeys made by feminist pioneers into backwoods and frontiers, or door to door in the towns to speak about the issues or to collect signatures for petitions that were laughed right out of the Assemblies. Nor do they know that Elizabeth Cady Stanton and Susan B. Anthony, the most militant feminists of the movement, were among the first to stress the importance of organizing women workers, founding the Working Woman's Association in September, 1868. (Delegates to the National Labor Union Convention as early as 1868, they later fell out over the short-changing of women workers by the

2. Hereafter abbreviated WRM.

24

– hasn't changed – male chauvinist labour movement.) Other pioneer female labour organizers such as Augusta Lewis and Kate Mullaney were in the feminist movement.

This radical movement was built by women who had literally no civil status under the law; who were pronounced civilly dead upon marriage, or who remained legal minors if they did not marry; who could not sign a will or even have custody of their own children upon divorce; who were not taught even to read, let alone admitted to college (the most privileged of them were equipped with a knowledge of embroidery, china painting, French, and harpsichord); who had no political voice whatever. Thus, even after the Civil War, more than half the USA's population was still legally enslaved, literally not owning even the bustles on their backs.

The first stirrings of this oppressed class, the first simple demands for justice, were met by a disproprotionate violence, a resistance difficult to understand today when the lines of sexual class have been blurred over. For, as often happens, the revolutionary potential of the first awakening was recognized more clearly by those in power than it was by the crusaders themselves. From its very beginning the feminist movement posed a serious threat to the established order, its very existence and long duration testifying to fundamental inequalities in a system that pretended to democracy. Working first together, later separately, the Abolitionist Movement and the WRM threatened to tear the country apart. If, in the Civil War, the feminists hadn't been persuaded to abandon their cause to work on 'more important' issues, the early history of feminist revolution might have been less dismal.

As it was, although the Stanton–Anthony forces struggled on in the radical feminist tradition for twenty years longer, the back of the movement had been broken. Thousands of women, at the impetus of the Civil War, had been allowed out of the home to do charity work. The only issue on which these very different camps of organized women could unite was the desirability of the vote – but predictably, they did not agree upon *why* it was desirable. The conservatives formed the American Woman Suffrage Association, or joined the sprouting women's clubs, such as the pious Woman's Christian Temperance Union. The radicals separated into the National Woman's Suffrage Association, concerned with the vote only as a symbol of the political power they needed to achieve larger ends.

By 1890, further legal reforms had been won, women had entered the labour force in the service capacity that they still hold today, and they had begun to be educated in larger numbers. In lieu of true political power they had been granted a token, segregated place in the public sphere as clubwomen. But though indeed this was a greater political power than before, it was only a newfangled version of female 'power' of the usual sort: behind the throne – a traditional *influence on power* which took modern form in lobbying and embarrassment tactics. When, in 1890, with their leaders old and discouraged, the radical feminist National merged with the conservative American to form the National American Woman Suffrage Association (NAWSA), all seemed lost. Conservative feminism, with its concentration on broad, unitive, single-issues like suffrage, with its attempt to work within and placate the white male power structure – trying to convince men who knew better, with their own fancy rhetoric yet – had won. Feminism, sold out, languished.

Even worse than the conservative feminists were the increasing number of women who, with their new-found bit of freedom, jumped enthusiastically into all the radicalisms of the day, the various social reform movements of the Progressive Era, even when at odds with feminist interests. (Consider the old debate about discriminatory 'protective' labour laws for women.) Margaret Rhondda, Britain's leading post-First World War feminist, put it this way:

One may divide the women in the woman's movement into two groups: the Feminists and the reformers who are not in the least Feminists; who do not care tuppence about equality for itself . . . Now almost every women's organization recognizes that reformers are far more common than Feminists, that the passion to decide to look after your fellowmen, to do good to them in your way, is far more common than the desire to put into everyone's hand the power to look after themselves.

26

These 'reformers', the women 'radicals' of their day, were at best influenced by feminism. They were neither true feminists nor true radicals because they did not yet see the woman's cause as a legitimate radical issue in itself. By seeing the WRM as only tangent to another, more important politics, they were in a sense viewing themselves as defective men: women's issues seemed to them 'special', 'sectarian', while issues that concerned men were 'human', 'universal'. Developing politically in movements dominated by men, they became preoccupied with reforming their position within those movements rather than getting out and creating their own. The Woman's Trade Union League is a good example: women politicos in this group failed at the most basic undertakings because they were unable to sever their ties with the strongly male chauvinist AFL, under Samuel Gompers, which sold them out time and again. Or, in another example, like so many VISTA volunteers bent on slumming it with an ungrateful poor, they rushed into the young settlement movement, many of them giving their lives without reward – only to become the rather grim, embittered, but devoted spinster social workers of the stereotype. Or the Woman's Peace Party founded to no avail by Jane Addams on the eve of American intervention in the First World War, which later split into, ironically, either jingoist groups working for the war effort, or radical pacifists as ineffective as they were extreme.

This frenzied feminine organizational activity of the Progressive Era is often confused with the WRM proper. But the image of the frustrated, bossy battle-axe derives less from the radical feminists than from the non-feminist politicos, committee women for the various important causes of their day. In addition to the now defunct movements we have mentioned – the Woman's Trade Union League, the National Federation of Settlements, and the Woman's International League for Peace and Freedom (formerly the Woman's Peace Party, begun by Jane Addams) – the whole spectrum of Organized Ladyhood was founded in the era between 1890 and 1920: The General Federation of Women's Clubs, the League of Women Voters, the American Association of Collegiate Alumnae, the National

Consumer's League, the PTA, even the DAR. Although these organizations were associated with the most radical movements of their day, that in fact their politics were reactionary, and finally fatuous and silly, was indicated at first solely by their non-feminist views.

Thus the majority of organized women in the period between 1890–1920 – a period usually cited as a high point of feminist activity – had nothing to do with feminism. On the one hand, feminism had been constricted to the single issue of the vote – the WRM was (temporarily) transformed into a suffrage movement – and on the other, women's energies were diffused into any other radical cause but their own.

But radical feminism was only dormant: the awakening began with the return of Harriet Stanton Blatch, the daughter of Elizabeth Cady Stanton, from England, where she had joined the militant Woman's Social and Political Union – the English Suffragettes of whom the Pankhursts are perhaps the best known – in opposing the Constitutionalists (conservative feminists). Believing that militant tactics were needed to achieve the radical goals espoused by her mother, she recommended attacking the problem of the vote with the discarded strategy of the Stanton–Anthony faction: pressure to amend the *federal* Constitution. Soon the American militants split off from the conservative NAWSA to form the Congressional Union (later the Woman's Party), beginning the daring guerrilla tactics and uncompromisingly tough line for which the whole suffrage movement is often incorrectly credited.

It worked. Militants had to undergo embarrassment, mobbings, beatings, even hunger strikes with forced feeding, but within a decade the vote was won. The spark of radical feminism was just what the languishing suffrage movement needed to push through their single issue. It provided a new and sound approach (the pressure for a national amendment rather than the tedious state-by-state organizing method used for over thirty years), a militancy that dramatized the urgency of the woman issue, and above all, a wider perspective, one in which the vote was seen as only the first of many goals, and therefore to be won as quickly as possible. The mild demands of the conservative feminists, who had all but pleaded that if they won the vote they wouldn't use it, were welcomed as by far the lesser of two evils in comparison with the demands of the Woman's Party.

But with the granting of the vote the establishment co-opted the woman's movement. As one gentleman of that period, quoted by William O'Neill in *Everyone Was Brave*, summarized it, 'Nevertheless woman suffrage is a good thing if only to have it over with.' Mrs Oliver Hazard Perry Belmont of the Woman's Party urged women to boycott the elections: 'Husband your new power. Suffragists did not fight for your emancipation for seventy years to have you become servants to men's parties.' Charlotte Perkins Gilman seconded this:

The power women will be able to exercise lies with their not joining a party system of men. The party system of politics is a trick of men to conceal the real issues. Women should work for the measures they want outside of party politics. It is because the old political parties realize that woman's influence will be so negligible on the inside that they are so eager to get women to join them.

But none of this was to any avail. Even the formation of a new Woman's Party on 18 February 1921, as an alternative to the major parties that were so rapidly absorbing woman's new political strength, could not resuscitate the dying movement.[3]

The granting of the vote to the suffrage movement killed the WRM. Though the antifeminist forces appeared to give in, they did so in name only. They never lost. By the time the vote was granted, the long channelling of feminist energies into the limited goal of suffrage – seen initially as only one step to political power – had thoroughly depleted the WRM. The monster Ballot had swallowed everything else. Three generations had elapsed from the time of the inception of the WRM; the master-planners all were dead. The women who later joined the feminist movement to work for the single issue of the vote had

3. The Woman's Party struggled on through a depression and several wars, campaigning for the next big legal boost to women's freedom, an Equal Rights Amendment to the Constitution. Fifty years later those who are still alive are still campaigning. The stereotype of the crotchety old lady with her umbrella, obsessed with a cause already won, is the 'comic' product of the ossification of feminism created by the Fifty-Year Ridicule.

never had time to develop a broader consciousness: by then they had forgotten what the vote was for. The opposition had had its way.

*

Of all that struggle what is even remembered? The fight for suffrage alone – not worth much to women, as later events bore out – was an endless war against the most reactionary forces in America at the time, which, as Eleanor Flexner shows in *Century of Struggle*, included the biggest capitalist interests of the North, i.e. oil, manufacturing, railroad, and liquor interests; the racist bloc of southern states (which, in addition to their own bigotry about women, were afraid to grant the woman's vote because it would enfranchise another *half* of the Negro race, as well as draw attention to the hypocrisy of 'universal' male suffrage), and, finally, the machine of government itself. The work involved to achieve this vote was staggering. Carrie Chapman Catt estimated that:

> to get the word 'male' out of the constitution cost the women of this country 52 years of pauseless campaign ... During that time they were forced to conduct 56 campaigns of referenda to male voters, 480 campaigns to get legislatures to submit suffrage amendments to voters, 47 campaigns to get state constitutional conventions to write woman suffrage into state constitutions, 277 campaigns to get state party conventions to include woman suffrage planks, 30 campaigns to get presidential party conventions to adopt woman suffrage planks in party platforms and 19 successive campaigns with 19 successive Congresses.

Thus defeat was so frequent, and victory so rare – and then achieved by such bare margins – that even to read about the struggle for suffrage is exhausting, let alone to have lived through it and fought for it. The lapse of historians in this area is understandable, if not pardonable.

But, as we have seen, suffrage was only one small aspect of what the WRM was all about. A hundred years of brilliant personalities and important events have also been erased from American history. The women orators who fought off mobs, in the days when women were not allowed to speak in public, to attack Family, Church, and State, who travelled on poor railways to cow towns of the West to talk to small groups of socially starved women, were quite a bit more dramatic than the Scarlett O'Haras and Harriet Beecher Stowes and all the Little Women who have come down to us. Sojourner Truth and Harriet Tubman, freed slaves who went back time and again, with huge prices on their heads, to free other slaves on their own plantations, were more effective in their efforts than the ill-fated John Brown. But most people today have never even heard of Myrtilla Miner, Prudence Crandall, Abigail Scott Duniway, Mary Putnam Jacobi, Ernestine Rose, the Claflin sisters, Crystal Eastman, Clara Lemlich, Mrs O. H. P. Belmont, Doris Stevens, Anne Martin. And this ignorance is nothing compared to ignorance of the lives of women of the stature of Margaret Fuller, Fanny Wright, the Grimké sisters, Susan B. Anthony, Elizabeth Cady Stanton, Harriet Stanton Blatch, Charlotte Perkins Gilman, Alice Paul.

And yet we know about Louisa May Alcott, Clara Barton, and Florence Nightingale, just as we know about, rather than Nat Turner, the triumph of Ralph Bunche, or George Washington Carver and the peanut. The omission of vital characters from standard versions of American history in favour of such goody-good models cannot be tossed off. Just as it would be dangerous to inspire still-oppressed black children with admiration for the Nat Turners of their history, so it is with the WRM: the suspicious blanks in our history books concerning feminism – or else the confusion of the whole WRM with the (conservative) suffrage movement or the reformist women's groups of the Progressive Era – is no accident.

It is part of a backlash we are still undergoing in reaction to the first feminist struggle. The few strong models allowed girls growing up in the fifty-year silence have been carefully chosen ones, women like Eleanor Roosevelt, of the altruistic feminine tradition, as opposed to the healthily selfish giants of the radical feminist rebellion. This cultural backlash was to be expected. Men of those days grasped immediately the true nature of a feminist movement, recognizing it as a serious threat to their open and unashamed power over woman. They may have been forced to buy off the women's movement with confusing surface reforms – a correction of the most blatant inequalities on the books, a few changes of dress, sex, style ('you've come a long way, baby'), all of which coincidentally benefited men. But the power stayed in their hands.

II
THE FIFTY-YEAR RIDICULE

How did the Myth of Emancipation operate culturally over a fifty-year period to anaesthetize women's political consciousness?

In the twenties eroticism came in big. The gradual blurring together of romance with the institution of marriage began ('Love and marriage, Love and marriage, go together like a horse and carriage . . .'), serving to repopularize and reinforce the failing institution, weakened by the late feminist attack. But the convalescence didn't last long: women were soon reprivatized, their new class solidarity diffused. The conservative feminists, who at least had viewed their problems as social, had been co-opted, while the radical feminists were openly and effectively ridiculed; eventually even the innocuous committee women of other movements came to appear ridiculous. The cultural campaign had begun: emancipation was one's private responsibility; salvation was personal, not political. Women took off on a long soul-search for 'fulfilment'.

Here, in the twenties, is the beginning of that obsessive modern cultivation of 'style', the search for glamour (You too can be Theda Bara), a cultural disease still dissipating women today – fanned by women's magazines of the *Vogue*, *Glamour*, *Mademoiselle*, *Cosmopolitan* variety. The search for a 'different', personal, style with which to 'express' oneself replaced the old feminist emphasis on character development through responsibility and learning experience.

In the thirties, after the Depression, women sobered. Flapperism was obviously not the answer: they felt more hung up and neurotic than ever before. But with the myth of emancipation going full blast, women dared not complain. If they had gotten what they wanted, and were *still* dissatisfied, then something must be wrong with them. Secretly they suspected that maybe they really *were* inferior after all. Or maybe it was just the social order: they joined the Communist party, where once again they empathized mightily with the underdog, unable to acknowledge that the strong identification they felt with the exploited working class came directly from their own experience of oppression.

In the forties there was another world war to think about. Personal hangups were temporarily overshadowed by the spirit of the war effort – patriotism and self-righteousness, intensified by a ubiquitous military propaganda, were their own kind of high. Besides, the cats were away. Better yet, their thrones of power were vacant. Women had substantial jobs for the first time in several decades. Genuinely needed by society to their fullest capacity, they were temporarily granted human, as opposed to female, status. (In fact, feminists are forced to welcome wars as their only chance.)

The first long stretch of peace and affluence in some time occurred in the late forties and the fifties. But instead of the predictable resurgence of feminism, after so many blind alleys, there was only 'The Feminine Mystique', which Betty Friedan has documented so well. This sophisticated cultural apparatus was hauled out for a specific purpose: women had gotten hired during the war, and now had to be made to quit. Their new employment gains had come only because they had been found to make a convenient surplus labour force, for use in just such time of crisis – and yet, one couldn't now just openly fire them. That would give the lie to the whole carefully cultivated myth of emancipation. A better idea was to have them quit of their own volition. The Feminine Mystique suited the purpose admirably. Women, still frantic, still searching (after all, a factory job is no man's idea of heaven either, even if it is preferable to woman's caged hell), took yet another false road.

This one was perhaps worse than any of the others. It offered neither the (shallow) sensuality of the twenties, the commitment to a (false) ideal of the thirties, nor the collective spirit (propaganda) of the forties. What it did offer women was respectability and upward mobility – along with Disillusioned Romance, plenty of diapers and PTA meetings (Margaret Mead's Mother Nurture), family arguments, endless and ineffective diets, TV

33

soap operas and commercials to kill the boredom, and, if the pain still persisted, psychotherapy. *Good Housekeeping* and *Parents' Magazine* spoke for every woman of the middle class, just as *True Confessions* did for the working class. The fifties was the bleakest decade of all, perhaps the bleakest in some centuries for women. According to the 1950 version of the Myth, women's emancipation had already been tried and found wanting (by women themselves, no doubt). The first attempt to break away from a stifling Creative Motherhood seemed to have failed utterly. All authentic knowledge of the old feminist movement by this time had been buried, and with it the knowledge that woman's present misery was the product of a still-virulent backlash.

For the youth of the fifties there was an even more sophisticated cultural apparatus: 'teenagerism', the latest guise of that persevering romanticism so bent on shoring up, by cultural fiat, a crumbling family structure (see Chapter 7, 'The Culture of Romance'). Young girls of all ages dreamed of escaping the dull homes of their mothers through Teenage Romance. The parked car, an established tradition since the era of the flappers, became an urgent necessity, perhaps the one prop that best characterized the passions of the fifties (see Edward Keinholz's 'environment' of 'The Parked Car'). The rituals of the high school dating game compared in formality with the finest of Deep South chivalric tradition, its twentieth-century 'belle' now a baton-twirling, Sweet Sixteen cheerleader. The highest goal that a girl could achieve was 'popularity', the old pleasing 'grace' in modern form.

But the boys couldn't take it. The cloying romanticism and sentimentality designed to keep women in their place had side effects on the men involved. If there was to be a ritual of girl-chasing, some males too would have to be sacrificed to it. Barbie needed a Ken. But dating was a drag ('Can I borrow the car tonight, Dad?'). Surely there must be an easier way to get sex. Frankie Avalon and Paul Anka crooned to teenage girls; the boys were tuned out.

In the sixties the boys split. They went to college and Down South. They travelled to Europe in droves. Some joined the

Peace Corps; others went underground. But wherever they went they brought their camp followers. Liberated men needed groovy chicks who could swing with their new life style: women tried. They needed sex: women complied. But that's all they needed from women. If the chick got it into her head to demand some old-fashioned return commitment, she was 'uptight', 'screwed up', or worse yet, a 'real bringdown'. A chick ought to learn to be independent enough not to become a drag on her old man (trans. 'clinging'). Women couldn't register fast enough: ceramics, weaving, leather talents, painting classes, lit. and psych. courses, group therapy, anything to get off his back. They sat in front of their various easels in tears.

Which is not to suggest that the 'chicks' themselves did not originally want to escape from Nowheresville. There was just no place they could go. Wherever they went, whether Greenwich Village c. 1960, Berkeley or Mississippi c. 1964, Haight-Ashbury or the East Village c. 1967, they were still only 'chicks', invisible as people. There was no marginal society to which they could escape: the sexual class system existed everywhere. Culturally immunized by the antifeminist backlash – if, in the long blackout, they had heard of feminism at all, it was only through its derogation – they were still afraid to organize around their own problem. Thus they fell into the same trap that had swallowed up the women of the twenties and thirties: the search for 'the private solution'.

The 'private solution' of the sixties, ironically, was as often the 'bag' of politics (radical politics, thus more marginal and idealistic than the official – segregated – arenas of power) as it was art or academia. Radical politics gave every woman the chance to do her thing. Many women, repeating the thirties, saw politics not as a means towards a better life, but as an end in itself. Many joined the peace movement, always an acceptable feminine pastime: harmless because politically impotent, it yet provided a vicarious outlet for female anger.

Others got involved in the civil rights movement: but though often no more directly effective than was their participation in the peace movement, white women's numbered days in the black movement of the early sixties proved to be a more valuable experience in terms of their own political development. This is easy to detect in the present-day women's liberation movement. The women who went South are often much more politically astute, flexible, and developed than women who came in from the peace movement, and they tend to move towards radical feminism much faster. Perhaps because this concern for the suffering of the blacks was white women's closest attempt since 1920 to face their own oppression: to champion the cause of a more conspicuous underdog is a euphemistic way of saying you yourself are the underdog. So just as the issue of slavery spurred on the radical feminism of the nineteenth century, the issue of racism now stimulated the new feminism: the analogy between racism and sexism had to be made eventually. Once people had admitted and confronted their own racism, they could not deny the parallel. And if racism was expungable, why not sexism?

*

I have described the fifty-year period between the end of the old feminist movement and the beginning of the new in order to examine the specific ways in which the Myth of Emancipation operated in each decade to defuse the frustrations of modern women. The smear tactic was effectively used to reprivatize women of the twenties and the thirties, and thereafter it combined with a blackout of feminist history to keep women hysterically circling through a maze of false solutions: the Myth had effectively denied them a legitimate outlet for their frustration. Therapy proved a failure as an outlet (see the following chapter). To return to the home was no solution either – as the generation of the forties and the fifties proved.

By 1970 the rebellious daughters of this wasted generation no longer, for all practical purposes, even knew there had been a feminist movement. There remained only the unpleasant residue of the aborted revolution, an amazing set of contradictions in their roles: on the one hand, they had most of the legal freedoms, the literal assurance that they were considered full political citizens of society – and yet they had no power. They had educational opportunities – and yet were unable, and not expected, to employ them. They had the freedoms of clothing and sex mores that they had demanded – and yet they were still sexually exploited. The frustrations of their trapped position were exacerbated by the development of mass media (see Chapter 7), in which these contradictions were nakedly exposed, the ugliness of women's roles emphasized by precisely that intensive character which made of the new media such a useful propaganda organ. The cultural indoctrinations necessary to reinforce sex role traditions had become blatant, tasteless, where before they had been insidious. Women, everywhere bombarded with hateful or erotic images of themselves, were at first bewildered by such distortion (could that be Me?), and, finally, angered. At first, because feminism was still taboo, their anger and frustration bottled up in complete withdrawal (Beatnik Bohemia and the Flower/Drug Generation) or was channelled into dissent movements other than their own, particularly the civil rights movement of the sixties, the closest women had yet come to recognizing their own oppression. But eventually the obvious analogy of their own situation to that of the blacks, coupled with the general spirit of dissent, led to the establishment of a women's liberation movement proper. The anger spilled over, finally, into its proper outlet.

But it would be false to attribute the resurgence of feminism only to the impetus generated by other movements and ideas. For though they may have acted as a catalyst, feminism, in truth, has a cyclical momentum all its own. In the historical interpretation we have espoused, feminism is the inevitable female response to the development of a technology capable of freeing women from the tyranny of their sexual-reproductive roles – both the fundamental biological condition itself, and the sexual class system built upon, and reinforcing, this biological condition.

The increasing development of science in the twentieth century should have only accelerated the initial feminist reaction to the Industrial Revolution. (Fertility control alone, for example, a problem for which the early feminists had no answer, has reached, in the period since 1920, its highest level of development in history.) The dynamics of the counter-revolution which – in conjunction with temporal crises such as war and depression – obstructed the growth of feminism I have attempted to describe. Because of such obstruction, new scientific developments that could have greatly helped the feminist cause stayed in the lab, while social-sexual practices not only continued as before but were actually intensified, in reaction to the threat. Scientific advances which threaten to further weaken or sever altogether the connection between sex and reproduction have scarcely been realized culturally. That the scientific revolution has had virtually no effect on feminism only illustrates the political nature of the problem: the goals of feminism can never be achieved through evolution, but only through revolution. Power, however it has evolved, whatever its origins, will not be given up without a struggle.

III

THE WOMEN'S LIBERATION[4] MOVEMENT

In three years, we have seen the whole political spectrum of the old women's movement recreated. The broad division between the radical feminists and the two types of reformists, the conservative feminists and the politicos, has reappeared in modern guise. There are roughly three major camps in the movement now, themselves sub-divided. Let us summarize them briefly, keeping in mind that in such a formative period the politics, as well as the membership, of any one group is in a continual state of flux.

(1) *Conservative feminists.* This camp, though now proliferating into myriads of similar organizations, is perhaps still best exemplified by its pioneer (and thus more hard-core feminist than is generally believed) NOW, the National Organization of Women, begun in 1965 by Betty Friedan after her reverberating publication of *The Feminine Mystique.* Often called the NAACP of the woman's movement (and indeed, because it too is full of older professionals – career women who have 'made it' – it is similarly attacked by the younger liberation groups for its 'careerism'), NOW concentrates on the more superficial

4. 'Liberation' as opposed to 'emancipation' to denote freedom from sexual classification altogether rather than merely an equalizing of sex roles. Nevertheless, I have always found the name heavy, too flavoured with New Left rhetoric, and ashamed to acknowledge any relation to feminism. I prefer to use 'radical feminism'.

38

symptoms of sexism – legal inequities, employment discrimination, and the like.

Thus in its politics it most resembles the suffragist movement of the turn of the century, Carrie Chapman Catt's National American Woman Suffrage Association, with its stress on equality with men – legal, economic, etc., within the given system – rather than liberation from sex roles altogether, or radical questioning of family values. Like the NAWSA, it tends to concentrate on the winning of single-issue political gains, whatever the cost to political principles. Like the NAWSA, it has attracted a wide membership, which it controls by traditional bureaucratic procedures.

However, already in the young movement, it is apparent that this position, untenable even in terms of immediate political gains – as witnessed by the failure of the last conservative feminist movement – is more a leftover of the old feminism (or, if you prefer, the forerunner) rather than a model of the new. The many women who had joined for lack of a better place to go soon shifted to radical feminism – and in doing so have forced NOW into an increasing radicalism, cf., where once the organization didn't dare officially endorse even abortion law repeal for fear of alienating those who could go no further than reform, now abortion law repeal is one of its central demands.

(2) *Politicos.* The politicos of the contemporary women's movement are those women whose primary loyalty is to the Left ('The Movement') rather than to the Women's Liberation Movement proper. Like the politicos of the Progressive Era, contemporary politicos see feminism as only tangent to 'real' radical politics, instead of central, directly radical in itself; they still see male issues, e.g., the draft, as universal, and female issues, e.g., abortion, as sectarian. Within the contemporary politico category is still a smaller spectrum, which can be roughly broken down as follows:

(a) *Ladies' auxiliaries of the Left.* Every major faction on the left, and even some unions, by now – after considerable resistance – have their women's lib caucuses, which agitate against male chauvinism within the organization, and for greater decision-making power for women. The politicos of these caucuses are reformist in that their main objective is to improve their own situation within the limited arena of leftist politics. Other women are, at best, their foremost 'constituency', strictly women's issues no more than a useful 'radicalizing ' tool to recruit women into the 'Larger Struggle'. Thus their attitude towards other women tends to be patronizing and evangelistic, the 'organizer' approach. Here are some (female) Black Panthers in an interview in *The Movement*, an underground paper, stating it in a way that is perhaps embarrassing to the white left in its blatancy, but that nevertheless is typical of (because lifted from?) most white revolutionary rhetoric on the subject:

It's very important that women *who are more advanced*, who already understand revolutionary principles, go to them and explain it to them and struggle with them. We have to recognize that women are backwards politically and that we must struggle with them. (Italics mine)

Or again, concerning an independent women's movement:

They lose sight of the *Primary Struggle*. Some special organizing of women's groups is possible, perhaps, but dangerous: in terms of turning in on themselves, in terms of becoming petit bourgeois little cliques where they just talk about *taking care of the kids* all the time, or become a *gripe session*. (Italics mine)

We have here a complete denial by blacks (and women, no less) of their own principles of Black Power as applied to another group: the right of the oppressed to organize around their oppression *as they see and define it*. It is sad that the Black Power movement, which taught women so much about their political needs through the obvious parallels, should be the last to see that parallel in reverse. (For a deeper analysis of why this is so, see Chapter 5.) Grass-roots organizing, around one's own oppression, the end of leadership and power plays, the need for a mass base prior to bloody struggle, all the most important principles of radical politics suddenly do not apply to women, in a double standard of the worst order.

The women's liberation groups still attempting to work within the larger leftist movement haven't a chance, for their line is dictated from above, their analysis and tactics shaped by the very class whose illegitimate power they are protesting. And thus they rarely succeed in doing more than increasing the tension that already threatens their frayed leftist groups with extinction. If ever they do become powerful they are bought off with tokens, or, if necessary, the larger group quietly disintegrates and re-organizes without them. Often, in the end, they are forced to split off and join the independent women's movement after all.

(b) *Middle-of-the-road politicos.* Working separately from, but still under the protection of the male umbrella, these groups are ambivalent and confused. They vacillate. Their obvious imitation of traditional (male) left analysis, rhetoric, tactics, and strategy, whether or not they are suited to the achievement of their own distinct goals, is compensated for by a lot of sentimentalizing about the Oppressed Sisters Out There. Their own politics tends to be ambiguous, because their loyalties are: if they are no longer so sure that it is capitalism which directly causes the exploitation of women, they do not go so far as to intimate that *men* might have anything to do with it. Men are Brothers. Women are Sisters. If one must talk about enemies at all, why not leave it open and call it The System?

(c) *The feminist politicos.* This position describes perhaps the largest proportion of the anonymous cell groups of the women's liberation movement across the country: it is the position towards which many of the Middle-of-the-Roaders eventually drift. Basically it is a conservative feminism with leftist overtones (or perhaps, more accurately, it is a leftism with feminist over-tones). While the feminist politicos admit that women must organize around their own oppression as they feel it, that they can best do this in independent groups, and that the primary concentration of any *women's* group should be on women's issues, every effort is still made to fit such activities into the existing leftist analysis and framework of priorities – in which, of course, Ladies never go first.

Despite the seeming diversity within such a spectrum, the three positions can be reduced to one common denominator: feminism is secondary in the order of political priorities, and must be tailored to fit into a pre-existent (male-created) political framework. The fear that if it isn't watched feminism will go off the deep end, to become divorced from The Revolution, gives away the politicos' fear that feminism is not a legitimate issue in itself, one that will (unfortunately) *require* a revolution to achieve its ends.

And here we have the crux of it: politico women are unable to evolve an authentic politics because they have never truly confronted their oppression *as women* in a gut way. Their inability to originate a feminist leftist analysis of their own, their need to tie their issue at all times to some 'primary struggle' rather than seeing it as revolutionary in itself, let alone central to all revolution, is derived directly from their lingering feelings of inferiority as women. Their inability to put their own needs first, their need for male approval – in this case anti-establishment male approval – to legitimate them politically, renders them incapable of breaking from other movements when necessary, and thus consigns them to mere left reformism, lack of originality, and, ultimately, political sterility.

However, the contrast of radical feminism, the more militant position in the women's liberation movement, has forced the politicos, as well as the conservative feminists, into a growing defensiveness, and, finally, into an increasing radicalism. At first Cuban and NLF women were the unquestioned models, their freedom idolized; now there is a let's-wait-and-see attitude. Last year purely feminist issues were never brought up without tacking on a tribute to the blacks, workers, or students. This year spokesmen on the left instead talk pompously and importantly of the abolition of the nuclear family. For the Left Brotherhood have been quick to jump in to see what they could co-opt – coming up with a statement against monogamy, at which clear sign of male-at-work, feminists could only laugh bitterly. But still, where SDS didn't care a damn about a silly woman's movement a few years ago, it now has taken to giving its women a more and more glamorous role to keep them from bolting, e.g., first place on the *Ten Most Wanted* list of Weathermen and assorted guerrillas. There are the beginnings of the official leftist acknowledgement of women as an important oppressed group in their own right; some shallow understanding of the need for an independent feminist movement; some degree of consideration of women's issues and complaints, e.g., abortion or day-care centres; and the growing tokenism. And, as with the early stages of Black Power, there is the same attempt to appease, the same nervous liberal laughter, the same insensitivity to how it feels to be a woman, disguised under a we're-trying-give-us-a-kiss grin.

(3) *Radical feminism.* The two positions we have described usually generate a third, the radical feminist position: the women in its ranks range from disillusioned moderate feminists from NOW to disillusioned leftists from the women's liberation movement, and include others who had been waiting for just such an alternative, women for whom neither conservative bureaucratic feminism nor warmed-over leftist dogma had much appeal.

The contemporary radical feminist position is the direct descendant of the radical feminist line in the old movement, notably that championed by Stanton and Anthony, and later by the militant Congressional Union subsequently known as the Woman's Party. It sees feminist issues not only as *women's* first priority, but as central to any larger revolutionary analysis. It refuses to accept the existing leftist analysis not because it is too radical, but because *it is not radical enough*: it sees the current leftist analysis as outdated and superficial, because this analysis does not relate the structure of the economic class system to its origins in the sexual class system, the model for all other exploitative systems, and thus the tapeworm that must be eliminated first by any true revolution. In the following chapters I shall explore the ideology of radical feminism and its relation to other radical theory, in order to illustrate how it alone succeeds in pulling into focus the many troubled areas of the leftist analysis, providing for the first time a comprehensive revolutionary solution.

Offhand we may note that the radical feminist movement has many political assets that no other movement can claim, a revolutionary potential far higher, as well as qualitatively different, from any in the past:

(1) *Distribution. Unlike minority groups (a historical accident), or the proletariat (an economic development), women have always made up an oppressed majority class (51 per cent), spread evenly*

43

throughout all other classes. The most analogous movement in America, Black Power, even could it instantly mobilize every black in the country, would command only 15 per cent of the population. Indeed, all the oppressed minorities *together*, generously assuming no factional infighting, would not make up a majority – unless you included women. That women live with men, while on some levels our worst disadvantage – the isolation of women from each other has been responsible for the absence or weakness of women's liberation movements in the past – is, in another sense, an advantage: a revolutionary in every bedroom cannot fail to shake up the status quo. And if it's your wife who is revolting, you can't just split to the suburbs. Feminism, when it truly achieves its goals, will crack through the most basic structures of our society.

(2) *Personal politics.* The feminist movement is the first to combine effectively the 'personal' with the 'political'. It is developing a new way of relating, a new political style, one that will eventually reconcile the personal – always the feminine prerogative – with the public, with the 'world outside', to restore that world to its emotions, and literally to its senses.

The dichotomy between emotions and intellect has kept the established movement from developing a mass base: on the one hand, there are the orthodox leftists, either abstract university intellectuals out of touch with concrete reality, or, in their activist guise, militantly into *machismo*, self-indulgent in their action with little concern for political effectiveness. On the other, there is Woodstock Nation, the Youth Revolt, the Flower and Drug Generation of Hippies, Yippies, Crazies, Motherfuckers, Mad Dogs, Hog Farmers, and the like, who, though they understand that the old leafletting and pamphletting and Marxist analysis are no longer where it's at – that the problem is much deeper than merely the struggle of the proletariat, which, in any case, is hardly the American vanguard – yet have no solid historical analysis of their own with which to replace it; indeed, who are apolitical. Thus the Movement is foundering, either marginal, splintered, and ineffective due to its rigid and out-dated analysis or, where it does have mass movement appeal, lacking a solid base in history and economics, 'drop out' rather than revolutionary. The feminist movement is the urgently needed solder.

(3) *The end of power psychology.* Most revolutionary movements are unable to practise among themselves what they preach. Strong leadership cults, factionalism, 'ego-tripping', backbiting are the rule rather than the exception. The woman's movement, in its short history, has a somewhat better record than most in this area. One of its major stated goals is internal democracy – and it goes to (often absurd) lengths to pursue this goal.

Which is not to claim that it is successful. There is much more rhetoric than reality on the subject, often disguising hypocritically the same old games and power plays – often with new and complex feminine variations. But it is too much to expect that, given its deep roots in sexual class and family structure, anyone born today would be successful at eliminating the power psychology. And though it is true that many females have never assumed the dominant (power over others) role, there are many others who, identifying all their lives with men, find themselves in the peculiar position of having to eradicate, at the same time, not only their submissive natures, but their dominant natures as well, thus burning their candle at both ends.

But if any revolutionary movement can succeed at establishing an egalitarian structure, radical feminism will. To question the basic relations between the sexes and between parents and children is to take the psychological pattern of dominance-submission to its very roots. Through examining politically this psychology, feminism will be the first movement ever to deal in a materialist way with the problem.

3   Freudianism: The Misguided Feminism

If we had to name the one cultural current that most characterizes America in the twentieth century, it might be the work of
Freud and the disciplines that grew out of it. There is no one
who remains unexposed to his vision of human life, whether
through courses in it ('psych'); through personal therapy, a
common cultural experience for children of the middle class;
or generally, through its pervasion of popular culture. The new
vocabulary has crept into our everyday speech, so that the
ordinary man thinks in terms of being 'sick', 'neurotic', or
'psycho'; he checks his 'id' periodically for a 'death wish',
and his 'ego' for 'weakness'; people who reject him are 'ego-
centric'; he takes for granted that he has a 'castration complex',
that he has 'repressed' a desire to sleep with his mother, that
he was and maybe still is engaged in 'sibling rivalry', that women
'envy' his penis; he is likely to see every banana or hotdog as a
'phallic symbol'. His marital arguments and divorce-court
proceedings are conducted in this psychoanalese. Most of the
time he is unclear about what these terms mean, but if he doesn't
know, at least he is certain that his 'shrink' does. The spectacled
and goateed little Viennese dozing in his armchair is a cliché of
(nervous) modern humour. It would take some time to tabulate
the number of cartoons that refer to psychoanalysis. We have
built a whole new symbology around the couch alone.

Freudianism has become, with its confessionals and penance,
its proselytes and converts, with the millions spent on its up-
keep, our modern Church. We attack it only uneasily, for you
never know, on the day of final judgement, whether they *might
be right*. Who can be sure that he is as healthy as he can get?
Who is functioning at his highest capacity? And who not scared

out of his wits? Who doesn't hate his mother and father? Who doesn't compete with his brother? What girl at some time did not wish she were a boy? And for those hardy souls who persist in their scepticism, there is always that dreadful word *resistance*. They are the ones who are sickest: it's obvious, they fight it so much.

There has been a backlash. Books have been written, careers have bloomed, on the contradictions within Freud's work alone: some have made a name for themselves simply on one small section of his work (e.g., by disproving the death wish, or penis envy), and others, braver, or more ambitious, have attacked the absurdities of the whole. Critical theories abound at every cocktail party: some intellectuals go so far as to relate the demise of the intellectual community in America to the importation of psychoanalysis. In opposition to the religiosity of Freudianism, a whole empirical school of behaviourism has been founded (though experimental psychology suffers from its own kind of bias). And gradually, with all this, Freudian thought has been unwound, its most essential tenets sloughed off one by one until there is nothing left to attack.

And yet it does not die. Though psychoanalytic therapy has been proven ineffective, and Freud's ideas about women's sexuality literally proven wrong (e.g., Masters and Johnson on the myth of the double orgasm), the old conceptions still circulate. The doctors go on practising. And at the end of each new critique we find a guilty paean to the Great Father who started it all. They can't quite do him in.

But I don't think it is solely a lack of courage to admit after all these years that the emperor had no clothes on. I don't think it is entirely because they might work themselves out of a job. I think that in most cases it is the same integrity that made them question it all that keeps them from destroying it all. 'Intuitively' their 'conscience' tells them they dare not drop that final axe.

For while it is true that Freud's theories are not verifiable empirically, that Freudianism in clinical practice has led to real absurdities, that in fact as early as 1913 it was noted that psychoanalysis itself is the disease it purports to cure, creating a new neurosis in place of the old (we have all observed that those undergoing therapy seem more preoccupied with themselves than ever before, having advanced to a state of 'perceptive' neurosis now, replete with 'regressions', lovesick 'transferences', and agonized soliloquies), still we sense there is something to it. Though those undergoing therapy are overcome with confusion when asked pointblank 'Does it help?' or 'Is it worth it?' it can't be dismissed entirely.

Freud captured the imagination of a whole continent and civilization for a good reason. Though on the surface inconsistent, illogical, or 'way out', his followers, with their cautious logic, their experiments and revisions have nothing comparable to say. *Freudianism is so charged, so impossible to repudiate because Freud grasped the crucial problem of modern life : sexuality.*

I

THE COMMON ROOTS OF FREUDIANISM AND FEMINISM

(1) *Freudianism and feminism grew from the same soil.* It is no accident that Freud began his work at the height of the early feminist movement. We underestimate today how important feminist ideas were at the time. The parlour conversations about the nature of men and women, the possibility of artificial reproduction (babies in glass bottles) recorded in D. H. Lawrence's *Lady Chatterley's Lover* were not imaginary. Sexism was the hottest topic of the day: Lawrence was merely picking up on it, adding his own views. Sexism also determined nearly the whole of G. B. Shaw's material. Ibsen's Nora in *The Doll's House* was no freak: such arguments were splitting up many real-life marriages. Henry James's nasty description of feminist women in *The Bostonians* and Virginia Woolf's more sympathetic ones in *The Years* and *Night and Day* were drawn from real life. The culture reflected prevailing attitudes and concerns: feminism was an important literary theme because it was then a vital problem. For writers wrote about what they saw: they described the cultural milieu around them. And in this milieu there was concern for the issues of feminism. The question of the eman-

cipation of women affected every woman, whether she developed through the new ideas or fought them desperately. Old films of the time show the growing solidarity of women, reflecting their unpredictable behaviour, their terrifying and often disastrous testing of sex roles. No one remained untouched by the up-heaval. And this was not only in the West: Russia at this time was experimenting at doing away with the family.

At the turn of the century, then, in social and political think-ing, in literary and artistic culture, there was a tremendous ferment of ideas regarding sexuality, marriage and family, and women's role. Freudianism was only one of the cultural products of this ferment. Both Freudianism and feminism came as reactions to one of the smuggest periods in Western civilization, the Victorian Era, characterized by its family-centredness, and thus its exaggerated sexual oppression and repression. Both movements signified awakening: but Freud was merely a diagnostician for what feminism purports to cure.

(2) *Freudianism and feminism are made of the same stuff.* Freud's achievement was the rediscovery of sexuality. Freud saw sexuality as the prime life force; the way in which this libido was organized in the child determined the psychology of the individual (which, moreover, re-created that of the historic species). He found that in order to adjust to present civilization the sexuate being must undergo a repression process in child-hood. While every individual undergoes this repression, some undergo it less successfully than others, producing greater (psychosis) or lesser (neurosis) maladjustment, often severe enough to cripple the individual altogether.

Freud's proposed remedy is less significant, and indeed has caused actual damage: by a process of bringing to the surface the crippling repressions, of conscious recognition and open examination, the patient is supposed to be able to come to terms with, to consciously reject, rather than subconsciously repress, the troubling wishes of the *id*. This therapy process is entered into with the help of a psychoanalyst through 'transference', in which the psychoanalyst substitutes for the original authority figure at the origins of the repressive neurosis. Like religious healing or hypnosis (which, indeed, Freud studied and was much

49

influenced by), 'transference' proceeds by emotional involvement rather than by reason. The patient 'falls in love' with his analyst; by 'projecting' the problem on to the supposedly blank page of the therapeutic relationship, he draws it out in order to be cured of it. Only it doesn't work.[1]

For Freud, in the tradition of 'pure' science, observed psychological structures without ever questioning their social context. Given his own psychic structure and cultural prejudices – he was a petty tyrant of the old school, for whom certain sexual truths may have been expensive – he can hardly have been expected to make such an examination part of his life work. (Wilhelm Reich was one of the few who followed that path.) In addition, just as Marx could not take fully into account the future advent of cybernetics. Freud then did not have the mindbending knowledge of technological possibility that we now have. But whether or not we can blame Freud personally, his failure to question society itself was responsible for massive confusion in the disciplines that grew up around this theory. Beset with the insurmountable problems that resulted from trying to put into practice a basic contradiction – the resolution of a problem within the environment that created it – his followers began to attack one component after another of his theory, until they had thrown the baby out with the bath.

But was there any value in these ideas? Let us re-examine some of them once again, this time from a radical feminist view. I believe Freud was talking about something real, though perhaps his ideas, taken literally, lead to absurdity – for his genius was poetic rather than scientific; his ideas are more valuable as metaphors than as literal truths.

1. R. P. Knight in 'Evaluation of the Results of Psychoanalytic Therapy', *American Journal of Psychiatry*, 1941, found that psychoanalysis was a failure with 56·7 per cent of the patients he studied, and a success with only 43·3 per cent. Thus psychoanalysis failed somewhat more often than it succeeded. In 1952 in a different study Eysenck showed an improvement rate in patients who had received psychoanalysis of 44 per cent; in patients who had received psychotherapy of 64 per cent; and in those who had received no treatment at all an improvement rate of 72 per cent. Other studies (Barron and Leary, 1955; Bergin, 1963; Cartwright and Vogel, 1960; Truax, 1963; Powers and Witmer, 1951) confirm these negative results.

In this light let us first examine the Oedipus Complex,[2] a cornerstone of Freudian theory, in which the male child is said to want to possess his mother sexually and to kill his father, fear of castration by the father forcing him to repress this wish. Freud himself said in his last book, 'I venture to assert that if psychoanalysis could boast of no other achievement than the discovery of the repressed Oedipus Complex, that alone would give it claim to be counted among the precious new acquisitions of mankind.' Contrast this with Andrew Salter in *The Case Against Psychoanalysis*:

Even those most sympathetic to Freud find the contradictions in the Oedipus Complex somewhat confusing. Says the Psychiatric Dictionary of the passing of the Oedipus Complex, 'The fate of the Oedipus Complex is not yet clearly understood.' I think we can talk with certainty about the fate of the Oedipus Complex. The fate of the Oedipus Complex will be the fate of alchemy, phrenology, and palmistry. The fate of the Oedipus Complex will be oblivion.

For Salter is plagued by all the usual contradictions in a theory that assumes the social context, the cause of the complex, to be immutable:

Freud's thought about the 'normal' disappearance of the Oedipus Complex suffers from a critical inconsistency in logic. If we grant that the disappearance of the Oedipus Complex is achieved *through castration fear*, does it not appear as if *normality is acquired as a result of fear and repression exerted on the boy*? And is not the achievement of mental health by repression in flagrant contradiction of the most elementary Freudian doctrines? (Italics mine)

I submit that the only way that the Oedipus Complex can make full sense is in terms of power. We must keep in mind that Freud observed this complex as common to every normal individual who grows up in the nuclear family of a patriarchal society, a form of social organization that intensifies the worst effects of

2. If I deal with the male child before the female that is because Freud – indeed our whole culture – deals with the male child first. Even in order properly to criticize Freud we shall have to follow the priorities he has set up in his own work. Also, as Freud himself saw, the Oedipus Complex had much greater cultural significance than the Electra; I too shall attempt to show that indeed it *is* more psychologically damaging, if only because in a male-dominated culture the damage done to the male psyche has vaster consequences.

the inequalities inherent in the biological family itself. There is some evidence to prove that the effects of the Oedipus Complex decrease in societies where males hold less power, and that the weakening of patriarchalism produces many cultural changes that perhaps can be traced to this relaxation.

Let us take a look at this patriarchal nuclear family in which the Oedipus Complex appears so markedly. In the prototypical family of this kind the man is the breadwinner; all other members of this family are thus his dependents. He agrees to support a wife in return for her services: housekeeping, sex, and reproduction. The children whom she bears for him are even more dependent. They are legally the property of the father (one of the first campaigns of the early WRM was against the deprivation of women, upon divorce, of their children), whose duty it is to feed them and educate them, to 'mould' them to take their place in whatever class of society to which he belongs. In return for this he expects that continuation of name and property which is often confused with immortality. His rights over them are complete. If he is not a kind father/master, tough luck. They cannot escape his clutches until they are grown, and by then the psychological moulding has been accomplished: they are now ready to repeat his performance.

It is important to remember that more recent versions of the nuclear family, though they may blur this essential relationship beyond recognition, reproduce essentially the same triangle of dependencies: father, mother, son. For even if the woman is equally educated, even when she is working (we need to be reminded that until the hard-won advances of the WRM of Freud's time women were not educated, nor could they find jobs), she is rarely able, given the inequality of the job market, to make as much money as her husband (and woe betide the marriage in which she does). But even if she could, later, when she bears children and takes care of infants, she is once again totally incapacitated. To make both women and children totally independent would be to eliminate not just the patriarchal nuclear family, but the biological family itself.

This then is the oppressive climate in which the normal child grows up. From the beginning he is sensitive to the hierarchy of power. He knows that in every way, physically, economically, emotionally, he is completely dependent on, thus at the mercy of, his two parents, whoever they may be. Between the two of them, though, he will certainly prefer his mother. He has a bond with her in oppression: while he is oppressed by both parents, she, at least, is oppressed by one. The father, so far as the child can see, is in total control. ('Just you wait till your father gets home from the office. Boy, will you get a spanking!') The child then senses that his mother is half-way between authority and helplessness. He can run to his father if his mother tries anything unjust; but if his father beats him there is little his mother can offer except tea and sympathy. If his mother is sensitive to injustice, she may use her wiles and tears to spare him. But he uses wiles and tears himself at that age, and he knows that tears don't compare to solid force. Their effectiveness, at any rate, is limited, dependent on many variables ('bad day at the office'). Whereas physical force or the threat of it is a sure bet.

In the traditional family there exists a parental polarity: the mother is expected to love the child devotedly, even unconditionally, whereas the father, on the other hand, seldom takes an active interest in infants – certainly not in their intimate care – and later, when the son is older, loves him conditionally, in response to performance and achievement. Erich Fromm in *The Art of Loving*:

We have already spoken about motherly love. Motherly love is by its very nature unconditional. Mother loves the newborn infant because it is her child, not because the child has fulfilled any specific condition, or lived up to any specific expectation ... The relationship to the father is quite different. Mother is the home we come from, she is nature, soil, the ocean; father does not represent any such natural home. He has little connection with the child in the first years of its life, and his importance for the child in this early period cannot be compared with that of the mother. But while father does not represent the natural world, he represents the other pole of human existence; the world of thought, of man-made things, of law and order, of discipline, of travel and adventure. Father is the one who teaches the child, who shows him the road into the world ... Fatherly love is conditional love. Its principle is 'I love you *because* you fulfil my expectations, because you do your duty, because you are like me' ... In this development from mother-centred to father-centred attachment, and their eventual synthesis, lies the basis for mental health and the achievement of maturity.

If this were not the case when he wrote it, it certainly would be by now: Fromm's book on love has been translated into seventeen languages, selling – as it says on the jacket – 1,500,000 copies in English alone. Later on I shall deal in greater detail with the nature of mother love that such a quote espouses, and the kind of damage such an ideal does to both mother and child. Here I'll try to show only in what way this traditional polarity relates to the Oedipus Complex.

Freud, unlike others, did not underestimate what goes on in a child before the age of six. If an infant's basic needs are taken care of by his mother, if he is fed, dressed, and coddled by her, if he is loved by her 'unconditionally' as opposed to 'conditionally' by his father – seldom seeing him and then only for punishment or 'manly approval' – and if moreover he senses that he and his mother are united against the more powerful father whom they both must please and appease, then it is true that every normal male first identifies with the female.

As for desiring his mother – yes, this too. But it is absurd what Freud's literalism can lead to. The child does not actively dream of penetrating his mother. Chances are he cannot yet even imagine how one would go about such an act. Nor is he physically developed enough to have a need for orgasmic release. It would be more correct to view this sexual need in a generalized, more negative fashion: that is, only later, due to the structuring of the family around the incest taboo, must the sexual separate from other kinds of physical and emotional responses. At first they are integrated.

What happens at the age of six when the boy is suddenly expected to start 'shaping up', acting like a little man? Words like 'male identification' and 'father image' are thrown around. Last year's cuddly toys are snatched away. He is led out to start playing baseball. Trucks and electric trains multiply. If he cries he is called a 'sissy'; if he runs to his mother, a 'mama's boy'. Father suddenly takes an active interest in him ('You spoiled him'). The boy fears his father, rightly. He knows that between the two of them, his mother is far more on his side. In most cases he has already observed very clearly that his father makes his mother unhappy, makes her cry, doesn't talk to her very much, argues with her a lot, bullies (this is why, if he has seen intercourse, he is likely to interpret it on the basis of what he has already gathered of the relationship: that is, that his father is attacking his mother). However, suddenly now he's expected to identify with this brutish stranger. Of course he doesn't want to. He resists. He starts dreaming of bogeymen. He becomes afraid of his shadow. He cries when he goes to the barber. He expects his father to cut off his penis: he's not behaving like the Little Man he had better learn to be.

This is his 'difficult transitional phase'. What finally convinces the normal child to reverse his identification? Fromm puts it so well:

But while father does not represent the natural world, he represents the other pole of human existence; the world of thought, of man-made things, of law and order, of discipline, of travel and adventure. Father is the one who teaches the child, who shows him *the road into the world* . . .

What finally convinces him is the offer of *the world* when he grows up. He is asked to make a transition from the state of the powerless, women and children, to the state of the potentially powerful, son (ego extension) of his father. Most children aren't fools. *They* don't plan to be stuck with the lousy limited lives of women. They want that travel and adventure. But it is hard. Because deep down they have a contempt for the father with all his power. They sympathize with their mother. But what can they do? They 'repress' their deep emotional attachment to their mother, 'repress' their desire to kill their father, and emerge into the honourable state of manhood.

It is no wonder that such a transition leaves an emotional residue, a 'complex'. The male child, in order to save his own hide, has had to abandon and betray his mother and join ranks with her oppressor. He feels guilty. His emotions towards women in general are affected. Most men have made an all-too-beautiful transition into power over others; some are still trying.

55

Other components of Freudian theory open up just as well when examined in power, i.e. political, terms; the antidote of feminism cancels the sex bias that produced the initial distortion.

It is generally believed that the Electra Complex is less profound a discovery than the Oedipus Complex, because, like all Freud's theories about women, it analyses the female only as negative male: the Electra Complex is an inverse Oedipus Complex. The Electra Complex, with its interwoven castration complex, is briefly as follows: the little girl, just like the little boy, begins with a fixation on the mother. Towards the age of five, when she discovers that she has no penis, she begins to feel castrated. To compensate, she tries to make an alliance with her father through seduction, thus developing a rivalry with, and a subsequent hostility to, her mother. The superego develops in response to repression by the father: but because he is the object of her seduction, he does not repress her as he does his son, who is his sexual rival for the affection of the mother, and thus the young girl's basic psychic organization differs from, is weaker than, that of her brother. A girl who persists in strongly identifying with her father is said to be retarded at the 'clitoral' stage of female sexuality, likely to be frigid or a lesbian.

The most remarkable feature of this description, restated in feminist terms, is that *the little girl, also, is first attached to her mother* (which, incidentally, disproved a biologically determined heterosexuality). Like the little boy, the little girl loves her mother more than her father, and for precisely the same reasons: the mother cares for her more closely than the father, and shares her oppression with her. At about the age of five, along with the boy, she consciously begins to observe the father's greater power, his access to that interesting wider world that is denied her mother. At this point she rejects her mother as dull and familiar, and begins to identify with her father. The situation is complicated further if she has brothers, for then she observes that the father is more than willing to allow her brother to share his world, his power, and yet that world is still denied *her*. She now has two alternatives: (1) Realistically sizing up the situation, she can start using female wiles for all they're worth in the attempt to rob the father of his power (she will then have to compete with her mother for the favours of the powerful) or (2) She can refuse to believe that the physical difference between her and her brother will forever imply a corresponding power inequity. In this case she rejects everything identified with her mother, i.e. servility and wiles, the psychology of the oppressed, and imitates doggedly everything she has seen her brother do that gains *for him* the kind of freedom and approval she is seeking. (Notice I do not say she *pretends* masculinity. These traits are not sexually determined.) But though she tries desperately to gain her father's favour by behaving more and more in the manner in which he has openly encouraged her brother to behave, it doesn't work *for her*. She tries harder. She becomes a tomboy – and is flattered to be called one. This obstinacy in the face of an unpalatable reality may even succeed. For a time. Until puberty perhaps. Then she is really stuck. She can no longer deny her sex: it is confirmed by lustful males all around her. This is when she often develops a female identification, with a vengeance. (Teenage girls, so 'difficult', 'secretive', 'giggly'; with boys it's the brat stage.)

As for the 'penis envy', again it is safer to view this as a metaphor. Even when an actual preoccupation with genitals does occur it is clear that anything that physically distinguishes the envied male will be envied. For the girl can't really understand how it is that when she does exactly the same thing as her brother, his behaviour is approved and hers isn't. She may or may not make a confused connection between his behaviour and the organ that differentiates him. Her hostility towards her mother is, again, only possibly tied up with an observed genital similarity: anything that identifies her with the mother she is trying so hard to reject is also rejected. But that a small girl on her own will see herself as of the same sex as her mother is much less likely than that she will see herself as asexual. She may even be proud of it. After all, she has no obvious protrusions, like the breasts that mark the female for her. And as for her genitals, her innocent slit appears to bear no resemblance to the hairy mound that her mother has: she is seldom even

57

aware that she *has* a vagina because it is sealed. Her body as yet is as limber and functional as her brother's, and she is at one with it: they are only equally oppressed by the greater strength of adults. Without specific direction, she could fool herself a long time that she will not end up like her mother. This is why she is so encouraged to play with dolls, to 'play house', to be pretty and attractive. It is hoped that she will not be one of those to fight off her role till the last minute. It is hoped she will slip into it early, by persuasion, artificially, rather than by necessity; that the abstract promise of a baby will be enough of a lure to substitute for that exciting world of 'travel and adventure'.[3]

In the light of this feminist interpretation, many peripheral Freudian doctrines that had seemed absurd now make sense. For example, Ernest Jones, in *Papers on Psychoanalysis*:

With very many children there is a lively desire to become the parents of their own parents . . . This curious construction of the imagination . . . is evidently closely connected with incestuous wishes, since it is an exaggerated form of the *commoner desire* to be one's own father.

Feminist translation: children fantasy being in a position of power over their parent masters, particularly the one who has really got the power: father.

Or, here is Freud on fetishism: 'The object is the substitute for the mother's phallus which the little boy believed in and does not wish to forego.' Really, Freud can be embarrassing. Wouldn't it be a lot more sensible to talk about the mother's power? Chances are the little boy has not even seen his mother undressed, let alone closely observed the difference between the penis and the clitoris. What he does not know is that he is attached to his mother and does not want to reject her on the grounds of her powerlessness. The chosen object is merely the symbol of this attachment.

3. A booming doll business capitalizes on this parental anxiety. As for the kid, she likes presents, whatever the obscure reasoning of adult minds. Though once they realize what the dolls are for, many sharp little girls hastily decide they want a different kind of toy, or at least a 'Barbie' doll; after all, they'd rather sharpen their weapons against 'Ken' than play already-conquered Mama.

Other such examples are abundant, but I have made my point: with a feminist analysis the whole structure of Freudianism – for the first time – makes thorough sense, clarifying such important related areas as homosexuality, even the nature of the repressive incest taboo itself – two causally related subjects which have been laboured for a long time with little unanimity. We can understand them, finally, only as symptoms of the power psychology created by the family.

Durkheim, at the turn of the century, with his foundation work on incest, like Freud, triggered off a train of contradictory opinion that has lasted till our present day. Durkheim thought that the incest taboo originated in the structure of the clan:

[Many facts tend to prove] that at the beginning of human societies, incest was not forbidden until division into at least two primary clans; for the first form of this prohibition that we know, namely exogamy, seems above all to be correlative to this organization. The latter is certainly not primitive.

And:

As the basic structure of the clan was a stage through which all human societies seem to have passed, and exogamy was strictly linked to the constitution of the clan, it is not surprising that the moral state the clan inspired and left behind it was itself general throughout humanity. At least it was necessary in order to triumph over it, to have particularly pressing social necessities; and this explains both how incest was legitimized among certain peoples and why these people remained the exception.

Once the family had become the centre of religious moralism, and all free passions had come to be tied up outside it, with women and sex, the taboo against incest became firmly established, self-perpetuating. For:

by the time the origins of this duality (between morality and passion) disappeared, it was firmly entrenched in the culture. The entire moral life had been organized as a result of this development: it would have been necessary to overthrow the whole morality to return to the previous status.

Durkheim adds, strikingly, 'Without the origins in exogamy, passion and love between the sexes would not have become synonymous.'

So that to eliminate the incest taboo we would have to eliminate the family, and sexuality as it is now structured.

Not such a bad idea. For this traditional and by now almost universal proscription on incest has caused us to accept as 'normal' a sexuality in which individual potential remains unfulfilled. Freud described the psychological penalties of sexual repression caused by the incest taboo, discovering particularly the existence of the Oedipus Complex in every normal male child, and its counterpart, the Electra, in every normal female.

Homosexuality is only what happens when these repressions don't 'take' as they ought to – that is, rather than being thoroughly suppressed, allowing the individual to at least function in society, they remain on the surface, seriously crippling that individual's sexual relationships, or even his total psyche. A system in which the first person to whom the child responds emotionally will require of him that he repress a substantial part of those responses is bound to misfire most of the time. As Ruth Hirschberger notes in *Adam's Rib*:

It is significant that the same woman who awakens the boy's affection (and few deny the sexual component in all demonstrativeness) is also the first to issue the taboo against his sexuality ... Suppression of sexuality becomes the ticket to the mother's affection.

Or, male homosexuality could result from the refusal by the child at five or six to make the transition from 'mother-centredness' to 'father-centredness' – often from a genuine love for the mother and a real contempt for the father. (In the case of the missing 'father figure', such a transition is never clearly demanded of the child.) Very often, it is true, given the war between the sexes as it presents itself in most marriages, the mother encourages such an attachment out of spite, to get even with the father by denying him the progeny for the sake of which he tolerates her. But I think it would be more accurate to say that the child has simply taken the place of the indifferent, often philandering father in her affections. Every mother, even the most 'well adjusted', is *expected* to make motherhood a central focus of her life. Often the child is her only substitute for all that she has been denied in the larger world, in Freud's terms, her 'penis' substitute. How can we then demand that she not be 'possessive', that she give up suddenly, without a struggle – to the world of 'travel and adventure' – the very son who was meant to compensate her for her lifelong loss of this world?

Female homosexuality, though it too has its sources in unsuccessful repression (the Electra Complex), is considerably more complicated. Remember that the little girl also is first attached to her mother. She may never, out of later rivalry, learn to repress this attachment. Or she may attempt to act like a boy also in order to win her mother's approval (unfortunately women, too, prefer male children). Conversely, in cases where she does identify very strongly with her father, she may refuse to give up the desired male privilege even beyond puberty; in extreme cases she imagines herself really to *be* the male whose part she is playing.

And even those women who appear to be sexually adjusted seldom really are. We must remember that a woman can go through intercourse with almost no response; a man can't. Though few women, due to the excessive pressure on them to conform, actually repudiate their sexual role altogether by becoming actively lesbian, this does not mean that most women are sexually fulfilled by interaction with men. (However, a damaged female sexuality is relatively harmless in social terms; whereas the male sexual sickness, the confusion of sexuality with power, hurts others.) This is one reason why in Victorian society as well as a long time before and after, including today, women's interest in sex is less than men's. This fact is so bafflingly obvious that it led a well-known psychoanalyst, Theodor Reik, to conclude (in 1966!) 'that the very sexual drive itself is masculine, even in women, because on a lower evolutionary level reproduction is possible without males'.

Thus we see that in a family-based society, repressions due to the incest taboo make a totally fulfilled sexuality impossible for anyone, and a well-functioning sexuality possible for only a few. Homosexuals in our time are only the extreme casualties of the system of obstructed sexuality that develops in the family. But though homosexuality at present is as limited and sick as our heterosexuality, a day may soon come in which a healthy transexuality would be the norm. For if we grant that the sexual drive is at birth diffuse and undifferentiated from the total personality (Freud's 'polymorphous perversity') and, as we have seen, becomes differentiated only in response to the incest taboo; and that, furthermore, the incest taboo is now necessary only in order to preserve the family; then if we did away with the family we would in effect be doing away with the repressions that mould sexuality into specific formations. All other things being equal, people might still prefer those of the opposite sex simply because it is physically more convenient. But even this is a large assumption. For if sexuality were indeed at no time separated from other responses, if one individual responded to the other in a total way that merely *included* sexuality as one of its components, then it is unlikely that a purely physical factor could be decisive. However, we have no way of knowing that now.

The end of the compartmentalization of personality through reintegration of the sexual with the whole could have important cultural side-effects. At the present time the Oedipus Complex, originating in the now almost universal incest taboo, demands that the child soon distinguish between the 'emotional' and the 'sexual': one is considered by the father to be an appropriate response to the mother, the other is not. If the child is to gain his mother's love he must separate out the sexual from his other feelings (Freud's 'aim-inhibited' relationships). One cultural development that proceeds directly from such an unnatural psychological dichotomy is the good/bad women syndrome, with which whole cultures are diseased. That is, the personality split is projected outwards on to the class 'women': those who resemble the mother are 'good', and consequently one must not have sexual feelings towards them; those unlike the mother, who don't call forth a total response, are sexual, and therefore 'bad'. Whole classes of people, e.g., prostitutes, pay with their lives for this dichotomy; others suffer to different degrees. A good portion of our language degrades women to the level where it is permissible to have sexual feelings for them. ('Cunt. Your brain is between your legs.') This sexual schizophrenia is rarely overcome totally in the individual. And in the larger culture,

62

whole historical developments, the history of art and literature itself, have been directly moulded by it. Thus the courtly honour of the Middle Ages, exalting women only at the expense of their flesh-and-blood humanity – making sex a lowly act, divorced from true love – developed into Marcianism, the cult of the virgin in art and poetry.

A song from the period illustrates the division:

> I care not for these ladies
> Who must be wooed and prayed,
> Give me kind Amaryllis,
> The wanton country maid,
> Nature Art disdaineth,
> Her beauty is her own,
> For when we hug and kiss she cries
> 'Forsooth, let us go'
> But when we come where comfort is
> She never will say no.

The separation of sex from emotion is at the very foundations of Western culture and civilization. If early sexual repression is the basic mechanism by which character structures supporting political, ideological, and economic serfdom are produced, then an end to the incest taboo, through abolition of the family, would have profound effects: sexuality would be released from its straitjacket to eroticize our whole culture, changing its very definition.

*

To summarize briefly my second point, that Freud and feminism dealt with the same material: Freud's fundamental hypothesis, the nature of the libido and its conflict with the reality principle, makes a great deal more sense when seen against the social backdrop of the (patriarchal nuclear) family. I have attempted to reanalyse in feminist terms those components of Freud's theory that most directly relate to sexuality and its repression within the family system: the incest taboo and the resulting Oedipus and Electra Complexes, and their common misfiring into sexual malfunctioning, or, in severe cases, into what is now sexual deviation. I have pointed out that this sexual repression, demanded of every individual in the interests of family integrity, makes not only for individual neurosis, but also for widespread cultural illnesses.

Admittedly more than a sketchy presentation is beyond the scope of this chapter: a thorough restatement of Freud in feminist terms would make a valuable book in itself. Here I have submitted only that Freudianism and feminism sprang up at the same time, in response to the same stimuli, and that essentially they are made of the same substance: in carefully examining the basic tenets of Freudianism, I have shown that these are also the raw material of feminism. The difference lies only in that radical feminism does not accept the social context in which repression (and the resulting neurosis) must develop as immutable. If we dismantle the family, the subjection of 'pleasure' to 'reality', i.e. sexual repression, has lost its function; and is no longer necessary.

II
FREUDIANISM SUBSUMES FEMINISM

To the two main points of this chapter, first, that Freudianism and feminism grew out of the same historical conditions, and second, that Freudianism and feminism are based on the same set of realities, I shall add a third: *Freudianism subsumed the place of feminism as the lesser of two evils.*

We have shown how Freudianism hit the same nerve that feminism did: both at once were responses to centuries of increasing privatization of family life, its extreme subjugation of women, and the sex repressions and subsequent neuroses this caused. Freud too was once considered a sex maniac, destructive to society – he was ridiculed and despised as much as were the militant feminists. It was only much later that Freudianism became as sacred as an established religion. How did this reversal come about?

Let us first consider the social context of the development of both feminism and Freudianism. We have seen that the ideas of the early radical feminists contained the seeds of the coming sexual revolution. We have seen that though in many cases the feminists themselves did not clearly grasp the importance of what they had stumbled into, though often they did not have down a thorough and consistent radical feminist critique of society – and given the political climate at that time, it is no wonder – the reaction of society to them indicates that their enemies knew what they were about, if they themselves weren't sure: the virulent antifeminist literature of the time, often written by men well respected and honest in their own fields of endeavour, illustrates the threat the feminists presented to the establishment. I have also shown in the past chapter how the movement was redirected into an all-consuming effort to obtain the vote, and how in this way it was sidetracked and destroyed. Following the end of the feminist movement, with the granting of the vote, came the era of the flappers, an era that in its pseudo-liberated sexuality much resembles our own. The widespread female rebellion stirred up by the feminist movement now had nowhere to go. Girls who had cut their hair, shortened their skirts, and gone off to college no longer had a political direction for their frustration; instead they danced it away in marathons, or expended themselves swimming the Channel and flying aeroplanes across the Atlantic. They were a roused class who did not know what to do with their consciousness. They were told then as we are still told now, 'You've got civil rights, short skirts, and sexual liberty. You've won your revolution. What more do you want?' But the 'revolution' had been won within a system organized around the patriarchal nuclear family. And as Herbert Marcuse in *Eros and Civilization* shows, within such a repressive structure only a more sophisticated repression can result ('repressive de-sublimation').

In a repressive society, individual happiness and productive development are in contradiction to society; if they are defined as values to be realized within the society, they become themselves repressive . . . [The concept of repressive de-sublimation is] the release of sexuality in modes and forms which reduce and weaken erotic energy. In this process sexuality spreads into formerly tabooed dimensions and relations. However, instead of recreating these dimensions and relations in the images of the Pleasure Principle, the opposite tendency asserts itself: the Reality Principle extends its hold over Eros. The most telling illustration is provided by the methodical introduction of sexiness into business, politics, propaganda, etc.

Here in the twenties began the stereotypes of the American 'career girl', the 'coed', and the 'butchy' businesswoman. This image of the supposedly 'liberated' woman went around the world via Hollywood, the unbalancing effects on women of pseudo-liberation giving antifeminists new ammunition, and further bolstering the resistance of the still openly male supremacist societies to setting 'their' women free. ('We like our women the way they are – *womanly*.') American servicemen came back from the Second World War with stories of those great continental women who still knew how to make a man feel good. The word *castration* began to circulate. And finally in America, in the forties, Freudianism came in big.

Meanwhile, Freudianism itself had undergone deep internal changes. Emphasis had shifted from the original psychoanalytic theory to clinical practice. In the final chapter of *Eros and Civilization*, Marcuse discusses the reactionary implications of this shift, showing how the contradiction between Freud's ideas and the possibility of any effective 'therapy' based on them – psychoanalysis cannot effect individual happiness in a society the structure of which can tolerate no more than severely controlled individual happiness – finally caused the assimilation of the theory to suit the practice:

The most speculative and 'metaphysical' concepts not subject to clinical verification ... were minimized and discarded altogether. Moreover, in the process, some of Freud's most decisive concepts (such as the relation between the id and the ego, the function of the unconscious, and the scope and significance of sexuality) were redefined in such a way that their explosive content was all but eliminated ... The revisionists have converted the weakening of Freud's theory into a new theory.

The term that perhaps best characterizes this neo-Freudian revisionism is 'adjustment'. But adjustment to what? The underlying assumption is that one must accept the reality in which one finds oneself. But what happens if one is a woman, a black, or a member of any other especially unfortunate class of society? Then one is doubly unlucky. Then one not only has to achieve a normalcy that even for the privileged is, as we have shown, difficult and precarious at best, but one must also 'adjust' to the specific racism or sexism that limits one's potential from the very beginning. One must abandon all attempts at self-definition or determination. Thus, in Marcuse's view, the process of therapy becomes merely 'a course in resignation', the difference between health and neurosis only 'the degree and effectiveness of the resignation'. For, as in the often-quoted statement of Freud to his patient (*Studies in Hysteria*, 1895), '[A great deal will be gained if we succeed through therapy in] transforming your hysterical misery into everyday unhappiness.'

And as all those who have undergone therapy can attest, that's just about the size of it. Cleaver's description of his analysis in *Soul on Ice* speaks for the experience of any other oppressed person as well:

I had several sessions with a psychiatrist. His conclusion was that I hated my mother. How he arrived at this conclusion I'll never know because he knew nothing about my mother, and when he'd ask me questions I would answer him with absurd lies. What revolted me about him was that he had heard me denouncing whites, yet each time he deliberately guided the conversation back to my family life, to my childhood. That in itself was alright, but he deliberately blocked all my attempts to bring out the racial question, and he made it clear that he was not interested in my attitudes towards whites. This was a Pandora's box he did not care to open.

Theodor Reik, perhaps the prototype of the crackerbarrel layman's Freud, exemplifies the crassness and insensitivity of most psychoanalysts to the real problems of their patients. It is remarkable that, with so many writings on the emotional differences between men and women, Reik should never have discovered the objective difference in their social situations. For example, he observes in passing differences like the following without ever drawing the right conclusions:

Little girls sometimes whisper to each other 'Men do' this or that. Little boys almost never speak of women in this way.

A woman gives much more thought to being a woman than a man to being a man.

Most women, when they ask a favour of a man, smile. In the same situation men rarely smile.

To be a ladies' man means somewhere not to be much of a man.

Almost all women are afraid that the man they love will leave them. But hardly a man is afraid that a woman will leave him.

Women in groups sometimes say, 'My lord and master let me out of the house tonight.' Men say, 'My ball-and-chain.'

And here is a random sampling of his neo-Freudian contributions to sexual understanding:

The first impression one gets of a young woman entering a room full of people is that of concealed or well-disguised insecurity. It seems that being the possessor of a penis protects men against such over self-awareness.

Men are not at home in the universe and therefore have to explore it. Women who form the chain of all organic beings are at home in the world and do not feel the urge to find out all about it.

It seems to me that psychoanalytic research in emphasizing the physical deficiency in the genitals region which the little girl experiences has neglected the aesthetic value and its significance in the development of the feminine attitude. I assume that the little girl who compares her genitals to those of the little boy finds her own ugly. Not only the greater modesty of women, but their never ceasing striving towards beautifying and adorning their bodies is to be understood as displacement and extension of their effort to overcompensate for their original impression that their genitals are ugly.

I believe that cleanliness has a double origin: the first in the taboos of tribes, and the second another matter coming thousands of years later, namely in women's awareness of their own odor, specifically the bad smells caused by the secretion of their genitals.

And a typical therapeutic interpretation:

[A patient was afraid to show me her book.] It occurred to me: this patient, who had during the preceding transference shown clear indications of transference love for me, now acts as if the book were a child she had gotten by me. She acts the way a woman does who has to show her child to her husband for the first time. She is afraid he might not like the newborn baby.

It reads like a Freudian jokebook.

Reik's female patients, in contrast, were often touchingly perceptive, even brilliantly astute. They were far more in touch with the reality of their situation than he was ever able to be:

A woman seems incapable of expressing her strong negative feelings and explains her incapacity in a psychoanalytic session: 'I am afraid to show these emotions because if I did, it would be like opening Pandora's box . . . I am afraid that my aggressiveness would destroy all.'

Before she left I took her to the window and showed her the stores across the street, and their signs in neon letters, and said, 'Isn't it a woman's world?' But she was not much impressed by this and replied, 'Walk down Wall Street and you'll see it's a man's world.'

[A patient notes that] Men are odd. They do not permit us to be only women, I mean women with all their weaknesses; but they do not for a moment let us forget that we are only women.

How can these women stand Reik's stupid misogyny? They can't:

When I told a patient in her forties that she had wanted to be a boy like her brother she began to curse and abuse me, saying 'Fuck you' and 'Go to hell!' and other unladylike expressions.

But the doctor wins:

When it was time for her to leave, she stood for a while longer than usual before the mirror in my anteroom, putting her hair in order. I smilingly remarked, 'I am glad to see a remnant of femininity.'

Here are a few other female reactions:

When you listen to me a long time without saying anything, I often have the impression that what I say is silly woman's stuff and without value. It is as if you do not consider it worth your while to speak to me.

Woman criticizing her psychoanalyst: 'Even your spontaneity is artificial.'

The patient had been silent for a longer time than usual and then said in a quiet manner: 'Goddam, I don't know why I am here. Go fuck yourself!'

It is not that these women were unaware of their situation: on the contrary, they were in Reik's office because of their awareness. There was no other way to handle their frustration because there *is* no way to handle it, *short of revolution*.

We have arrived at our final point: the importation of clinical Freudianism to stem the flow of feminism. Girls in the twenties and thirties found themselves half-way in and half-way out of the traditional roles. Thus they were neither insulated and protected from the larger world as before, nor were they equipped to deal with it. Both their personal and work lives suffered. Their frustration often took hysterical forms, complicated by the fact that they were despised the world over for even the little false liberation they had achieved. Mass confusion sent them in droves to the psychoanalysts. And where had all the psychoanalysts come from? By this time a war was going on in Europe, and much of the German and Austrian intelligentsia had settled here in search of a practice. It was ideal: a whole class of suffering people awaited them. And it was not just a few bored, rich women who were sucked into the new religion. For America was undergoing serious cramps from withholding a sexual revolution already well beyond the beginning stages. Everyone suffered, men as well as women. Books came out with such titles as *How to Live with a Neurotic* (because that oppressed class is right there in your kitchen, whining and complaining and nagging). Soon men, too, were turning up at the psychoanalysts'. Well-educated, responsible citizens, not just psychos. And children. Whole new fields were opened to deal with the influx: child psychology, clinical psychology, group therapy, marriage counselling services, any variation you can think of, name it and there it was. And none of it was enough. The demand multiplied faster than new departments could be opened up in colleges.

That these new departments were soon filled up with women is no wonder. Masses of searching women studied psychology with a passion in the hope of finding a solution to their 'hangups'. But women who had grown interested in psychology because its raw material touched them where they lived soon were spouting jargon about marital adjustment and sex-role responsibility. Psychology departments became half-way houses to send women scurrying back 'adjusted' to their traditional roles as wives and mothers. Those women who persisted in demanding careers became in their turn instruments of the repressive educational system, their new-found psychological 'insight' – that babble of Child Psych., Social Work 301 and El. Ed. – serving to keep a fresh generation of women and children down. Psychology became reactionary to its core, its potential as a serious discipline undermined by its usefulness to those in power.

And psychology was not the only new discipline to be corrupted. Education, social work, sociology, anthropology, all the related behavioural sciences, remained for years pseudo-sciences, overburdened with a double function: the indoctrination of women, as well as the study of 'human behaviour'. Reactionary schools of thought developed: social science became 'functional', studying the operation of institutions only within the given value system, thus promoting acceptance of the status quo.

It is not surprising that these remained 'women's fields'. Men soon fled to (exclusively male) 'pure' science; women, still only semi-educated, awed with their new entrance into academia, were left to be snowed with the pseudo-scientific bullshit. For, in addition to role indoctrination, the behavioural sciences served as a dyke to keep the hordes of questing nouveaux intellectuelles from entering the 'real' sciences – physics, engineering, biochemistry, etc., sciences that in a technological society bore an increasingly direct relation to control of that society.

As a result, even access to higher education, one of the few victories of the early WRM, was subverted. More average women went to college than ever before, with less effect. Often the only difference between the modern college-educated housewife and her traditional prototype was the jargon she used in describing her marital hell.

*

In short, Freudian theory, regroomed for its new function of 'social adjustment', was used to wipe up the feminist revolt. Patching up with band-aids the casualties of the aborted feminist revolution, it succeeded in quieting the immense social unrest and role confusion that followed in the wake of the first attack on the rigid patriarchal family. It is doubtful that the sexual revolution could have remained paralysed at half-way point for half a century without its help; for the problems stirred up by the first wave of feminism are still not resolved today. D. H. Lawrence and Bernard Shaw are no less relevant than they were in their own time; Wilhelm Reich's *The Sexual Revolution* could have been written yesterday.

Freudianism was the perfect foil for feminism, because, though it struck the same nerve, it had a safety catch that feminism didn't – it never questioned the given reality. While both at their cores are explosive, Freudianism was gradually revised to suit the pragmatic needs of clinical therapy: it became an applied science complete with white-coated technicians, its contents subverted for a reactionary end – the socialization of men and women to an artificial sex-role system. But there was just enough left of its original force to serve as a lure for those seeking their way out of oppression – causing Freudianism to go in the public mind from extreme suspicion and dislike to its current status: psychoanalytic expertise is the final say in everything from marital breakups to criminal court judgements. Thus Freudianism gained the ground that feminism lost: it flourished at the expense of feminism, to the extent that it acted as a container of its shattering force.

Only recently have we begun to feel the generations of drugging; half a century later women are waking up. There is a new emphasis on objective social conditions in psychology as well as in the behavioural sciences; these disciplines, only now, decades after the damage has been done, are reacting to their long prostitution with demands for scientific verification – but an end to 'objectivity' and a reintroduction of 'value' judgements'. The large numbers of women in these fields may soon start using this fact to their advantage. And a therapy that has proven worse than useless may eventually be replaced with the only thing that can do any good: political organization.

4   Down with Childhood

FOR NECHEMIA
who will outgrow childhood before it is eliminated

Women and children are always mentioned in the same breath ('Women and children to the forts!'). The special tie women have with children is recognized by everyone. I submit, however, that the nature of this bond is no more than shared oppression. And that moreover this oppression is intertwined and mutually reinforcing in such complex ways that we will be unable to speak of the liberation of women without also discussing the liberation of children, and – vice versa. The heart of woman's oppression is her child-bearing and child-rearing role. And in turn children are defined in relation to this role and are psychologically formed by it; what they become as adults and the sorts of relationships they are able to form determine the society they will ultimately build.

*

I have tried to show how the power hierarchies in the biological family, and the sexual repressions necessary to maintain it – especially intense in the patriarchal nuclear family – are destructive and costly to the individual psyche. Before I go on to describe how and why it created a cult of childhood, let us see how this patriarchal nuclear family developed.

In every society to date there has been some form of the *biological* family and thus there has always been oppression of women and children to varying degrees. Engels, Reich, and others point to the primitive matriarchies of the past as examples, attempting to show how authoritarianism, exploitation, and sexual repression originated with monogamy. However, turning

73

to the past for ideal states is too facile. Simone de Beauvoir is more honest when, in *The Second Sex*, she writes:

The peoples who have remained under the thumb of the goddess mother, those who have retained the matrilineal régime, are also those who are arrested at a primitive stage of civilization . . . The devaluation of women [under patriarchy] represents a necessary stage in the history of humanity, for it is not upon her positive value but upon man's weakness, that her prestige is founded. In woman are incarnated all the disturbing mysteries of nature, and man escapes her hold when he frees himself from nature . . . Thus the triumph of the patriarchate was neither a matter of chance nor the result of violent revolution. From humanity's beginnings their *biological advantage* has enabled the males to affirm their status as sole and sovereign subjects; they have never abdicated this position; they once relinquished a part of their independent existence to Nature and to Woman; but afterwards they won it back. (Italics mine)

She adds:

Perhaps however, *if productive work had remained within her strength*, woman would have accomplished *with man* the conquest of nature . . . through *both* male and female . . . but because she did not share his way of working and thinking, *because she remained in bondage to life's mysterious processes*, the male did not recognize in her a being like himself. (Italics mine)

Thus it was woman's reproductive biology that accounted for her original and continued oppression, and not some sudden patriarchal revolution, the origins of which Freud himself was at a loss to explain. Matriarchy is a stage on the way to patriarchy, to man's fullest realization of himself; he goes from worshipping Nature through women to conquering it. Though it's true that woman's lot worsened considerably under patriarchy, she never had it good; for despite all the nostalgia it is not hard to prove that matriarchy was never an answer to women's fundamental oppression. Basically it was no more than a different means of counting lineage and inheritance, one which, though it might have held more advantages for women than the later patriarchy, did not allow women into the society as equals. To be worshipped is not freedom.[1] For worship still takes place in someone else's head, and that head belongs to Man. Thus throughout

1. The misery of the goddess has been portrayed admirably in Satyajit Ray's film *Devi*.

history, in all stages and types of culture, women have been oppressed due to their biological functions.

Turning to the past, while it offers no true model, is, however, of some value in understanding the *relativity* of the oppression: though it has been a fundamental human condition, it has appeared to differing degree in different forms.

The *patriarchal family* was only the most recent in a string of 'primary' social organizations, all of which defined woman as a different species due to her unique child-bearing capacity. The term *family* was first used by the Romans to denote a social unit the head of which ruled over wife, children, and slaves – under Roman law he was invested with rights of life and death over them all; *famulus* means domestic slave, and *familia* is the total number of slaves belonging to one man. But though the Romans coined the term, they were not the first to develop the institution. Read the Old Testament: for example, the description of Jacob's family train as after a long separation he travels to meet his twin brother Esau. This early patriarchal household was only one of many variations on the patriarchal family taking place in many different cultures up to the present time.

However in order to illustrate the relative nature of children's oppression, rather than comparing these different forms of the patriarchal family throughout history we need only examine the development of its most recent version, the *patriarchal nuclear* family. For even its short history, roughly from the fourteenth century on, is revealing: the growth of our most cherished family values was contingent on cultural conditions, its foundations in no sense absolute. Let's review the development of the nuclear family – and its construct 'childhood' – from the Middle Ages to the present, basing our analysis on Philippe Ariès's *Centuries of Childhood : A Social History of Family Life*.

The modern nuclear family is only a recent development. Ariès shows that the family as we know it did not exist in the Middle Ages, only gradually evolving from the fourteenth century on. Until then one's 'family' meant primarily one's legal heredity line, the emphasis on blood ancestry rather than the conjugal unit. With respect to such legalities as the passing on of property, its primary function, there was joint estate of the husband and wife, and joint ownership by the heirs; only towards the end of the Middle Ages, with the increasing of paternal authority in the bourgeois family, was joint estate by the conjugal couple abolished, with joint ownership by all the sons giving way to the laws of primogeniture. Ariès shows how iconography reflected the current values of society in the Middle Ages: either solitary compositions or large convivial groupings of people in public places were the standard; there is a dearth of interior scenes, for life did not take place inside a 'home'. For at that time there was no retreat into one's private 'primary group'. The family group was composed of large numbers of people in a constant state of flux and, on the estates of noblemen, whole crowds of servants, vassals, musicians, people of every class as well as a good many animals, in the ancient patriarchal household tradition. Though the individual might retire from this constant social interaction to the spiritual or academic life, even in this there was a community in which he could participate.

This medieval family – lineal honour of the upper classes, in the lower nothing more than the conjugal pair planted in the midst of the community – gradually developed into the matchbox family that we know. Ariès describes the change: 'It was as if a rigid polymorphous body had broken up and had been replaced by a host of little societies, the families, and by a few massive groups, the classes.'

Such a transformation caused profound cultural changes, as well as affecting the very psychological structure of the individual. Even the view of the life cycle of the individual has culturally evolved, e.g., 'adolescence', which had never existed before, came in. Most important of these new concepts of the stages of life was childhood.

I

THE MYTH OF CHILDHOOD

In the Middle Ages there was no such thing as childhood. The medieval view of children was profoundly different from ours. It was not only that it was not 'child-centred', it literally was not

76

conscious of children as distinct from adults. The child-men and child-women of medieval iconography are miniature adults, reflecting a wholly different social reality: children then *were* tiny adults, carriers of whatever class and name they had been born to, destined to rise into a clearly outlined social position. A child saw himself as the future adult going through his stages of apprenticeship; he was his future powerful self 'when I was little'. He moved into the various stages of his adult role almost immediately.

Children were so little differentiated from adults that there was no special vocabulary to describe them: they shared the vocabulary of feudal subordination; only later, with the introduction of childhood as a distinct state, did this confused vocabulary separate. The confusion was based on reality: children differed socially from adults only in their economic dependence. They were used as another transient servant class, with the difference that because all adults began in this class, it was not seen as degrading (an equivalent would be the indentured servant of American history). *All* children were literally servants; it was their apprenticeship to adulthood. (Thus for a long time after, in France, waiting on table was not considered demeaning because it had been practised as an art by all the youthful aristocracy.) This experience held in common by children and servants and the resulting intimacy that grew up between them has been bemoaned right down to the twentieth century: as the classes grew more and more isolated from each other, this lingering intimacy was considered the cause of considerable moral corruption of children from the upper and middle classes.

The child was just another member of the large patriarchal household, not even essential to family life. In every family the child was wetnursed by a stranger, and thereafter sent to another home (from about the age of seven until fourteen to eighteen) to serve an apprenticeship to a master – as I have mentioned, usually composed of or including domestic service. Thus he never developed a heavy dependence on his parents: they were responsible only for his minimal physical welfare. And they in turn did not 'need' their children – certainly children were not doted upon. For in addition to the infant mortality rate, which would

77

discourage this, parents reared *other people's children* for adult life. And because households were so large, filled with many genuine servants as well as a constant troupe of visitors, friends and clients, a child's dependence on, or even contact with, any specific parent was limited; when a relationship did develop it might better be described as avuncular.

Transmission from one generation to the next was ensured by the everyday participation of children in adult life – children were never segregated off into special quarters, schools, or activities. Since the aim was to ready the child for adulthood as soon as possible, it was felt quite reasonably that such a segregation would delay or stymie an adult perspective. In every respect the child was integrated into the total community as soon as possible: there were no special toys, games, clothes, or classes designed just for children. Games were shared by all age groups; children took part in the festivities of the adult community. Schools (only for specialized skills) imparted learning to anyone who was interested, of whatever age: the system of apprenticeship was open to children as well as adults.

After the fourteenth century, with the development of the bourgeoisie and empirical science, this situation slowly began to evolve. The concept of childhood developed as an adjunct to the modern family. A vocabulary to describe children and childhood was articulated (e.g., the French *le bébé*) and another vocabulary was built especially for addressing children: 'childrenese' became fashionable during the seventeenth century. (Since then it has been expanded into an art and a way of life. There are all kinds of modern refinements on baby talk: some people never go without it, using it especially on their girlfriends, whom they treat as grown-up children.) Children's toys did not appear until 1600 and even then were not used beyond the age of three or four. The first toys were only childsize replicas of adult objects: the hobby horse took the place of the real horse that the child was too small to ride. But by the late seventeenth century special artifacts for children were common. Also in the late seventeenth century we find the introduction of special children's games. (In fact these signified only a division: certain games formerly shared by both children and adults were abandoned by the adults to children and the lower class, while other games were taken over from then on exclusively for adult use, becoming the upper-class adult 'parlour games'.)

Thus, by the seventeenth century childhood as a new and fashionable concept was 'in'. Ariès shows how the iconography too reflects the change, with, for example, the gradual increase of glorified depictions of the mother/child relationship, e.g., the Infant in the Arms of Mary, or, later, in the fifteenth and the sixteenth centuries, of depictions of interiors and family scenes, including even individualized portraits of children and the paraphernalia of childhood. Rousseau among others developed an ideology of 'childhood'. Much was made of children's purity and 'innocence'. People began to worry about their exposure to vice. 'Respect' for children, as for women, unknown before the sixteenth century, when they were still part of the larger society, became necessary now that they formed a clear-cut oppressed group. Their isolation and segregation had set in. The new bourgeois family, child-centred, entailed a constant supervision; all earlier independence was abolished.

The significance of these changes is illustrated by the history of children's costume. Costume was a way of denoting social rank and prosperity – and still is, especially for women. The consternation even now, especially in Europe, at any clothing impropriety is due primarily to the impropriety of 'breaking rank'; and in the days when garments were expensive and mass production unheard of, this function of clothing was even more important. Because clothing customs so graphically describe disparities of sex and class, the history of child fashion gives us valuable clues to what was happening to children.

The first special children's costumes appeared at the end of the sixteenth century, an important date in the formation of the concept of childhood. At first children's clothing was modelled after archaic adult clothing, in the fashion of the lower class, who also wore the hand-me-downs of the aristocracy. These archaisms symbolized the growing exclusion of children and the proletariat from contemporary public life. Before the French Revolution, when special trousers of naval origin were introduced, further distinguishing the lower class, we find the same custom spreading to upper-class male children. This is important because it illustrates quite clearly that children of the upper class formed a lower class within it. That differentiation of costume functions to increase segregation and make clear class distinctions is also borne out by an otherwise unexplainable custom of the seventeenth and the eighteenth centuries: two broad ribbons had to be worn by both male and female children fastened to the robe under each shoulder and trailing down the back. These ribbons apparently had no other function than to serve as sartorial indications of childhood.

The male child's costume especially reveals the connection of sex and childhood with economic class. A male child went through roughly three stages: the male infant went from swaddling clothes into female robes; at about the age of five he switched to a robe with some elements of the adult male costume, e.g., the collar; and finally, as an older boy, he advanced to full military regalia. The costume worn by the older male child in the period of Louis XVI was at once archaic (Renaissance collar), lower-class (naval trousers), and masculinely military (jacket and buttons). Clothing became another form of initiation into manhood, with the child, in modern terms, begging to advance to 'long pants'.

These stages of initiation into manhood reflected in the history of child costume neatly tie in with the Oedipus Complex as I have presented it in the previous chapter. Male children begin life in the lower class of women. Dressed as women, they are in no way distinguished from female children; both identify at this time with the mother, the female; both play with dolls. Attempts are made at about the age of five to wean the child from its mother, to encourage it by slow degrees, e.g., the male collar, to imitate the father: this is the transitional period of the Oedipus Complex. Finally the child is rewarded for breaking away from the female and transferring his identifications to the male by a special 'grown-up' costume, its military regalia a promise of the full adult male power to come.

What about girls' costumes? Here is an astonishing fact: *childhood did not apply to women.* The female child went from swaddling clothes right into adult female dress. She did not go to school, which, as we shall see, was the institution that structured childhood. At the age of nine or ten she acted, literally, like a 'little lady'; her activity did not differ from that of adult women. As soon as she reached puberty, as early as ten or twelve, she was married off to a much older male.

The class basis of childhood is exposed: both girls and working-class boys did not have to be set apart by distinctive dress, for in their adult roles they would be servile to upper-class men; no initiation into freedom was necessary. Girls had no reason to go through costume changes, when there was nothing for them to grow up *to*: adult women were still in a lower class in relation to men. Children of the working class, even up to the present day, were freed of clothing restrictions, for their adult models, too, were 'children' relative to the ruling class. While boys of the middle and upper classes temporarily shared the status of women and the working class, they gradually were elevated out of these subjected classes; women and lower-class boys stayed there. It is no coincidence, either, that the effeminization of little boys' dress was abolished at the same time that the feminists agitated for an end to oppressive women's clothes. Both dress styles were integrally connected to class subjection and the inferiority of women's roles. Little Lord Fauntleroy went the way of the petticoat. (Though my own father remembers his first day in long pants, and even today, in some European countries, these clothing initiation customs are still practised.)

We can also see the class basis of the emerging concept of childhood in the system of child education that came in along with it. If childhood was only an abstract concept, then the modern school was the institution that built it into reality. (New concepts about the life cycle in our society are organized around institutions, e.g., adolescence, a construction of the nineteenth century, was built to facilitate conscription for military service.) The modern school education was, indeed, the articulation of the new concept of childhood. Schooling was redefined: no longer confined to clerics and scholars, it was widely extended to become the normal instrument of social initiation – in the progress from childhood to *man*hood. (Those for whom true adulthood never would apply, e.g., girls and working-class boys, did not go to school for many centuries.)

For contrary to popular opinion, the development of the modern school had little connection with the traditional scholarship of the Middle Ages, nor with the development of the liberal arts and humanities in the Renaissance. (In fact the humanists of the Renaissance were noted for the inclusion in their ranks of many precocious children and learned women; they stressed the development of the individual, of whatever age or sex.) According to Ariès, literary historians exaggerate the importance of the humanist tradition in the structure of our schools. The real architects and innovators were the moralists and pedagogues of the seventeenth century, the Jesuits, the Oratorians, and the Jansenists. These men were at the origins of both the concept of childhood and its institutionalization, the modern concept of schooling. They were the first espousers of the weakness and 'innocence' of childhood; they put childhood on a pedestal just as femininity had been put on a pedestal; they preached the segregation of children from the adult world. 'Discipline' was the keynote to modern schooling, much more important finally than the imparting of learning or information. For to them discipline was an instrument of moral and spiritual improvement, adapted less for its efficiency in directing large groups to work in common than for its intrinsic moral and ascetic value. That is, repression itself was adopted as a spiritual value.

Thus, the function of the school became 'child-rearing', complete with disciplinary 'child psychology'. Ariès quotes the *Regulations for Boarders at Port-Royal*, a forerunner of our teacher training manuals:

A close watch must be kept on the children, and they must never be left alone anywhere, whether they are ill or in good health . . . this constant supervision should be exercised gently and with a certain trustfulness *calculated* to make them think one loves them, and that it is only to enjoy their company that one is with them. This will make them love their supervision rather than fear it. (Italics mine)

This passage, written in 1612, already exhibits the mincing tone characteristic of modern child psychology, and the peculiar distance – at that time rehearsed, but by now quite unconscious – between adults and children.

The new schooling effectively segregated children off from the adult world for longer and longer periods of time. But this segregation of child from adult, and the severe initiation process demanded to make the transition to adulthood, indicated a growing disrespect for, a systematic underestimation of, the abilities of the child.

The precocity so common in the Middle Ages and for some time after has dwindled almost to zero in our own time.[2] Today, for example, Mozart's feats as a child composer are hardly credible; in his own time he was not so unusual. Many children played and wrote music seriously then and also engaged in a good many other 'adult' activities. Our piano lessons of today are in no way comparable. They are, in fact, only indications of child oppression – in the same way that the traditional 'women's accomplishments' such as embroidery are superficial activity – telling us only about the subjugation of the child to adult whims. And it is significant that these 'talents' are more often cultivated in girls than in boys; when boys study piano it is most often because they are exceptionally gifted or because their parents are musical.

Ariès quotes Heroard, *Journal sur l'enfance et la jeunesse de Louis XIII*, the detailed account of the Dauphin's childhood years written by his doctor, that the Dauphin played the violin and sang all the time at the age of *seventeen months*. But the Dauphin was no genius, later proving himself to be certainly no more intelligent than any average member of the aristocracy. And playing the violin wasn't all he did: the record of the child life of the Dauphin, born in 1601 – of only average intelligence – tells us that we underestimate the capabilities of children. We find that at the same age that he played the violin, he also played mall, the equivalent of golf for adults of that period, as well as tennis; he talked; he played games of military strategy. At three and four respectively, he learned to read and write. At four and

2. In the orthodox Jewish milieu in which I grew up, considered anachronistic by outsiders, many little boys still begin serious study before the age of five, and as a result Talmudic prodigies are common.

five, though still playing with dolls (!), he practised archery, played cards and chess (at six) with adults, and played many other adult games. At all times, just as soon as he was able to walk, he mixed as an equal with adults in all their activities (such as they were), professionally dancing, acting, and taking part in all amusements. At the age of seven the Dauphin began to wear adult male clothes, his dolls were taken away, and his education under male tutors began; he began hunting, riding, shooting, and gambling. But Ariès says:

We should beware of exaggerating [the importance of this age of seven]. For all that he had stopped playing, or should have stopped playing, with his dolls, the Dauphin went on leading the same life as before ... Rather more dolls and German toys before seven, and more hunting, riding, fencing, and possibly playgoing after seven; the change was almost imperceptible in that long succession of pastimes which the child shared with the adult.

What seems most clear to me from this description is this: that before the advent of the nuclear family and modern schooling, childhood was as little as possible distinct from adult life. The child learned directly from the adults around him, emerging as soon as he was able into adult society. At about the age of seven there was some sex-role differentiation – it had to happen sometime, given the patriarchy in operation, but this was not yet complicated by the lower-class position of children. The distinction as yet was only between men and women, not yet between children and adults. In another century, this had begun to change, as the oppression of women and children increasingly intertwined.

In summary, with the onset of the child-centred nuclear family, an institution became necessary to structure a 'childhood' that would keep children under the jurisdiction of parents as long as possible. Schools multiplied, replacing scholarship and a practical apprenticeship with a theoretical education, the function of which was to 'discipline' children rather than to impart learning for its own sake. Thus it is no surprise that *modern schooling retards development rather than escalating it.* By sequestering children away from the adult world – adults are, after all, simply larger children with worldly experience – and by artificially subjecting them to an adult/child ratio of one to twenty-plus, how could the final effect be other than a levelling of the group to a median (mediocre) intelligence? As if this weren't enough, after the eighteenth century a rigid separation and distinction of ages took place ('grades'). Children were no longer able to learn even from older and wiser children. They were restricted in most of their waking hours to a chronological finely-drawn[3] peer group, and then spoon-fed a 'curriculum'. Such a rigid gradation increased the levels necessary for the initiation into adulthood and made it hard for a child to direct his own pace. His learning motivation became outer-directed and approval-conscious, a sure killer of originality. Children, once seen simply as younger people – the way we now see a half-grown puppy in terms of its future maturity – were now a clear-cut class with its own internal rankings, encouraging competition: the 'biggest guy on the block', the 'brainiest guy in school', etc. Children were forced to think in hierarchical terms, all measured by the supreme 'When I grow up . . .' In this the growth of the school reflected the outside world which was becoming increasingly segregated according to age and class.

*

In conclusion: the development of the modern family meant the breakdown of a large, integrated society into small, self-centred units. The child within these conjugal units now became important; for he was the product of that unit, the reason for its maintenance. It became desirable to keep one's children at home for as long as possible to bind them psychologically, financially, and emotionally to the family unit until such time as they were ready to create a new family unit. For this purpose the Age of Childhood was created. (Later, extensions were added, such as adolescence, or in twentieth-century American terms, 'Teen-agerdom', 'Collegiate Youth', 'Young Adulthood'.) The concept of childhood dictated that children were a species different not just in age, but in kind, from adults. An ideology was

3. This is carried to extremes in contemporary public schools where perfectly ready children are turned away for a whole year because their birthdays fall a few days short of an arbitrary date.

developed to prove this, fancy tractates written about the innocence of children and their closeness to God ('little angels'), with a resulting belief that children were asexual, child sex play an aberration – all in strong contrast to the period preceding it, when children were exposed to the facts of life from the beginning.[4] For any admission of child sexuality would have accelerated the transition into adulthood, and this now had to be retarded at all cost: the development of special costumes soon exaggerated the physical differences distinguishing children from adults or even from older children; children no longer played the same games as adults, nor did they share in their festivities (children today do not normally attend fancy dinner parties) but were given special games and artifacts of their own (toys); storytelling, once a community art, was relegated to children, leading to in our own time a special child literature; children were spoken to in a special language by adults and serious conversation was never indulged in their presence ('Not in front of the children'); the 'manners' of subjection were instituted in the home ('Children should be seen and not heard'). But none of this would have worked to effectively make of children an oppressed class if a special institution hadn't been created to do the job thoroughly: the modern school.

The ideology of school was the ideology of childhood. It operated on the assumption that children needed 'discipline', that they were special creatures who had to be handled in a special way (child psych., child ed., etc.) and that to facilitate this they should be corralled in a special place with their own kind, and with an age group as restricted to their own as possible. The school was the institution that structured childhood by effectively segregating children from the rest of society, thus retarding their growth into adulthood and their development of specialized skills for which the society had use. As a result they remained economically dependent for longer and longer periods of time; thus family ties remained unbroken.

4. See Ariès, *Centuries of Childhood: A Social History of Family Life*, Ch. V, 'From Immodesty to Innocence', for a detailed description of this exposure, based on the sexual experiences of the Dauphin as recorded in the Heroard Journal.

I have pointed out that there is a strong relationship between the hierarchies of the family and economic class. Engels has observed that within the family the husband is the bourgeois and the wife and children are the proletariat. Similarities between children and all working-class or other oppressed groups have been noted, studies done to show that they share the same psychology. We have seen how the development of the proletarian costume paralleled that of children's costume, how games abandoned by upper-class adults were played by both children and 'yokels'; both were said to like to 'work with their hands' as opposed to the higher cerebrations of the adult male, abstractions beyond them; both were considered happy, carefree, and good-natured, 'more in touch with reality'; both were reminded that they were lucky to be spared the worries of responsible adulthood – and both wanted it anyway. Relations with the ruling class were tinged in both cases by fear, suspicion, and dishonesty, disguised under a thin coating of charm (the adorable lisp, the eyeroll and the shuffle).

The myth of childhood has an even greater parallel in the myth of femininity. Both women and children were considered asexual and thus 'purer' than man. Their inferior status was ill-concealed under an elaborate 'respect'. One didn't discuss serious matters nor did one curse in front of women and children; one didn't *openly* degrade them, one did it behind their backs. (As for the double standard about cursing: a man is allowed to blaspheme the world because it belongs to him to damn – but the same curse out of the mouth of a woman or a minor, i.e. an incomplete 'man' to whom the world does not yet belong, is considered presumptuous, and thus an impropriety or worse.) Both were set apart by fancy and nonfunctional clothing and were given special tasks (housework and homework respectively); both were considered mentally deficient ('What can you expect from a woman?' 'He's too little to understand'). The pedestal of adoration on which both were set made it hard for them to breathe. Every interaction with the adult world became for children a tap dance. They learned how to use their childhood to get what they wanted indirectly ('He's throwing another tantrum!'), just as women learned how to use their femininity ('There she goes, crying again!'). All excursions into the adult world became terrifying survival expeditions. The difference between the natural behaviour of children in their peer group as opposed to their stilted and/or coy behaviour with adults bears this out – just as women act differently among themselves than when they are around men. In each case a physical difference had been enlarged culturally with the help of special dress, education, manners, and activity until this cultural reinforcement itself began to appear 'natural', even instinctive, an exaggeration process that enables easy stereotyping: the individual eventually appears to be a different kind of human animal with its own peculiar set of laws and behaviour ('I'll never understand women!' . . . 'You don't know a thing about child psychology!').

Contemporary slang reflects this animal state: children are 'mice', 'rabbits', 'kittens', women are called 'chicks', 'birds' (in England), 'hens', 'dumb clucks', 'silly geese', 'old mares', 'bitches'. Similar terminology is used about males as a defamation of character, or more broadly only about *oppressed* males: stud, wolf, cat, stag, jack – and then it is used much more rarely, and often with a specifically sexual connotation.

Because the class oppression of women and children is couched in the phraseology of 'cute' it is much harder to fight than open oppression. What child can answer back when some inane aunt falls all over him or some stranger decides to pat his behind and gurgle baby talk? What woman can afford to frown when a passing stranger violates her privacy at will? If she responds to his, 'Baby you're looking good today!' with 'No better than when I didn't know you', he will grumble, 'What's eating that bitch?' Or worse. Very often the real nature of these seemingly friendly remarks emerges when the child or the woman does not smile as she should: 'Dirty old scum bag. I wouldn't screw you even if you *had* a smile on your puss!' . . . 'Nasty little brat. If I were your father I would spank you so hard you wouldn't know what hit you!' . . . Their violence is amazing. Yet these men feel that the woman or the child is to blame for not being 'friendly'. Because it makes them uncomfortable to know that the woman or the child or the black or the workman is grumbling, the oppressed groups must also appear to *like* their oppression – smiling and simpering though they may feel like hell inside. The smile is the child/woman equivalent of the shuffle; it indicates acquiescence of the victim to her own oppression.

In my own case, I had to train myself out of that phony smile, which is like a nervous tic on every teenage girl. And this meant that I smiled rarely, for in truth, when it came down to real smiling, I had less to smile about. My 'dream' action for the women's liberation movement: *a smile boycott*, at which declaration all women would instantly abandon their 'pleasing' smiles, henceforth smiling only when something pleased *them*. Likewise children's liberation would demand an end to all fondling not welcomed by the child itself. (This of course would predicate a society in which fondling in general was no longer frowned upon; often the only demonstration of affection a child now receives is of this phony kind, which he may still consider better than nothing.) Many men can't understand that their easy intimacies come as no privilege. Do they ever consider that the real person inside that baby or female animal may not choose to be fondled then, or by them, or even noticed? Imagine this man's own consternation were some stranger to approach him on the street in a similar manner – patting, gurgling, muttering baby talk – without respect for his profession or his 'manhood'.

In sum, if members of the working class and minority groups 'act like children', it is because children of every class *are* lower-class, just as women have always been. The rise of the modern nuclear family, with its adjunct 'childhood', tightened the noose around the already economically dependent group by extending and reinforcing what had been only a brief dependence, by the usual means: the development of a special ideology, of a special indigenous life style, language, dress, mannerisms, etc. And with the increase and exaggeration of children's dependence, woman's bondage to motherhood was also extended to its limits. Women and children were now in the same lousy boat. Their oppressions began to reinforce one another. To the mystique of the glories of childbirth, the grandeur of 'natural' female creativity, was now added a new mystique about the glories of childhood itself and the 'creativity' of child-*rearing*. ('Why, my dear, what could be more *creative* than raising a child?') By now people have forgotten what history has proven: that 'raising' a child is tantamount to retarding his development. The best way to raise a child is to LAY OFF.

II
OUR TIME: THE MYTH IS MAGNIFIED

We have seen how the increasing privatization of family life brought ever more oppression to its dependents, women and children. The interrelated myths of femininity and childhood were the instruments of this oppression. In the Victorian Era they reached such epic proportions that finally women rebelled – their rebellion peripherally affecting childhood. But the rebellion was destroyed before it could eliminate these myths. They went underground to reappear in a more insidious version, complicated by mass consumerism. For in fact nothing had changed. In Chapter 2 I described how the emancipation of women was subtly sabotaged; the same thing occurred in the corollary oppression 'childhood'.

The pseudo-emancipation of children exactly parallels the pseudo-emancipation of women: though we have abolished all the superficial signs of oppression – the distinct and cumbrous clothing, the schoolmaster's rod – there is no question that the myth of childhood is flourishing in epic proportions, twentieth-century style: whole industries are built on the manufacture of special toys, games, baby food, breakfast food, children's books and comic books, candy with child appeal, etc.; market analysts study child psychology in order to develop products that will appeal to children of various ages; there is a publishing, movie, and TV industry built just for them, with its own special literature, programmes and commercials, and even censorship boards to decide just which cultural products are fit for their consumption; there is an endless proliferation of books and magazines instructing the layman in the fine art of child care (Dr Spock, *Parents' Magazine*); there are specialists in child psychology, child education methods, pediatrics, and all the special branches of learning that have developed recently to study this peculiar animal. Compulsory education flourishes and is now widespread enough to form an inescapable net of social-ization (brainwashing) from which even the very rich can no longer entirely escape. Gone are the days of Huckleberry Finn: today the malingerer or dropout has a full-time job just in warding off the swarm of specialists studying him, the proliferating government programmes, the social workers on his tail.

Let's look more closely at the modern form this ideology of childhood takes: visually it is as beefy, blonde, and smiling as a Kodak advertisement. As is the case with the exploitation of women as a ready-made, consumer class, there are many indus-tries eager to profit from children's physical vulnerability (e.g., St Joseph's Aspirin for children); but even more than their health, the key word to the understanding of modern childhood is *happiness*. You are only a child once, and this is it. Children must be living embodiments of happiness (sulky or upset or dis-turbed children are immediately disliked; they make of the myth a lie); it is every parent's duty to give his child a childhood to remember (swing sets, inflated swimming pools, toys and games, camping trips, birthday parties, etc.). This is the Golden Age that the child will remember when he grows up to become a robot like his father. So every father tries to give his son whatever it was he missed most himself in what should have been a most glorious stage of his own life. The cult of childhood as the Golden Age is so strong that all other ages of life derive their value from how closely they resemble it, in a national cult of youth; 'grownups' make asses of themselves with their jealous apologetics ('Of course I'm twice your age, dear, but . . .'). There is the general belief that progress has been made because at least in our time children have been freed from the ugly toils of child labour and many other traditional exploitations of past generations. In fact there is even the envious moan that children are getting too much attention. They are spoiled. ('When I was your age . . .' parallels 'Women have it easy . . .')

A major bulwark for this myth of happiness is the continued rigid segregation of children from the rest of society; the exager-ation of their distinctive features has made of them, as it was designed to, almost another race. Our parks provide the perfect metaphor for our larger age-segregated society: a special playground for the Tender Untouchables, mothers and young children (one seldom finds anyone else here, as if by decree), an athletic field or swimming pool for the youth, a shady knoll for young couples and students, and a bench section for the elderly. This age segregation continues throughout the life of every modern individual; people have very little contact with children once they have outgrown their own childhood. And even within their own childhood, as we have seen, there are rigid age segregations, so that an older child will be embarrassed to be seen with a younger one. ('Tagalong! Why don't you go play with someone your own age!') Throughout school life, and that is a rather long time in our century, a child remains with others only a year or two in age from himself. The schools themselves reflect these increasingly rigid gradations: junior junior high, senior junior high, etc., marked by a complex system of promotions and 'graduations'; lately even graduations from nursery school and/or kindergarten are common.

So by the time a child grows old enough to reproduce himself he has no contact whatever with those outside his own narrow adult age group, and certainly not with children. Because of the cult surrounding it he can barely remember even his own childhood, often blocking it entirely. Even as a child he may have attempted to mould himself to the myth, believing that all other children were happier than he; later, as a teenager, he may have indulged in a desperate joyousness, flinging himself into 'fun' – when really adolescence is a horror to live through – in the spirit of 'you're only young once'. (But true youth is unaware of age – 'youth is wasted on the young' – and is marked by real spontaneity, the absence of precisely this self-consciousness. The storing up of happiness in this manner to think of when you no longer have it is an idea only old age could have produced.) Such an absence of contact with the reality of childhood makes every young adult ripe for the same sentimentalization of children that he himself probably despised as a child. And so it goes, in a vicious circle: young adults dream of having their own children in a desperate attempt to fill up the void produced by the artificial cutoff from the young, but it is not until they are mired in pregnancies and Pampers, babysitters and school problems, favouritism and quarrelling that they again, for a short period, are forced to see that children are just human like the rest of us.

So let's talk about what childhood is *really* like, and not of what it is like in adult heads. It is clear that the myth of childhood happiness flourishes so wildly not because it satisfies the needs of children but because it satisfies the needs of adults. In a culture of alienated people, the belief that everyone has at least one good period in life free of care and drudgery dies hard. And obviously you can't expect it in your old age. So it must be you've already had it. This accounts for the fog of sentimentality surrounding any discussion of childhood or children. Everyone is living out some private dream in their behalf.

*

Thus segregation is still operating full blast to reinforce the oppression of children as a class. What constitutes this oppression in the twentieth century?

Physical and Economic dependence. The natural physical inferiority of children relative to adults – their greater weakness, their smaller size – is reinforced, rather than compensated for, by our present culture: children are still 'minors' under the law, without civil rights, the property of an arbitrary set of parents. (Even when they have 'good' parents, there are just as many 'bad' people in the world as 'good' – and the 'bad' people are considerably more likely to bear children.) The number of child beatings and deaths every year testifies to the fact that merely unhappy children are lucky. A lot worse could happen. It is only recently that doctors saw fit to report these casualties, so much were children at the mercy of their parents. Those children without parents, however, are even worse off (just as single women, women without the patronage of a husband, are still worse off than married women). There is no place for them but the orphanage, a dumping ground for the unwanted.

But the oppression of children is most of all rooted in economic dependence. Anyone who has ever observed a child wheedling a nickel from its mother knows that economic dependence is the basis of the child's shame. (Relatives who bring money are often the best liked. But make sure you give it *directly* to the kid!) Though he may not be starving to death (neither would he be if children had their own employment; black children who shine shoes, beg, and cultivate various rackets, and working-class white boys who sell papers, are envied in their neighbour-hood) he is dependent for his survival on *patronage*, and that's a bad state to be in. Such extreme dependence is hardly worth the bread.

It is in this area that we find one of the pivots of the modern myth: we are told that childhood represents great progress – immediately calling to mind Dickensian images of poor, gaunt children struggling in a coal pit. We have shown, however, in the brief history of childhood presented earlier in this chapter, that middle-class and upper-class children were not labouring at the dawn of the Industrial Era, but were safely ensconced in some dull schoolhouse studying Homer and Latin grammar. The children of the lower class, it is true, were not considered any more privileged than their fathers, sharing the inhuman tortures to which all members of their class had to submit; so that at the same time as there were idle Emma Bovarys and Little Lord Fauntleroys, there were also women destroying their lives and lungs in early textile mills and children roaming, begging. This difference between the lives of children of the different economic classes persisted right up until the days of the women's vote and into our own time. Children who were the reproductive chattel of the middle class were enduring soul-squeezing worse than our own; so were women. But they, to offset this, had economic *patronage*. Children of the lower class were exploited, not particularly as children, but generally, on a class basis: the myth of childhood was too fancy to waste on them. Here again we see illustrated just how arbitrary a myth childhood was, ordered expressly for the needs of the middle-class family structure.

Yes, you say, but surely it would have been better for the children of the working class could they too have lived sheltered by this myth. At least they would have been spared their lives.

So that they could sweat out their spiritual lives in some school-room or office? The question is rhetorical, like wondering whether the suffering of the blacks in America is authentic because they would be considered rich in some other country. Suffering is suffering. No, we have to think in broader terms here. Like, why were their parents being exploited in the first place: what is *anybody* doing down in that coal mine? What we ought to be protesting, rather than that children are being exploited just *like* adults, is that *adults* can be so exploited. We need to start talking not about sparing children for a few years from the horrors of adult life, but about eliminating those horrors. In a society free of exploitation, children could be like adults (with no exploitation implied) and adults could be like children (with no exploitation implied). The privileged slavery (patronage) that women and children undergo is not freedom. For self-regulation is the basis of freedom, and dependence the origin of inequality.

Sexual repression. Freud depicts the early contentment of the child: the satisfaction of the infant at the breast of the mother, which it then tries to regain for the rest of its life; how, due to adult protection, the child is freer from the 'reality principle' and is allowed to play (activity done for the pleasure of it, and not to achieve any other end); how, sexually, the child is poly-morphous and only later is so directed and repressed as to make him fit only for adult genital sex pleasure.

Freud also showed the origins of the adult neurosis to be built into the very processes of childhood. Though the prototypical child may have the *capacity* for pure pleasure, that does not mean that he can fully indulge it. It would be more correct to say that though by nature inclined to pleasure, to the degree that he becomes socialized (repressed) he loses this inclination. *And that begins right away*.

The 'reality principle' is not reserved for adults. It is intro-duced into the child's life almost immediately on his own small scale. For as long as such a reality principle exists, the notion of sparing the child its unpleasantness is a sham. At best he can go through a retarded repressive process; but more often the repres-sion takes place as soon as he can handle it, at all levels. It is not as though there is ever a blessed period when 'reality' lays off. For in truth the repression begins as soon as he is born – the well-known formula-by-clock feedings only an extreme example. Before the age of eighteen months, says Robert Stoller, the basic sex differentiation has set in, and as we have seen, this process in itself demands inhibition of the sex drive towards the mother. So from the beginning his polymorphous sexuality is denied free play. (Even now, with a campaign to recognize masturbation as normal, many infants are kept from playing with themselves while still in their cribs.) The child is weaned and toilet trained, the sooner the better – both traumatic in child terms. Repressions increase. The mother love that ideally is meant to be such perfect fulfilment ('unconditional') is used in the manner of father love: to better direct the child into socially approved conduct. And finally an active identification with the father is demanded. (In fatherless homes the identification may occur somewhat later, when the child begins school.) From here until puberty the child must lead a sexless – or secretive – life, not even admitting any sexual needs. Such forced asexuality produces a frustration that is at least partially responsible for the extreme rambunctiousness and aggressiveness – or alternately the anaemic docility – that often make children so trying to be around.

Family repression. We don't need to elaborate on the subtle psychological pressures of family life. Think of your own family. And if that isn't enough, if you are actually that one-in-a-million who is truly convinced that you had a 'happy family', read some of the work of R. D. Laing, particularly the *Politics of the Family*, on the Game of Happy Families. Laing exposes the internal dynamics of the family, explaining its invisibility to the ordinary family member:

One thing is often clear to an outsider: there are concerted family *resistances* to discovering what is going on, and there are complicated stratagems to keep everyone in the dark, and in the dark that they are in the dark. The truth has to be expended to sustain a family image ... Since this fantasy exists only in so far as it is 'in' everyone who shares 'in' it, anyone who gives it up shatters the 'family' in everyone else.

And here are a few children speaking for themselves. Again we quote Reik:

I was told of a boy, who, until he was almost four years old, thought that his name was 'Shutup'.

A boy witnessed a furious quarrel between his parents and heard his mother threaten his father with divorce. When he returned home from school the next day, he asked his mother, 'Are you divorced yet?' He remembered later being very disappointed because she had not gotten divorced.

A boy of nine years was asked by his visiting father at camp if he felt homesick, and the boy replied, 'No.' The father then asked if the other boys felt homesick. 'Only a few,' said the child, 'those who have dogs at home.'

What is amusing about these anecdotes, if indeed they are amusing, is the candour of children unable to understand or accept the masochistic hell of it all.

Educational repression. It is at school that the repression is cemented. Any illusions of freedom remaining are quickly wiped out now. All sexual activity or physical demonstrativeness is barred. Here is the first heavily supervised play. Children's natural enjoyment of play is now co-opted to better socialize (repress) them. ('Larry did the best fingerpainting. What a good boy! Your mother will be proud of you!') In some liberal schools all the way up, it is true, good teachers try to find subjects and activities that will truly interest children. (It's easier to keep the class in order that way.) But as we have seen, the repressive structure of the segregated classroom itself guarantees that any natural interest in learning will finally serve the essentially disciplinary interests of the school. Young teachers entering the system idealistic about their jobs suddenly are up against it: many give up in despair. If they had forgotten what a jail school was for them, it all comes back now. And they are soon forced to see that though there are liberal jails and not-so-liberal jails, by definition they are jails. The child is forced to go to them: the test is that he would never go of his own accord. ('School's out, School's out, Teachers let the fools out, No more pencils, No more books, No more teacher's dirty looks.') And though enlightened educators have devised whole systems of inherently interesting disciplined activities to lure and bribe the child into an acceptance of school, these can never fully succeed, for a school that existed solely to serve the curiosity of children on their own terms and by their own direction would be a contradiction in terms – as we have seen, the modern school in its structural definition exists to implement repression.

The child spends most of his waking hours in this coercive structure or doing homework for it. The little time that is left is often taken up with family chores and duties. He is forced to sit through endless family arguments, or, in some 'liberal' families, 'family councils'. There are relatives at whom he must smile, and often church services that he must attend. In the little time left, at least in our modern middle class, he is 'supervised', blocking the development of initiative and creativity: his choice of *play materials* is determined for him (toys and games), his *play area* is defined (gyms, parks, playgrounds, camp-sites); often he is limited in his *choice of playmates* to children of the same economic class as himself, and in the suburbs, to his schoolmates, or children of his parents' friends; he is organized into more groups than he knows what to do with (Boy Scouts, Cub Scouts, Girl Scouts, Brownies, camps, after-school clubs and sports); his *culture* is chosen for him – on TV he is often allowed to watch only pap children's programmes (father knows best) and is barred from all adult (good) movies; his books and literature are often taken from corny children's lists. (*Dick and Jane. The Bobbsey Twins. The Partridge Family. The Annals of Babe Ruth. Robinson Crusoe. Lassie* ad nauseam.)

The only children who have the slightest chance of escape from this supervised nightmare – but less and less so – are children of the ghettos and the working class where the medieval conception of open community – living on the street – still lingers. That is, historically, as we have seen, many of these processes of childhood came late to the lower class, and have never really stuck. Lower-class children tend to come from large immediate families composed of people of many different ages. But even when they don't, often there are half-brothers and sisters, cousins, nieces, nephews, or aunts, in a constantly changing milieu of relatives. Individual children are barely noticed, let alone supervised: children are often allowed to roam far from home or play out on the streets until all hours. And on the street, if by chance their family size is limited, there are hundreds of kids, many of whom have formed their own social groupings (gangs).[5] They do not often receive toys, which means they create their own. (I have seen ghetto kids devise ingenious slides out of cardboard and put them up against old tenements with missing steps; I have seen others make go-carts and pulleys out of old tyre wheels and string and boxes. No middle-class child does that. He doesn't need to. But as a result he soon loses that ingenuity.) They explore far afield of their own few blocks, and much more often than their middle-class contemporaries make the acquaintance of adults on an equal level. In class they are wild and unruly, as indeed they ought to be – for the class-room is a situation that would make any even partially free person suspicious. There is a lingering disrespect for school in the lower class, for, after all, it is a middle-class phenomenon in origin.

Sexually, too, ghetto kids are freer. One fellow told me that he can't remember an age when he didn't have sexual intercourse with other kids as a natural thing; everyone was doing it. Those who teach in ghetto schools have remarked on the impossibility of restraining child sexuality: it's a groovy thing, the kids love it, and it far surpasses a lesson about the Great American Demo-cracy or the contribution of the Hebrews who developed Monotheism or coffee and rubber as the chief exports of Brazil. So they do it on the stairs. And stay away from school the next day. If, in modern America, free childhood exists in any degree, it exists in the lower class, where the myth is least developed.

Why then do they 'turn out' worse than middle-class kids? Perhaps this is obvious. But I shall answer from my experience living and teaching in the ghettos: ghetto kids are not lower in intelligence until they reach adulthood, and even this is debat-able; lower-class children are some of the brightest, brassiest, and most original children around. They are that way because *they are left alone*. (If they do not do well on tests, perhaps we

5. Gangs are the only modern children's groups that are self-directed: the term *gang* has an ominous sound for good political reasons.

ought to reexamine the tests and not the children.) Later, in confronting a 'reality principle' very different from the middle-class one, they are drained and smashed; they will never 'out-grow' their economic subjection. Thus it is day-by-day oppression that produces these listless and unimaginative adults, the ubiquitous restrictions on their personal freedom to expand – not their wild childhood.

But children of the ghettos are only relatively free. They are still dependent, and they are oppressed as an economic class. There is good reason that all children want to grow up. Then at least they can leave home, and (finally) have a chance to do what they want to do. (There is some irony in the fact that children imagine that parents can do what they want, and parents imagine that children do. 'When I grow up . . .' parallels 'Oh to be a child again . . .') They dream of love and sex, for they live in the driest period of their lives. Often when confronted with their parents' misery, they make firm vows that when *they* grow up, *that* won't happen to them; they build glorious dreams of perfect marriages, or of no marriage at all (smarter children, who realize the fault lies in the institution, not in their parents), of money to spend as they please, of plenty of love and acclaim; they want to appear older than they are and are insulted if told that they appear younger than they are. They try fiercely to disguise the ignorance of affairs that is the peculiar physical affliction of all children. Here is an example from Reik's *Sex in Man and Woman* of the little cruelties to which they are constantly subjected:

I had some fun with a boy four years old, whom I told that a certain tree in his parents' garden bore pieces of chewing gum. I had bought some chewing gum and had hung the sticks by strings on the lower bough of the tree. The boy climbed up and picked them. He did not doubt that they grew on the tree, nor did he consider that they were wrapped in paper. He willingly accepted my explanation that the sticks of gum, blossoming at different times, had various flavors. In the following year when I reminded him of the chewing-gum tree, he was very ashamed of his previous credulity and said, 'Don't mention that.'

Some children, in an attempt to fight this constant ridicule of their gullibility – when they see that their painful ignorance is considered 'cute' – try to cash in on it, in much the same way that women do. Hoping to elicit that hug and kiss, they purposely take things out of context, but it seldom works the second time, perplexing them: what they don't understand is that the ignorance itself is considered 'funny', not its specific manifestations. For most children don't understand the arbitrary adult order of things, inadequately explained even when there *is* a sound explanation. But, in almost every case given the amount of information the child begins with, his conclusions are perfectly logical. Similarly if an adult were to arrive on a strange planet to find the inhabitants building fires on their roofs, he might assume an explanation; but his conclusions, based on his dissimilar past, might cause the others some amusement. Every person in his first trip to a foreign country, where he knows neither the people nor the language, experiences childhood.

*

Children, then, are not freer than adults. They are burdened by a wish fantasy in direct proportion to the restraints of their narrow lives; with an unpleasant sense of their own physical inadequacy and ridiculousness; with constant shame about their dependence, economic and otherwise ('Mother, may I?'); and humiliation concerning their natural ignorance of practical affairs. Children are repressed at every waking minute. Childhood is hell.

The result is the insecure, and therefore aggressive/defensive, often obnoxious little person we call a child. Economic, sexual, and general psychological oppressions reveal themselves in coyness, dishonesty, spite, these unpleasant characteristics in turn reinforcing the isolation of children from the rest of society. Thus their rearing, particularly in its most difficult personality phases, is gladly relinquished to women – who tend, for the same reason, to exhibit these personality characteristics themselves. Except for the ego rewards involved in having children of one's own, few men show any interest in children. And fewer still grant them their due political importance.

So it is up to feminist (ex-child and still oppressed child-women) revolutionaries to do so. We must include the oppression of children in any programme for feminist revolution or we will be subject to the same failing of which we have so often accused men: of not having gone deep enough in our analysis, of having missed an important substratum of oppression merely because it didn't directly concern *us*. I say this knowing full well that many women are sick and tired of being lumped together with children: that they are no more our charge and responsibility than anyone else's will be an assumption crucial to our revolutionary demands. It is only that we have developed, in our long period of related sufferings, a certain compassion and understanding for them that there is no reason to lose now; we know where they're at, what they're experiencing, because we, too, are still undergoing the same kind of oppressions. The mother who wants to kill her child for what she has had to sacrifice for it (a common desire) learns to love that same child only when she understands that it is as helpless, as oppressed as she is, and by the same oppressor: then her hatred is directed outwards, and 'mother-love' is born. But we will go further: our final step must be the elimination of the very conditions of femininity and childhood themselves that are now conducive to this alliance of the oppressed, clearing the way for a fully human condition.

5 Racism: The Sexism of the Family of Man

The slave may be freed and woman be where she is, but women cannot be freed and the slave remain where he is.

Angelina Grimké, *in a letter to* Theodore Weld

What must be done, I believe, is that all these problems, particularly the sickness between the white woman and the black man, must be brought out into the open, dealt with, and resolved . . . I think all of us, the entire nation, will be better off if we bring it all out front.

Eldridge Cleaver, *On Becoming*

The first American book to deal specifically with the connection of sex and racism was Calvin Hernton's *Sex and Racism in America*. The immediate popularity of the book in both black and white communities confirmed what everyone had known all along: that sex and racism are intricately interwoven. However, Hernton, not sufficiently grasping the depth of the relationship, merely described the obvious: that white men have a thing for black women, that black men have a thing for white women, that black men can't respect black women and white men can't get turned on by white women, that white women have a secret sympathy and curiosity about black men, that black women hate and are jealous of white women, and so on. Even so, the book, as have the many such books and articles since, made instant waves. Why is this?

The early civil rights movement had hushed up the truth too long: suited and tied, it had tiptoed about speaking in low tones on the 'Negro Problem'; black people were 'coloured people', they wanted only the same simple things uncoloured people wanted ('we're just folks'). Whereupon whites obligingly filtered their vision to screen out the obvious physical, cultural, and psychological differences. Words like 'nigger' were dropped. Statements like, 'Would you want your sister to marry one?' became unforgivable bad taste, a sign of poor breeding. 'You're prejudiced!' was the accusation of the year. And Martin Luther King masterfully utilized this guilt, turning liberal Christian rhetoric back on itself.

But then came Black Power. A rumble of I-told-you-sos issued from the nation, especially from the working class, who were closest to the blacks: what they really want is our power – they're after our women. Eldridge Cleaver's honesty in *Soul on Ice* clinched it. The heavily sexual nature of the racial issue spilled out. Internally as well, the Black Power movement was increasingly involved in a special kind of *machismo*, as busy proclaiming manhood as protesting race and class injustice.

But it was not the *machismo* element of Black Power that shook up its enemies. This part of it was rarely questioned by the Establishment proper, by the liberal Establishment (in fact, Moynihan's paper on 'black matriarchy' can be said to have *created* that massive castration complex within the black community which he describes), or even by the New Left. It was eminently understandable, after all, that black men would eventually want what all men want: to be on top of their women. In fact this part of it was reassuring: black men might become interested in black beauty instead of white (the wave of recent articles bemoaning the black woman's 'double burden' and her lack of an appreciative mate are suspicious), a 'purity' of home and family would lead eventually, perhaps, to conservatism and predictability. No, it was not black manhood itself that got whites up-tight – it was what manhood means in action: power. Black men were now out in the open in the male power struggle: we want what you've got, no more tap dances. White men breathed with relief and began arming: they knew how to cope with *this*. For once again, it was men vs. men, one (rigged) power force against the other. They drew the battle lines with glee.

What is this truth that was censored in order to make the civil rights movement acceptable to white America? What is the connection between sex and racism that makes any book on it sell so well? Why are the fears of the common man so sexual in nature when it comes to the Negro? Why does just the sight of a Negro so often evoke strong sexual feelings in a white man? Why do black men lust after white women? Why is racial prejudice so often phrased in sexual terms? Why does lynching, often accompanied by castration, occur as the most extreme manifestation of racism?

The connection between sex and racism is obviously much deeper than anyone has cared to go. But though the connection has never been more than superficially explored, already in the one decade of the new movement we have a new set of platitudes concerning sex and race, a new dogma for the 'hips'. For example, in the Who's Who of Oppression, a ranking of white man–white woman–black woman–black man is still in circulation, despite recent statistics of the Department of Labor.[1] Then there is the Brains vs. Brawn Antagonism, as developed by Mailer, Podhoretz, et al., and continued by Cleaver, basically the mystique of the black man's greater virility. And the Black Womb of Africa, Big Black Mammy in African garb. But this superficial exposure of sex-racism was meant only to seal up the issue a different way, this time in the interests of the male Anti-Establishment.

In this chapter I shall attempt to show that *racism is a sexual phenomenon*. Like sexism in the individual psyche, we can fully understand racism only in terms of the power hierarchies of the family: in the Biblical sense, the races are no more than the various parents and siblings of the Family of Man; and as in the development of sexual classes, the physiological distinction of race became important culturally only due to the unequal distribution of power. Thus, *racism is sexism extended*.

1. In 1969, white men who worked full-time the year around earned a median income of $6,497; black men, $4,285; white women, $3,859; and black women, $2,674.

But in only a few radical circles affected by the Women's Liberation Movement has even the black woman been acknowledged to be at the bottom economically.

I

The Racial Family: Oedipus/Electra, the Eternal Triangle, the Brothel-Behind-the-Scenes

Let us look at race relations in America,[2] a macrocosm of the hierarchical relations within the nuclear family: the white man is father, the white woman wife-and-mother, her status dependent on his; the blacks, like children, are his property, their physical differentiation branding them the subservient class, in the same way that children form so easily distinguishable a servile class vis-à-vis adults. This power hierarchy creates the psychology of racism, just as, in the nuclear family, it creates the psychology of sexism.

Previously we have described the Oedipus Complex in the male as that neurosis resulting from enforced subservience to the power of the father. Let us apply this interpretation to the psychology of the black male. The black male at first makes a sympathetic identification with the white female, who is also visibly oppressed by the white man. Because both have been 'castrated' (i.e. made impotent, powerless) in the same way by the Father, there is much similarity in the types of psychological oppressions they each must endure, in the sex-repressive nature of these oppressions – and thus in their resulting character formations. They have a special bond in oppression in the same way that the mother and child are united against the father.

This accounts for the white woman's frequent identification with the black man personally, and in a more political form, from the abolitionist movement (cf. Harriet Beecher Stowe) to our present black movement. The vicarious nature of this struggle against the white man's dominion is akin to the mother's vicarious identification with the son against the father. The woman has no real hope of her own self-determined struggle, for her it's all lost from the beginning: she is defined *in toto* as the appendage of the white man, she lives under his day-to-day surveillance isolated from her sisters: she has less aggressive

2. I shall deal here only with the domestic race relations with which I am most familiar. though I have no doubt that the same metaphor could be applied equally well to international and Third World politics.

strength. But the mother (white female) knows that if not herself, then at least her son (black male) is potentially 'male', that is, powerful.

But while some women may still attempt to achieve their freedom vicariously through the struggle of the black man or other racially oppressed (also biologically distinct) groups, many other women have resigned from this struggle altogether. Instead they choose to embrace their oppression, identifying their own interests with those of their men in the vain hope that power may rub off; *their* solution has been to obliterate their own poor egos – often by love – in order to merge completely into the powerful egos of their men.

This hopeless identification is the racism of white women – which perhaps produces an even greater bitterness in black men than the more immediately understandable racism of these women's husbands; for it betokens a betrayal by the Mother. Yet it is an inauthentic form of racism, for it arises from a false class consciousness, from the threat to what is, after all, only an illusion of power. If and when it is as strong as or stronger than the white man's racism, it is still different in kind: it is characterized by a peculiar hysteria, which, like the conservatism of the black bourgeoisie – or like the wife screaming at her husband that he treats the children better than he treats her – is, in itself, directly the product of the precariousness of her own class(less) situation. Thus the black man may become a scapegoat for the venom the woman feels for her husband, but is incapable of admitting directly.

So the white woman tends to oscillate between either a vicarious identification with the black man or a hysterical (but inauthentic) racism. Radical women, who, like most women, suffer from benefit-of-the-doubtism towards men in general, especially tend to trust and sympathize with black men – and then are often bitterly disillusioned when black men take personal advantage of them, or when the black movement does not move quickly enough to support the woman's cause.

For it is seldom all love and sympathy on the part of the black male either. To return to our analogy: just as the child begins with a bond of sympathy with the mother, and is soon required to transfer his identification from the mother to the father, thus to eradicate the female in himself, so too the black male, in order to 'be a man', must untie himself from his bond with the white female, relating to her if at all only in a degrading way. In addition, due to his virulent hatred and jealousy of her Possessor, the white man, he may lust after her as a thing to be conquered in order to 'get whitey'. Thus, unlike the more clear-cut polarization of feelings in white women, the black man's feelings about the white woman are characterized by their ambivalence – their intense *mixture* of love and hate; but however he may choose to express this ambivalence, he is unable to control its intensity.

LeRoi Jones's early play *Dutchman* illustrates some of these psychological tensions and ambivalences in the relationship of the black man to the white woman. In a subway encounter. Clay, a young bourgeois black, and Lula, a blonde vampire, personify them: Clay's contempt for Lula as the white man's plaything mixed with a grudging erotic attraction, her deep and immediate understanding of him, and finally her betrayal ending with a literal backstab (after which she cries 'rape', getting off scot free – one must presume to destroy more young black men who were only minding their own business). This is a black man's inner view of the white woman. Lula never comes across as a real woman, so much is she a product of the racial Oedipus Complex I have described.

The relationship of the black man with the white man, similarly, duplicates the relationship of the male child to the father. We have seen how at a certain point, in order to assert his ego, the child must transfer his identification from the female (powerless) to the male (powerful). He hates the powerful father. But he is offered the alternative: if he does make that transition (on the father's terms, of course), he is rewarded; if he denies it, his 'manhood' (humanity) is called into question. A black man in America can do only one of the following:

(1) He can give in to the white man on the white man's terms, and be paid off by the white man (Uncle Tomism).

(2) He can refuse such an identification altogether, at which he often surrenders to homosexuality. Or he may continue des-

perately to try to prove that if not a 'man' in the eyes of white society, at least he is not a woman (the Pimp Complex): by treating 'the bitches' with open contempt, he demonstrates to all the world that he is in the superior sex class.

(3) He may attempt to overthrow the Father's power. Such an attempt may, but will not necessarily, encompass a wish to *become* the Father, through subsuming his position of power.

Unless the black man makes the first choice, identification with the Father on the Father's own terms, he is subject to castration (destruction of his maleness, his *illegitimate* 'male' power), particularly if he tampers with the Father's treasure, the cushion for and embodiment of the Father's power – his woman. This racial castration occurs not only metaphorically, but literally, in the form of lynching.

Let us now apply our political interpretation of the Electra Complex to the psychology of the black woman. If the black man is Son to the American family, then the black woman is Daughter. Her initial sympathy with the white woman (mother), her bond of oppression with her (mother) against the white man (father) is complicated by her later relationship with the white male (father). When she discovers that the white male *owns* that 'world of travel and adventure', she, in the subservient position of child, attempts to identify with him, to reject the female in herself. (This may be the cause of the greater aggressiveness of the black woman compared with the docility of her white sisters.) In the effort to reject the womanly (powerless) element in herself, she develops contempt for the Mother (white woman). Like the young girl, she may react to her powerlessness in one of two ways: she may attempt to gain power directly by imitating white men, thus becoming a 'big achiever', a woman of strong character who rises high ('especially for a black woman'), or she may attempt to gain power indirectly by seducing the Father (voilà the black sexpot), thus putting herself in sexual competition with the white woman for the Father's favour – causing her to hate and be jealous of the white woman, whom she now must attempt to imitate.

Meanwhile the relationship of the Brother (black man) and Sister (black woman) is one of rivalry and mutual contempt. Each sees the other as powerless, a lackey desperately trying to get in good with the Parents (white man and woman). Each is on to the other's sexual games. It is difficult for them to direct their erotic energies towards each other: they see through each other too well.

We can use the family in another way to illuminate the psychology of racism. Let us look at racism as a form of the Eternal Triangle. In this situation the white man is Husband, the white woman is Wife, and the black woman is the Other Woman. We have seen how this kind of dichotomy between the 'good' and the 'bad' woman is in itself a product of the Oedipus Complex. A man is unable to feel both sex and affection for the same object, so he must divide up his feelings: for his wife and mother of his children he feels respect and affection; for the 'other' woman, his sexual receptacle, he feels passion. The further exaggeration of this division through biological differentiation, e.g., colour,[3] or economic class distinctions, makes the acting out of the sexual schizophrenia itself very convenient: one does not have to bother actually degrading one's sex object to avoid the guilt of breaking the incest taboo; her attributes, by social definition, already render her degraded. (Perhaps the measure of corruption of the individual male psyche can be judged by the degree to which it lusts after black flesh as something exotic, erotic, because forbidden.) The black woman, while made to pay the sexploitation price of this schism, is at least freed of the enslavement of the family structure. The white woman, though revered in her role as Mother, is permanently chained to her own private tyrant.

How do the women of this racial triangle feel about each other? Divide and Conquer: both women have grown hostile to each other, white women feeling contempt for the 'sluts' with no morals, black women feeling envy for the pampered 'powder puffs'. The black woman is jealous of the white woman's legitimacy, privilege, and comfort, but she also feels

3 An interesting illustration of their common and interchangeable political function is the psychological substitution of the racial caste distinction for the sexual caste distinction, e.g., a black lesbian often automatically assumes the male role in a black–white lesbian relationship.

deep contempt: white women are 'frigid bitches' who have it too easy, leaving black women to do all their white woman's work – from supplying their husbands' sex/passion needs and taking care of their children to doing their literal dirty work ('help'). Similarly, the white woman's contempt for the black woman is mixed with envy: for the black woman's greater sexual licence, for her gutsiness, for her freedom from the marriage bind. For after all, the black woman is not under the thumb of a man, but is pretty much her own boss to come and go, to leave the house, to work (much as it is degrading work) or to be 'shiftless'. What the white woman doesn't know is that the black woman, not under the thumb of *one* man, can now be squashed by all. There is no alternative for either of them than the choice between being public or private property, but because each still believes that the other is getting away with something, both can be fooled into mischanneling their frustration on to each other, rather than on to the real enemy, 'The Man'.

If, in the white man's sex drama, the white woman plays Wife (his private property), and the black woman plays Whore (his public property), what role does the black man play? The black man plays Pimp. The black man is a pawn in the game of the white man's sexuality. For as we have seen, the black man is not a complete man, nor yet a homosexual (who has given up the struggle for male identity altogether), but a *degraded* male. (That pimp signifies 'degrading male' is borne out by the fact that in the male code to call someone a pimp is tantamount to setting up a duel. I have pointed out that degrading animal terms for the male as well as the female occur regularly only in ghetto slang – stud, cat, dude, spade, jack, etc.) The black man's malehood is so questioned by The Man that it registers only in terms of his power over and domination of women, who are at least more powerless than himself. Because women are his major weapon in the war of masculinity with the white man, his relation to them becomes corrupted – not like that of man over woman, husband over wife, but like that of pimp over whore. His patronage of the black woman is a false one: though he may even, at times, protect her from the evils of the marketplace, he does so for his own interests. But even when the black man most appears to be her primary exploiter, he is in reality only the indirect agent of her exploitation. For though he may play the mares of his 'stable' against each other, drink and gamble away their money (the hard-won fruits of their direct exploitation by the white man), beat them, and call them names, it will never qualify him as a real man. The *real* man, as they both know, is The Man. He alone can confer legitimacy on either the black male or the black female. And again, as in his Wife–Whore triangle, he keeps both the Pimp and the Whore dangling, fighting with him *through each other*. Most of the tensions of these overlapping triangles appear in the following short quote by a black woman addressed to her man:

Of course you will say, 'How can I love you and want to be with you when I come home and you're looking like a slob? Why, white women never open the door for their husbands the way you black bitches do.'

I should guess not, you ignorant man. Why should they be in such a state when they've got maids like me to do everything for them? There is no screaming at the kids for her, no standing over the hot stove; everything is done for her and whether her man loves her or not, he provides ... *provides* ... do you hear that, nigger? PROVIDES!

Gail A. Stokes in 'Black Woman to Black Man',
Liberator, December, 1968

But it is not only the black man's relation to black women that is corrupted by his preoccupation with the white man. For though the black woman may give her last dollar to buy the black man a drink, *her* real involvement, too, is with the white man. Here is The Infidel speaking, from Cleaver's 'Allegory of the Black Eunuchs':

Ever since then I always believed that marrying a white man, to a black woman, is like adding the final star to her crown. It's the apex of achievement in her eyes and in the eyes of her sisters. Look at how many family black celebrities marry white men. All of the Negro women who are not celebrities wish they were so that they too, could marry white men. Whitey is their dream boy. When they kiss you, it ain't really you they're kissing. They close their eyes and picture their white dream boy. Listen to the grapevine ... Jesus Christ the pure is the black woman's psychic bridegroom. You will learn before you die that during coition and at the moment of her orgasm, the black woman, in the first throes of her spasm, shouts out the name of Jesus. 'Oh Jesus, I'm coming!' she shouts to him. And to you it will hurt. It will be like a knife in your heart. It will be the same as if your woman, during orgasm, calls out the name of some sneaky cat who lives down the block.

Thus the black woman has as much contempt for the black man as he has for her – a *real* man could elevate her through marriage, by virtue of his superior class. She can't respect the black man, because she knows he has no power. The white man at least 'provides' for his women, and doesn't beat them. The white man is civil, kind, and polite at all times. She doesn't see that it is in his interests to be: that way neither the Pimp nor the Whore will suspect that their Polite White Customer is responsible for both their destructions.

Thus, the All-American Family is predicated on the existence of the black ghetto Whorehouse. The rape of the black community in America makes possible the existence of the family structure of the larger white community, just as sexual prostitution in general maintains the respectable middle-class family. The black community is the outgroup that supplies the sexual needs of the white human family, keeping it functioning. And *that's* why there is no family solidity in the ghetto.

The way this sex/race system is so often recreated in miniature in private life reveals the depth of the problem. The individual white household is sustained by the lifelong domestic, as well as sexual, exploitation of individual black women. Or, the average ghetto youth does some pimping or even whoring as a matter of course, his value as a 'man' measured by the way he is able to command his bitches – and how many he can command at once. He becomes a master of the smooth line, of doubletalk. If he is able to string along a white 'chick', this is an added notch on his belt – for it's a direct blow to the white man (Father). This explains the frequent pairing of the white whore with the black pimp: the white woman (Mother) is degraded to whore along with the black woman, a direct slap at the white man. She is the Father's most precious property, now sold back to him as damaged merchandise. As for the white whore herself – in those few cases where it was a matter of choice – she has expressed the ultimate in masochism. She becomes totally the prey of the white man, rubbing his nose in her acquiescence to the extreme humiliation: a black pimp.

II
'BLACK MANHOOD'

What is the attitude of the militant black community to this psychosexual degradation that is racism? I have stated that the black male has three choices in reacting to the white male's power over him.

(1) He can submit on the terms set up by the white male (at best to become a black celebrity – comedian, athlete, or musician – or a member of the black bourgeoisie).

(2) He can refuse the identification altogether, with all the consequences of being defined as less than 'a man' (the ravaged ghetto youth I have described).

(3) He can try to revolt and overthrow the Father, which *may* include stealing that power position for himself (political organization for revolution, especially the recent militance).

The black movement has chosen the third alternative, by far the healthiest. But how does it plan to accomplish this? One way is to unite with the white forces that are also attempting the same thing.[4] The Family once again: the white male left is the weakling Legitimate Son. The black male is the tough guy Bastard Brother, the illegitimate son wanting a chance at that power. The Half-Brothers have made a deal: the disinherited Brother's street 'smarts' and raw strength of discontent to aid the pampered neurotic Legitimate Son, in exchange for tactics, rhetoric, and, above all, for a promise of a portion of that son's birthright when he attains the throne. What the two brothers are really talking about is not justice and equality but (male) power.

And who is Little Sister? White women on the Left are allowed to tag along, occasionally, if they do the dirty work; but

4. Here, and throughout the chapter, I am assuming the position of the Black Panther Party as representative of Black Power, though I am well aware that the BPP has violent disputes with other Black Power groups over many things.

more often they get put down, and left out ('pests,' with their constant demands for inclusion, throwing tantrums at any little 'male chauvinist' remark). The Sister fools herself, identifying so strongly with Big Brother that she actually at times begins to believe herself just like him. She finds it harder and harder to identify with that dimming mass of ordinary women out there (Mother) whom she must kill in herself in order to win Big Brother's approval. He encourages her in this. He knows illusions of her coming power will make her more docile in the long run. She can be useful, especially in getting at the Father.

Moreover, the Brothers have made a blood pact: you give me your chicks (the Bastard Son fulfils his fantasies on Little Sister while His Lordship pretends not to notice), and I'll give you mine (the white boy gets his first real screw while the bastard brother snickers).

And the black sister? Black male militants, going for the 'legit' this time, are reordering their sexuality to conform with the going model. Attempts are now being made to institute the family in the black community, to transform the black community from Whorehouse for the white family to Black Family. The black woman is being converted from her previous role, Whore, to Revered-Black-Queen-Mother-of-My-Children. Thus, the Bastard Son has assumed the role of Father within his own community in anticipation of his coming power. Here is a much-circulated poster, tacked up in an East Village store window:

BLACK GOLD
[a large formidable profile of a black woman in an Afro]

I AM THE BLACK WOMAN, MOTHER OF CIVILIZATION, QUEEN OF THE UNIVERSE. THROUGH ME THE BLACK MAN PRODUCES HIS NATION.

If he does not protect his woman he will not produce a good nation.

It is my duty to teach and train the young, who are the future of the nation.

I teach my children the language, history, and culture when they are very young.

I teach them to love and respect their father, who works hard so that they may have adequate food, clothing, and shelter.

I care and make our home comfortable for my husband.

I reflect his love to the children as the moon reflects the light from the sun to the earth.

I sit and talk with my husband to work out the daily problems and necessities of running a stable and peaceful household.

The best that I can give my nation is strong, healthy, intelligent children who will grow to be the leaders of tomorrow.

I'm always aware that the true worth of a nation is reflected through the respect and protection of the woman, so I carry myself in a civilized manner at all times, and teach my children to do the same.

I am the Black Woman.

But such a transformation, when it succeeds, is based on fantasy, for as long as the white man is still in power, he has the privilege to define the black community as he chooses – they are dependent on him for their very survival – and the psychosexual consequences of this inferior definition must continue to operate. Thus the concept of the Dignified Black Family rarely penetrates beyond the circles of the Copycat Bourgeoisie or the True Believer Revolutionaries. Indeed, one would have to believe fanatically in the Revolution to fight off the mind sets resulting from the present sex/race system; one could embrace such a foreign structure only through steadfast visionary anticipation of a different world. That hard-core ghetto youth aren't eager to put such a family structure into practice is understandable: daily they are at the mercy of the real sexual needs of the White Family; they can't afford not to live with their unpleasant reality or to forget for a moment who has the power. In this respect black revolutionaries are as dangerous as a small band of Nat Turners trying to institute marriage in the slave quarters in anticipation of the coming rebellion. And, all exhortations to the contrary, even the revolutionaries have a hard time purging themselves of the sex/race psychology, finding themselves still irresistibly drawn to the 'white she-devils'. For it lies too deep in their psyches, backed up by the day-to-day realities of power. Here is Cleaver battling with himself:

One day I saw in a magazine a picture of the white woman who had flirted with [and thus caused the death of] Emmett Till. While looking at the picture, I felt a little tension in the center of my chest I experience when a woman appeals to me. I looked at the picture again and again and in spite of everything and against my will and my hate for the woman and everything she represented, she appealed to me. I flew into a rage at myself, at America, at white women, at the history that had placed those tensions of lust and desire in my chest. Two days later I had a 'nervous breakdown'.

Cleaver's greatest virtue as a writer is his honesty. In *Soul on Ice* we have the psychology of the black man, particularly the consuming love/hate for the 'Ogre' (white woman). In fact Cleaver's development contains most of the ambivalences we have described. We are given some idea of what his previous attitude towards (black) women was before he here falls in love with a (white) woman:

I even respect you behind your back. I have a bad habit, when speaking of women while only men are present, of referring to women as bitches. This bitch this and that bitch that, you know. A while back I was speaking of you to a couple of cutthroats and I said, 'this bitch . . .' And I felt very ashamed of myself about that. I passed judgement upon myself and suffered spiritually for days afterward. This may seem insignificant, but I attach great importance to it because of the chain of thought kicked off by it. I care about you, am concerned about you, which is all very new for, and a sharp departure from, Eldridge X.

('Prelude to Love—Three Letters')

In general, in these letters, originally written to San Francisco lawyer Beverly Axelrod, Cleaver attempts to rid himself of all the smooth talk, the clever come-on that is the trademark of the black man. He is not always successful. One senses that he has to fight with himself; he catches himself just in time (almost too cleverly) by admitting what he is doing: 'NOW TURN THE RECORD OVER AND PLAY THE OTHER SIDE: I have tried to mislead you. I am not humble at all.' But when Beverly expresses cynicism about his love, he assures her elaborately that she must 'open up' to him, trust him.

Beverly was right. Her female cynicism, as usual, was more than justified – she wasn't cynical *enough*. (Cleaver, to set an example, married just-black-enough Kathleen, leaving Beverly stranded. Latest pictures include an infant son.) His letters to Beverly, about as personalized and honest as probably he will ever get towards any woman, are followed by a florid letter (testimonial? doctrine?) To All Black Women From All Black Men. Its balls-and-womb imagery includes such gems as: 'Across the naked abyss of my negated masculinity, of four hundred years [!] minus my balls, we face each other today, my queen.' He reminds her that: 'Torrents of blood flow today from my crotch . . .' And finally, triumphantly: 'I have entered the den and seized my balls from the teeth of a roaring lion . . .' His pages-long incantations to the Black Womb of Africa are, to say the least, hardly the best way to go about flattering a woman.

For despite his address to Black Womanhood ('Queen-Mother-Daughter of Africa, Sister of My Soul, Black Bride of My Passion, My Eternal Love') Cleaver, in this supposed love letter, is hung up on himself, and on his 'masculinity'. There is no conception of the black woman as a human being in her own right; she is merely a buttress for his own (masculine) self-image. The same old trick in revolutionary guise: the male defining himself negatively as man-strong by distinguishing himself from woman-weak, through his control of her – like the pimp who rejects the female in himself, achieving a false sense of manhood (power) through domination of all females in his vicinity. The sexual nature of Cleaver's racial agonies is revealed in his attack on Baldwin, which is no more than the vicious attack of the Black Pimp on the Black Queen. The Queen has chosen to give up the male (power) identification altogether rather than accept the degrading sexual definition handed down by the white man, thus threatening the Pimp, who is fighting a losing battle. And if this attack weren't enough, Cleaver gives away his sexual insecurity through his superstud self-image – Norman Mailer in black. Some promotion, judging by the hysterics of his chestpounding.

The transformation of the black woman into the traditional passive female creates a useful negative backdrop against which the black male's own definition of himself as masculine (aggressive) can emerge. And in her capacity as springboard, or practice bouting-dummy, the black woman is valuable and must be 'humbly' wooed; her cooperation is important, for the black man can only be the 'man' if someone becomes the 'woman'.

118

Black women, so hip to 'lines', seem to have fallen for this one. Here is a rebuke written by another black woman in reply to the accusation of black men by Gail A. Stokes that I have quoted above. It is noted for its female antiwomanism:

Sure [black men] blunder and make mistakes, but don't we? This is normal for someone trying something new, i.e. leadership ... So how could you, Gail Stokes, scrounge up the audacity to prick the Black man's balloon! How could you dare to attempt to break his winning streak? Did it ever occur to you that it is you, in fact, who is inadequate? Check yourself, sister; a woman reflects her man.

She turns to the black man:

Black men: I too have heard your cry, ringing from within your new-found pride, and African garb. And to that cry I reply: Take your rightful place ahead of me, my love ... Yes, my Black man, you're a real man, a rare man. And in all your struggles I want you to know that I struggle only a few steps behind you, for that is my place in your life ... You are all I am here for.

She then assuages his pricked ego by assuring him of her undying loyalty to his balls:

Having your balls torn from you and still trying to be a man! Oh, those anguished moments of puberty ... those growing pains ... *Tell me how many men have been castrated only to defy that emasculation and grow new balls!* ... You need to be held and loved and told how wonderful you really are.

> Edith R. Hambrick, 'Black Woman to Black woman',
> *Liberator*, December, 1968.

(Italics hers. And notice the capitalization of the title: a warning to the sister to start toeing the line?)

But when she does toe the line, her reward will not be a personalized kind of love (as in the letters to Beverly Axelrod) but an impersonal one addressed through her to all Black Womanhood. Here is Bobby Seale from his much-published *Letter To My Wife* (like the budding poet's inscription on his girlfriend's Christmas gifts, inevitably appearing in the spring issue of the college poetry journal):

Artie Honey ...
Now if I ain't in love with you because I saw something on your face the other morning that said you were a revolutionary, then something is wrong ... What's Malik [their three-year-old son] doing? Teach

him how to serve the people by your examples, Artie ... Artie, I hope you are not being selfish and keeping this letter to yourself. Aw, I know you are reading it to the other party members ...

Why do black women, so shrewd about their men in general, settle for this patronizing, impersonal, and uninspired kind of love? Because of the triangle: as we have seen, the black woman has played Whore, used and abused by white men (her 'tricks') and black men (her 'pimps') for centuries. All this time she has looked with envy at the white woman's legitimacy and security. Now, offered that legitimacy, under whatever crude guise, she is tempted to set it up for herself, not knowing the horrors in store. The Wife is the only one who could tell her, but they are not on speaking terms. For, as we have seen, each has learned to focus her frustrations on the other. Their long antagonism makes it hard for them to trade the valuable (and painful) lessons they have learned about the Man. If they could, they might soon discover that neither Wife nor Whore grants freedom, for neither of these roles is self-determined. They might alert to Eldridge Cleaver's warning, as he anticipates his future male power, in one of his rare moments of honesty with women:

NOW TURN THE RECORD OVER AND PLAY THE OTHER SIDE: I have tried to mislead you. I am not humble at all. I have no humility and I do not fear you in the least. If I pretend to be shy, if I appear to hesitate, it is only a sham to deceive. By playing the humble part, I sucker my fellow men and seduce them of their trust. And then if it suits my advantage, I lower the boom mercilessly. I lied when I stated that I had no sense of myself. I am very well aware of my style. My vanity is as vast as the scope of a dream, my heart is that of a tyrant, my arm is the arm of the executioner. It is only the failure of my plots I fear.

6 Love

A book on radical feminism that did not deal with love would be a political failure. For love, perhaps even more than child-bearing, is the pivot of women's oppression today. I realize this has frightening implications: do we want to get rid of love?

The panic felt at any threat to love is a good clue to its political significance. Another sign that love is central to any analysis of women or sex psychology is its omission from culture itself, its relegation to 'personal life'. (And whoever heard of logic in the bedroom?) Yes, it is portrayed in novels, even metaphysics, but in them it is described, or better, re-created, not analysed. Love has never been understood, though it may have been fully experienced, and that experience communicated.

There is reason for this absence of analysis: *women and love are underpinnings. Examine them and you threaten the very structure of culture.*

The tired question 'What were women doing while men created masterpieces?' deserves more than the obvious reply: women were barred from culture, exploited in their role of mother. Or its reverse: women had no need for paintings since they created children. Love is tied to culture in much deeper ways than that. Men were thinking, writing, and creating, because women were pouring their energy into those men; women are not creating culture because they are preoccupied with love.

That women live for love and men for work is a truism. Freud was the first to attempt to ground this dichotomy in the individual psyche: the male child, sexually rejected by the first person in his attention, his mother, 'sublimates' his 'libido' – his reservoir of sexual (life) energies – into long-term projects, in the hope of gaining love in a more generalized form; thus he displaces his need for love into a need for recognition. This process does not occur as much in the female: most women never stop seeking direct warmth and approval.

There is also much truth in the clichés that 'behind every man there is a woman', and that 'women are the power behind [read: voltage in] the throne'. (Male) Culture was built on the love of women, and at their expense. Women provided the substance of those male masterpieces; and for millennia they have done the work, and suffered the costs, of one-way emotional relationships the benefits of which went to men and to the work of men. So if women are a parasitical class living off, and at the margins of, the male economy, the reverse too is true: (*male*) *culture is parasitical, feeding on the emotional strength of women without reciprocity.*

Moreover, we tend to forget that this culture is not universal, but rather sectarian, presenting only half the spectrum of experience. The very structure of culture itself, as we shall see, is saturated with the sexual polarity, as well as being in every degree run by, for, and in the interests of male society. But while the male half is termed all of culture, men have not forgotten there is a female 'emotional' half: they live it on the sly. As the result of their battle to reject the female in themselves (the Oedipus Complex as we have explained it) they are unable to take love seriously as a cultural matter; but they can't do without it altogether. Love is the underbelly of (male) culture just as love is the weak spot of every man, bent on proving his virility in that large male world of 'travel and adventure'. Women have always known how men need love, and how they deny this need. Perhaps this explains the peculiar contempt women so universally feel for men ('men are so dumb'), for they can see their men are posturing in the outside world.

I

How does this phenomenon 'love' operate?

Contrary to popular opinion, love is not altruistic. The initial attraction is based on curious admiration (more often today, envy and resentment) for the self-possession, the integrated unity, of

122

the other and a wish to become part of this Self in some way (today, read: intrude or take over), to become important to in that psychic balance. The self-containment of the other creates desire (read: a challenge); admiration (envy) of the other becomes a wish to incorporate (possess) its qualities. A clash of selves follows in which the individual attempts to fight off the growing hold over him of the other. Love is the final opening up to (or, surrender to the dominion of) the other. The lover demonstrates to the beloved how he himself would like to be treated. ('I tried so hard to make him fall in love with me that I fell in love with him myself.') Thus love is the height of selfishness: the self attempts to enrich itself through the absorption of another being. Love is being psychically wide-open to another. It is a situation of total emotional vulnerability. Therefore it must be not only the incorporation of the other, but an *exchange* of selves. Anything short of a mutual exchange will hurt one or the other party.

There is nothing inherently destructive about this process. A little healthy selfishness would be a refreshing change. Love between two equals would be an enrichment, each enlarging himself through the other: instead of being one, locked in the cell of himself with only his own experience and view, he could participate in the existence of another – an extra window on the world. This accounts for the bliss that successful lovers experience: lovers are temporarily freed from the burden of isolation that every individual bears.

But bliss in love is seldom the case: for every successful contemporary love experience, for every short period of enrichment, there are ten destructive love experiences, post-love 'downs' of much longer duration – often resulting in the destruction of the individual, or at least an emotional cynicism that makes it difficult or impossible ever to love again. Why should this be so, if it is not actually inherent in the love process itself?

Let's talk about love in its destructive guise – and why it gets that way, referring once more to the work of Theodor Reik. Reik's concrete observation brings him closer than many better minds to understanding the *process* of 'falling in love', but he is off insofar as he confuses love as it exists in our present society with love itself. He notes that love is a reaction formation, a cycle of envy, hostility, and possessiveness: he sees that it is preceded by dissatisfaction with oneself, a yearning for something better, created by a discrepancy between the ego and the ego-ideal; that the bliss love produces is due to the resolution of this tension by the substitution, in place of one's own ego-ideal, of the other; and finally that love fades 'because the other can't live up to your high ego-ideal any more than you could, and the judgement will be the harsher the higher are the claims on oneself'. Thus in Reik's view love wears down just as it wound up: dissatisfaction with oneself (whoever heard of falling in love the week one is leaving for Europe?) leads to astonishment at the other person's self-containment; to envy; to hostility; to possessive love; and back again through exactly the same process. This is the love process *today*. But why must it be this way?

Many, for example Denis de Rougemont in *Love in the Western World*, have tried to draw a distinction between romantic 'falling in love' with its 'false reciprocity which disguises a twin narcissism' (the Pagan Eros) and an unselfish love for the other person as that person really is (the Christian Agape). De Rougemont attributes the morbid passion of Tristan and Iseult (romantic love) to a vulgarization of specific mystical and religious currents in Western civilization.

I submit that love is essentially a much simpler phenomenon – it becomes complicated, corrupted, or obstructed by *an unequal balance of power*. We have seen that love demands a mutual vulnerability or it turns destructive: the destructive effects of love occur only in a context of inequality. But because sexual inequality has remained a constant – however its *degree* may have varied – the corruption 'romantic' love became characteristic of love between the sexes. (It remains for us only to explain why it has steadily increased in Western countries since the medieval period, which we shall attempt to do in the following chapter.)

How does the sex class system based on the unequal power distribution of the biological family affect love between the sexes? In discussing Freudianism, we have gone into the psychic structuring of the individual within the family and how this organization of personality must be different for the male and the female because of their very different relationships to the mother. At present the insular interdependency of the mother/ child relationship forces both male and female children into anxiety about losing the mother's love, on which they depend for physical survival. When later (Erich Fromm notwithstanding) the child learns that the mother's love is conditional, to be rewarded the child in return for approved behaviour (that is, behaviour in line with the mother's own values and personal ego gratification – for she is free to mould the child 'creatively', however she happens to define that), the child's anxiety turns into desperation. This, coinciding with the sexual rejection of the male child by the mother, causes, as we have seen, a schizophrenia in the boy between the emotional and the physical, and in the girl, the mother's rejection, occurring for different reasons, produces an insecurity about her identity in general, creating a lifelong need for approval. (Later her lover replaces her father as a grantor of the necessary surrogate identity – she sees everything through his eyes.) Here originates the hunger for love that later sends both sexes searching in one person after the other for a state of ego security. But because of the early rejection, to the degree that it occurred, the male will be terrified of committing himself, of 'opening up' and then being smashed. How this affects his sexuality we have seen: to the degree that a woman is like his mother, the incest taboo operates to restrain his total sexual/emotional commitment; for him to feel safely the kind of total response he first felt for his mother, which was rejected, he must degrade this woman so as to distinguish her from the mother. This behaviour reproduced on a larger scale explains many cultural phenomena, including perhaps the ideal love-worship of chivalric times, the forerunner of modern romanticism.

Romantic idealization is partially responsible, at least on the part of men, for a peculiar characteristic of 'falling' in love: the change takes place in the lover almost independently of the character of the love object. Occasionally the lover, though beside himself, sees with another rational part of his faculties that, objectively speaking, the one he loves isn't worth all this blind devotion; but he is helpless to act on this, 'a slave to love'.

More often he fools himself entirely. But others can see what is happening ('How on earth he could love her is beyond me!'). This idealization occurs much less frequently on the part of women, as is borne out by Reik's clinical studies. A man must idealize one woman over the rest in order to justify his descent to a lower caste. Women have no such reason to idealize men – in fact, when one's life depends on one's ability to 'psych' men out, such idealization may actually be dangerous – though a fear of male power in general may carry over into relationships with individual men, appearing to be the same phenomenon. But though women know to be inauthentic this male 'falling in love', all women, in one way or another, require proof of it from men before they can allow themselves to love (genuinely, in their case) in return. For this idealization process acts to equalize artificially the two parties, a minimum precondition for the development of an uncorrupted love – we have seen that love requires a mutual vulnerability that is impossible to achieve in an unequal power situation. *Thus 'falling in love' is no more than the process of alteration of male vision – through idealization, mystification, glorification – that renders void the woman's class inferiority.*

However, the woman knows that this idealization, which she works so hard to produce, is a lie, and that it is only a matter of time before he 'sees through her'. Her life is a hell, vacillating between an all-consuming need for male love and approval to raise her from her class subjection, to persistent feelings of inauthenticity when she does achieve his love. Thus her whole identity hangs in the balance of her love life. She is allowed to love herself only if a man finds her worthy of love.

But if we could eliminate the political context of love between the sexes, would we not have some degree of idealization remaining in the love process itself? I think so. For the process occurs in the same manner whoever the love choice: the lover 'opens up' to the other. Because of this fusion of egos, in which each sees and cares about the other as a new self, the beauty/character of the beloved, perhaps hidden to outsiders under layers of defences, is revealed. 'I wonder what she sees in him', then, means not only, 'She is a fool, blinded with romanticism', but,

'Her love has lent her x-ray vision. Perhaps we are missing something.' (Note that this phrase is most commonly used about women. The equivalent phrase about *men's* slavery to love is more often something like, 'She has him wrapped around her finger', she has him so 'snowed' that he is the last one to see through her.) Increased sensitivity to the real, if hidden, values of the other, however, is not 'blindness' or 'idealization' but is, in fact, deeper vision. It is only the *false* idealization we have described above that is responsible for the destruction. Thus it is not the process of love itself that is at fault, but its *political*, i.e. unequal *power* context: the who, why, when and where of it is what makes it now such a holocaust.

II

But sophisms about love are only one more symptom of its diseased state. (As one female patient of Reik so astutely put it, 'Men take love either too seriously or not seriously enough.') Let's look at it more concretely, as we now experience it in its corrupted form. Once again we shall quote from the Reikian Confessional. For if Reik's work has any value it is where he might least suspect, i.e. in his 'trivial feminine' urge to 'gossip'. Here he is, justifying himself (one supposes his Superego is troubling him):

A has-been like myself must always be somewhere and working on something. Why should I not occupy myself with those small questions that are not often posed and yet perhaps can be answered? The 'petites questions' have a legitimate place beside the great and fundamental problems of psychoanalysis.

It takes moral courage to write about certain things, as for example about a game that little girls play in the intervals between classes. Is such a theme really worthy of a *serious* psychoanalyst who has passed his 77th year? (Italics mine)

And he reminds himself: 'But in psychoanalysis there are no unimportant thoughts; there are only thoughts that pretend to be unimportant in order not to be told.' Thus he rationalizes what in fact may be the only valuable contribution of his work. Here are his patients of both sexes speaking for themselves about their love lives:

WOMEN:

Later on he called me a sweet girl . . . I didn't answer . . . what could I say? . . . but I knew I was not a sweet girl at all and that he sees me as someone I'm not.

No man can love a girl the way a girl loves a man.

I can go a long time without sex, but not without love.

It's like H_2O instead of water.

I sometimes think that all men are sex-crazy and sex-starved. All they can think about when they are with a girl is going to bed with her.

Have I nothing to offer this man but this body?

I took off my dress and my bra and stretched myself out on his bed and waited. For an instant I thought of myself as an animal of sacrifice on the altar.

I don't understand the feelings of men. My husband has me. Why does he need other women? What have they got that I haven't got?

Believe me, if all wives whose husbands had affairs left them, we would only have divorced women in this country.

After my husband had quite a few affairs, I flirted with the fantasy of taking a lover. Why not? What's sauce for the gander is sauce for the goose . . . But I was stupid as a goose: I didn't have it in me to have an extramarital affair.

I asked several people whether men also sometimes cry themselves to sleep. I don't believe it.

MEN (for further illustration, see *Screw*):

It's not true that only the external appearance of a woman matters. The underwear is also important.

It's not difficult to make it with a girl. What's difficult is to make an end of it.

The girl asked me whether I cared for her mind. I was tempted to answer I cared more for her behind.

'Are you going already?' she said when she opened her eyes. It was a bedroom cliché whether I left after an hour or after two days.

Perhaps it's necessary to fool the woman and to pretend you love her. But why should I fool myself?

When she is sick, she turns me off. But when I'm sick she feels sorry for me and is more affectionate than usual.

128

It's not enough for my wife that I have to hear her talking all the time – blah, blah, blah. She also expects me to hear what she is saying.

Simone de Beauvoir said it: 'The word love has by no means the same sense for both sexes, and this is one cause of the serious misunderstandings which divide them.' Above I have illustrated some of the traditional differences between men and women in love that come up so frequently in parlour discussions of the 'double standard', where it is generally agreed: that women are monogamous, better at loving, possessive, 'clinging', more interested in (highly involved) 'relationships' than in sex per se, and they confuse affection with sexual desire. That men are interested in nothing but a screw (Wham, bam, thank you M'am!), or else romanticize the woman ridiculously; that once sure of her, they become notorious philanderers, never satisfied; that they mistake sex for emotion. All this bears out what we have discussed – the difference in the psychosexual organizations of the two sexes, determined by the first relationship to the mother.

I draw three conclusions based on these differences:

(1) That men can't love. (Male hormones?? Women traditionally expect and accept an emotional invalidism in men that they would find intolerable in a woman.)

(2) That women's 'clinging' behaviour is necessitated by their objective social situation.

(3) That this situation has not changed significantly from what it ever was.

Men can't love. We have seen why it is that men have difficulty loving and that while men may love, they usually 'fall in love' – with their own projected image. Most often they are pounding down a woman's door one day, and thoroughly disillusioned with her the next; but it is rare for women to leave men, and then it is usually for more than ample reason.

It is dangerous to feel sorry for one's oppressor – women are especially prone to this failing – but I am tempted to do it in this case. Being unable to love is hell. This is the way it proceeds: as soon as the man feels any pressure from the other partner to commit himself, he panics and may react in one of several ways:

(1) He may rush out and screw ten other women to prove that the first woman has no hold over him. If she accepts this, he may continue to see her on this basis. The other women verify his (false) freedom; periodic arguments about them keep his panic at bay. But the women are a paper tiger, for nothing very deep could be happening with them anyway: he is balancing them against each other so that none of them can get much of him. Many smart women, recognizing this to be only a safety valve on their man's anxiety, give him 'a long leash'. For the real issue under all the fights about other women is that the man is unable to commit himself.

(2) He may consistently exhibit unpredictable behaviour, standing her up frequently, being indefinite about the next date, telling her that 'my work comes first', or offering a variety of other excuses. That is, though he senses her anxiety, he refuses to reassure her in any way, or even to recognize her anxiety as legitimate. For he *needs* her anxiety as a steady reminder that he is still free, that the door is not entirely closed.

(3) When he *is* forced into (an uneasy) commitment, he makes her pay for it: by ogling other women in her presence, by comparing her unfavourably to past girlfriends or movie stars, by snide reminders in front of friends that she is his 'ball and chain', by calling her a 'nag', a 'bitch', 'a shrew', or by suggesting that if he were only a bachelor he would be a lot better off. His ambivalence about women's 'inferiority' comes out: by being committed to one, he has somehow made the hated female identification, which he now must repeatedly deny if he is to maintain his self-respect in the (male) community. This steady derogation is not entirely put on: for in fact every other girl suddenly does look a lot better, he can't help feeling he has missed something – and, naturally, his woman is to blame. For he has never given up the search for the ideal; she has forced him to resign from it. Probably he will go to his grave feeling cheated, never realizing that there isn't much difference between one woman and the other, that it is the loving that *creates* the difference.

There are many variations of straining at the bit. Many men go from one casual thing to another, getting out every time it begins to get hot. And yet to live without love in the end proves intolerable to men just as it does to women. The question that remains for every normal male is, then, *how do I get someone to love me without her demanding an equal commitment in return?*

*

Women's 'clinging' behaviour is required by the objective social situation. The female *response* to such a situation of male hysteria at any prospect of mutual commitment was the development of subtle methods of manipulation, to force as much commitment as *could* be forced from men. Over the centuries strategies have been devised, tested, and passed on from mother to daughter in secret tetê-à-têtes, passed around at 'kaffee-klatsches' ('I never understand what it is women spend so much time talking about!'), or, in recent times, via the telephone. These are not trivial gossip sessions at all (as women prefer men to believe), but desperate strategies for survival. More real brilliance goes into one one-hour coed telephone dialogue about men than into that same coed's four years of college study, or for that matter, than into most male political manoeuvres. It is no wonder, then, that even the few women without 'family obligations' always arrive exhausted at the starting line of any serious endeavour. It takes one's major energy for the best portion of one's creative years to 'make a good catch', and a good part of the rest of one's life to 'hold' that catch. ('To be in love can be a full-time job for a woman, like that of a profession for a man.') Women who choose to drop out of this race are choosing a life without love, something that, as we have seen, most *men* don't have the courage to do.

But unfortunately the Manhunt is characterized by an emotional urgency beyond this simple desire for return commitment. It is compounded by the very class reality that produced the male inability to love in the first place. In a male-run society that defines women as an inferior and parasitical class, a woman who does not achieve male approval in some form is doomed. To legitimate her existence, a woman must be *more* than woman,

she must continually search for an out from her inferior definition;[1] and men are the only ones in a position to bestow on her
this state of grace. But because the woman is rarely allowed to
realize herself through activity in the larger (male) society – and
when she is, she is seldom granted the recognition she deserves –
it becomes easier to try for the recognition of one man than of
many; and in fact this is exactly the choice most women make.
Thus once more the phenomenon of love, good in itself, is
corrupted by its class context: women must have love not only
for healthy reasons but actually to validate their existence.

In addition, the continued *economic* dependence of women
makes a situation of healthy love between equals impossible.
Women today still live under a system of patronage: with few
exceptions, they have the choice, not between either freedom or
marriage, but between being either public or private property.
Women who merge with a member of the ruling class can at
least hope that some of his privilege will, so to speak, rub off. But
women without men are in the same situation as orphans: they
are a helpless sub-class lacking the protection of the powerful.
This is the antithesis of freedom when they are still (negatively)
defined by a class situation: for now they are in a situation of
magnified vulnerability.

To participate in one's subjection by choosing one's master
often gives the illusion of free choice; but in reality a woman is
never free to choose love without ulterior motives. For her at the
present time, the two things, love and status, must remain
inextricably intertwined.

Now assuming that a woman does not lose sight of these
fundamental factors of her condition when she loves, she will

1. Thus the peculiar situation that women never object to the insulting of
women as a class, *as long as* they individually are excepted. The worst insult
for a woman is that she is 'just like a woman', i.e. no better; the highest
compliment that she has the brains, talent, dignity, or strength of a man. In
fact, like every member of an oppressed class, she herself participates in the
insulting of others like herself, hoping thereby to make it obvious that *she*
as an individual is above their behaviour. Thus women as a class are set
against each other ['Divide and Conquer'], the 'other woman' believing
that the wife is a 'bitch' who 'doesn't understand him', and the wife believing that the other woman is an 'opportunist' who is 'taking advantage' of
him – while the culprit himself sneaks away free.

never be able to love gratuitously, but only in exchange for security:

(1) the emotional security which, we have seen, she is justified in demanding;

(2) the emotional identity which she should be able to find through work and recognition, but which she is denied – thus forcing her to seek her definition through a man;

(3) the economic class security that, in this society, is attached to her ability to 'hook' a man.

Two of these three demands are invalid conditions for love, but are imposed on it, weighing it down.

Thus, in their precarious political situation, women can't afford the luxury of spontaneous love. It is much too dangerous. The love and approval of men is all-important. To love thoughtlessly, before one has ensured return commitment, would endanger that approval. Here is Reik: 'It finally became clear during psychoanalysis that the patient was afraid that if she should show a man she loved him, he would consider her inferior and leave her.' For once a woman plunges in emotionally, she will be helpless to play the necessary games: her love would come first, demanding expression. To pretend a coolness she does not feel, *then*, would be too painful, and further, it would be pointless: she would be cutting off her nose to spite her face, for freedom to love is what she was aiming for. But in order to guarantee such a commitment, she *must* restrain her emotions, she *must* play games. For, as we have seen, men do not commit themselves to mutual openness and vulnerability until they are forced to.

How does she then go about forcing this commitment from the male? One of her most potent weapons is sex – she can work him up to a state of physical torment with a variety of games: by denying his need, by teasing it, by giving and taking back, by jealousy, and so forth. A woman under analysis wonders why: 'There are few women who never ask themselves on certain occasions "How hard should I make it for a man?" I think no man is troubled with questions of this kind. He perhaps asks himself only, "When will she give in?"' Men are right when they complain that women lack discrimination, that they seldom love a man for his individual traits but rather for what he has to offer (his class), that they are calculating, that they use sex to gain other ends, etc. For in fact women are in no position to love freely. If a woman is lucky enough to find 'a decent guy' to love her and support her, she is doing well – and usually will be grateful enough to return his love. About the only discrimination women *are* able to exercise is the choice between the men who have chosen them, or a playing off of one male, one power, against the other. But *provoking* a man's interest, and *snaring* his commitment once he has expressed that interest, is not exactly self-determination.

Now what happens after she has finally hooked her man, after he has fallen in love with her and will do anything? She has a new set of problems. Now she can release the vice, open her net, and examine what she has caught. Usually she is disappointed. It is nothing she would have bothered with were *she* a man. It is usually way below her level. (Check this out sometime: Talk to a few of those mousy wives.) 'He may be a poor thing, but at least I've got a man of my own' is usually more the way she feels. But at least now she can drop her act. For the first time it is safe to love – now she must try like hell to catch up to him emotionally, to really mean what she has pretended all along. Often she is troubled by worries that he will find her out. She feels like an imposter. She is haunted by fears that he doesn't love the 'real' her – and usually she is right. ('She wanted to marry a man with whom she could be as bitchy as she really is.')

This is just about when she discovers that love and marriage mean a different thing for a male than they do for her: though men in general believe women in general to be inferior, every man has reserved a special place in his mind for the one woman he will elevate above the rest by virtue of association with himself. Until now the woman, out in the cold, begged for his approval, dying to clamber onto this clean well-lighted place. But once there, she realizes that she was elevated above other women not in recognition of her real value, but only because she matched nicely his store-bought pedestal. Probably he doesn't even know who she is (if indeed by this time she herself knows).

He has let her in not because he genuinely loved her, but only because she played so well into his preconceived fantasies. Though she knew his love to be false, since she herself engineered it, she can't help feeling contempt for him. But she is afraid, at first, to reveal her true self, for then perhaps even that false love would go. And finally she understands that for him, too, marriage had all kinds of motivations that had nothing to do with love. She was merely the one closest to his fantasy image: she has been named Most Versatile Actress for the multi-role of Alter Ego, Mother of My Children, Housekeeper, Cook, Companion, in *his* play. She has been bought to fill an empty space in his life; but her life is nothing.

So she has not saved herself from being like other women. She is lifted out of that class only because she now is an appendage of a member of the master class; and he cannot associate with her unless he raises her status. But she has not been freed, she has been promoted to 'housenigger', she has been elevated only to be used in a different way. She feels cheated. She has gotten not love and recognition, but possessorship and control. This is when she is transformed from Blushing Bride to Bitch, a change that, no matter how universal and predictable, still leaves the individual husband perplexed. ('You're not the girl I married.')

*

The situation of women has not changed significantly from what it ever was. For the past fifty years women have been in a double bind about love: under the guise of a 'sexual revolution', presumed to have occurred ('Oh, c'mon Baby, where have you *been?* Haven't you heard of the sexual revolution?'), women have been persuaded to shed their armour. The modern woman is in horror of being thought a bitch, where her grandmother expected that to happen as the natural course of things. Men, too, in her grandmother's time, expected that any self-respecting woman would keep *them* waiting, would play all the right games without shame: a woman who did not guard her own interests in this way was not respected. It was out in the open.

But the rhetoric of the sexual revolution, if it brought no improvements for women, proved to have great value for men. By convincing women that the usual female games and demands were despicable, unfair, prudish, old-fashioned, puritanical, and self-destructive, a new reservoir of available females was created to expand the tight supply of goods available for traditional sexual exploitation, disarming women of even the little protection they had so painfully acquired. Women today dare not make the old demands for fear of having a whole new vocabulary, designed just for this purpose, hurled at them: 'fucked up', 'ballbreaker', 'cockteaser', 'a real drag', 'a bad trip' – to be a 'groovy chick' is the ideal.

Even now many women know what's up and avoid the trap, preferring to be called names rather than be cheated out of the little they can hope for from men (for it is still true that even the hippest want an 'old lady' who is relatively unused). But more and more women are sucked, only to find out too late, and bitterly, that the traditional female games had a point; they are shocked to catch themselves at thirty complaining in a vocabulary dangerously close to the old I've-been-used-men-are-wolves-they're-all-bastards variety. Eventually they are forced to acknowledge the old-wives' truth: a fair and generous woman is (at best) respected, but seldom loved. Here is a description, still valid today, of the 'emancipated' woman – in this case a Greenwich Village artist of the thirties – from *Mosquitoes*, an early Faulkner novel:

She had always had trouble with her men . . . Sooner or later they always ran out on her . . . Men she recognized as having potentialities all passed through a violent but temporary period of interest which ceased as abruptly as it began, without leaving even the lingering threads of mutually remembered incidence, like those brief thunderstorms of August that threaten and dissolve for no apparent reason without producing any rain.

At times she speculated with almost masculine detachment on the reason for this. She always tried to keep their relationships on the plane which the men themselves seemed to prefer – certainly no woman would, and few women could, demand less of their men than she did. She never made arbitrary demands on their time, never caused them to wait for her nor to see her home at inconvenient hours, never made them fetch and carry for her; she fed them and flattered herself that she was a good listener. And yet – She thought of the women she knew; how all of them had at least one obviously entranced male; she thought of the women she had observed; how they seemed to acquire a man at will, and if he failed to stay acquired, how readily they replaced him.

Women of high ideals who believed emancipation possible, women who tried desperately to rid themselves of feminine 'hangups', to cultivate what they believed to be the greater directness, honesty, and generosity of men, were badly fooled. They found that no one appreciated their intelligent conversation, their high aspirations, their great sacrifices to avoid developing the personalities of their mothers. For much as men were glad to enjoy their wit, their style, their sex, and their candlelight suppers, they always ended up marrying the Bitch, and then, to top it all off, came back to complain of what a horror she was. 'Emancipated' women found out that the honesty, generosity, and camaraderie of men was a lie: men were all too glad to use them and then sell them out, in the name of *true* friendship. ('I respect and like you a great deal, but let's be reasonable . . .' And then there are the men who take her out to discuss Simone de Beauvoir, leaving their wives at home with the diapers.) 'Emancipated' women found out that men were far from 'good guys' to be emulated; they found out that by imitating male sexual patterns (the roving eye, the search for the ideal, the emphasis on physical attraction, etc.), they were not only not achieving liberation, they were falling into something much worse than what they had given up. They were *imitating*. And they had inoculated themselves with a sickness that had not even sprung from their own psyches. They found that their new 'cool' was shallow and meaningless, that their emotions were drying up behind it that, they were ageing and becoming decadent: they feared they were losing their ability to love. They had gained nothing by imitating men: shallowness and callowness, and they were not so good at it either, because somewhere inside it still went against the grain.

Thus women who had decided not to marry because they were wise enough to look around and see where it led found that it was marry or nothing. Men gave their commitment only for a price: share (shoulder) his life, stand on his pedestal, become his appendage, or else. Or else – be consigned forever to that limbo of 'chicks' who mean nothing, certainly not what mother meant. Be the 'other woman' for the rest of one's life, used to provoke his wife, prove his virility and/or his independence, discussed by his friends as his latest 'interesting' conquest. (For even if she had given up those terms and what they stood for, no male had.) Yes, love means an entirely different thing to men than to women: it means ownership and control; it means jealousy, where he never exhibited it before – when she might have wanted him to (who cares if she is broke or raped until she officially belongs to him: then he is a raging dynamo, a veritable cyclone, because his property, his ego extension have been threatened); it means a growing lack of interest, coupled with a roving eye. Who needs it?

Sadly, women do. Here are Reik's patients once more: 'She sometimes has delusions of not being persecuted by men anymore. At those times of her nonpersecution mania she is very depressed.' And: 'All men are selfish, brutal and inconsiderate – and I wish I could find one.' We have seen that a woman needs love, first, for its natural enriching function, and second, for social and economic reasons which have nothing to do with love. To deny her need is to put herself in an extra-vulnerable spot socially and economically, as well as to destroy her emotional equilibrium, which, unlike most men's, is basically healthy. Are men worth that? Decidedly no. Most women feel that to do such tailspins for a man would be to add insult to injury. They go on as before, making the best of a bad situation. If it gets *too* bad, they head for a (usually male) shrink:

A young woman patient was once asked during a psychoanalytic consultation whether she preferred to see a man or woman psychoanalyst. Without the slightest hesitation she said, 'A woman psychoanalyst because I am too eager for the approval of a man.'

7   The Culture of Romance

So far we have not distinguished 'romance' from love. For there are no two kinds of love, one healthy (dull) and one not (painful) ('My dear, what you need is a mature love relationship. Get over this romantic nonsense'), but only less-than-love or daily agony. When love takes place in a power context, everyone's 'love life' must be affected. Because power and love don't make it together.

So when we talk about romantic love we mean love corrupted by its power context – the sex class system – into a diseased form of love that then in turn reinforces this sex class system. We have seen that the psychological dependence of women upon men is created by continuing real economic and social oppression. However, in the modern world the economic and social bases of the oppression are no longer *alone* enough to maintain it. So the apparatus of romanticism is hauled in. (Looks like we'll have to help her out. Boys!)

Romanticism develops in proportion to the liberation of women from their biology. As civilization advances and the biological bases of sex class crumble, male supremacy must shore itself up with artificial institutions, or exaggerations of previous institutions, e.g., where previously the family had a loose, permeable form, it now tightens and rigidifies into the patriarchal nuclear family. Or, where formerly women had been held openly in contempt, now they are elevated to states of mock worship.[1] Romanticism is a cultural tool of male power to keep women from knowing their conditions. It is especially needed – and therefore

1. Gallantry has been commonly defined as 'excessive attention to women without serious purpose', but the purpose is very serious: through a false flattery, to keep women from awareness of their lower-class condition.

strongest – in Western countries with the highest rate of industrialization. Today, with technology enabling women to break out of their roles for good – it was a near miss in the early twentieth century – romanticism is at an all-time high.

How does romanticism work as a cultural tool to reinforce sex class? Let us examine its components, refined over centuries, and the modern methods of its diffusion – cultural techniques so sophisticated and penetrating that even men are damaged by them.

(1) *Eroticism.* A prime component of romanticism is eroticism. All animal needs (the affection of a kitten that has never seen heat) for love and warmth are channelled into genital sex: people must never touch others of the same sex, and may touch those of the opposite sex only when preparing for a genital sexual encounter ('a pass'). Isolation from others makes people starved for physical affection; and if the only kind they can get is genital sex, that's soon what they crave. In this state of hypersensitivity the least sensual stimulus has an exaggerated effect, enough to inspire everything from schools of master painting to Rock 'n' Roll. Thus *eroticism is the concentration of sexuality – often into highly-charged objects ('Chantilly Lace') – signifying the displacement of other social/affection needs on to genital sex.* To be plain old needy-for-affection makes one a 'drip', to need a kiss is embarrassing, unless it is an erotic kiss; only 'sex' is OK, in fact it proves one's mettle. Virility and sexual performance become confused with social worth.[2]

Constant erotic stimulation of male sexuality coupled with its forbidden release through most normal channels are designed to encourage men to look at women as only things whose resistance to entrance must be overcome. For notice that this eroticism operates in only one direction. Women are the only 'love'

2. But as every woman has discovered, a man who seems to be pressuring for sex is often greatly relieved to be excused from the literal performance: his ego has been made dependent on his continuously proving himself through sexual conquest; but all he may have really wanted was the excuse to indulge in affection without the loss of manly self-respect. That men are more restrained than are women about exhibiting emotion is because, in addition to the results of the Oedipus Complex, to express tenderness to a woman is to acknowledge her equality. Unless, of course, one tempers one's tenderness – takes it back – with some evidence of domination.

objects in our society, so much so that women regard *themselves* as erotic.[3] This functions to preserve direct sex pleasure for the male, reinforcing female dependence: women can be fulfilled sexually only by vicarious identification with the man who enjoys them. Thus eroticism preserves the sex class system.

The only exception to this concentration of all emotional needs into erotic relationships is the (sometimes) affection within the family. But here, too, unless they are *his* children, a man can no more express affection for children than he can for women. Thus his affection for the young is also a trap to saddle him into the marriage structure, reinforcing the patriarchal system.

(2) *The sex privatization of women*. Eroticism is only the top-most layer of the romanticism that reinforces female inferiority. As with any lower class, group awareness must be deadened to keep them from rebelling. In this case, because the distinguishing characteristic of women's exploitation as a class is sexual, a special means must be found to make them unaware that they are considered all alike sexually ('cunts'). Perhaps when a man marries he chooses from this undistinguishable lot with care, for as we have seen, he holds a special high place in his mental reserve for 'The One', by virtue of her close association with himself; but in general, he can't tell the difference between chicks (blondes, brunettes, redheads).[4] And he likes it that way. ('A wiggle in your walk, a giggle in your talk, THAT'S WHAT I LIKE!') When a man believes all women are alike, but wants to keep women from guessing, what does he do? He keeps his beliefs to himself, and pretends, to allay her suspicions, that what she has in common with other women is precisely what makes her different. Thus her sexuality eventually becomes synonymous with her individuality. *The sex privatization of women is the process whereby women are blinded to their generality as a class which renders them invisible as individuals to the male eye*. Is not that strange Mrs Lady next to the President in his

3. Homosexuals are so ridiculed because in viewing the male as sex object they go doubly against the norm: even women don't read Pretty Boy magazines.
4. 'As for his other sports,' says a recent blurb about football hero Joe Namath, 'he prefers Blondes.'

entourage reminiscent of the discreet black servant at White House functions?

The process is insidious: When a man exclaims, 'I love Blondes!' all the secretaries in the vicinity sit up; they take it personally because they have been sex-privatized. The blonde one feels personally complimented because she has come to measure her worth through the physical attributes that differentiate her from other women. She no longer recalls that any physical attribute you could name is shared by many others, that these are accidental attributes not of her own creation, that her sexuality is shared by half of humanity. But in an authentic recognition of her individuality, her blondeness would be loved, but in a different way: she would be loved first as an irreplaceable totality, and then her blondeness would be loved as one of the characteristics of that totality.

The apparatus of sex privatization is so sophisticated that it may take years to detect – if detectable at all. It explains many puzzling traits of female psychology that take such form as:

Women who are personally complimented by compliments to their sex, i.e., 'Hats off to the Little Woman!'

Women who are not insulted when addressed regularly and impersonally as Dear, Honey, Sweetie, Sugar, Kitten, Darling, Angel, Queen, Princess, Doll, Woman.

Women who are secretly flattered to have their asses pinched in Rome. (Much wiser to count the number of times other girls' asses are pinched!)

The joys of 'prickteasing' (generalized male horniness taken as a sign of personal value and desirability).

The 'clotheshorse' phenomenon. (Women, denied legitimate outlets for expression of their individuality, 'express' themselves physically, as in 'I want to see something "different".')

These are only some of the reactions to the sex privatization process, the confusion of one's sexuality with one's individuality. The process is so effective that most women have come to believe seriously that the world needs their particular sexual contributions to go on. ('She thinks her pussy is made of gold.') But the love songs would still be written without them.

Women may be duped, but men are quite conscious of this as a valuable manipulative technique. That is why they go to great pains to avoid talking about women in front of them ('not in front of a lady') – it would give their game away. To overhear a bull session is traumatic to a woman: so all this time she has been considered only 'ass', 'meat', 'twat', or 'stuff', to be gotten a 'piece of', 'that bitch', or 'this broad' to be tricked out of money or sex or love! To understand finally that she is no better than other women but completely indistinguishable comes not just as a blow but as a total annihilation. But perhaps the time that women more often have to confront their own sex privatization is in a lover's quarrel, when the truth spills out: then a man might get careless and admit that the only thing he ever *really* liked her for was her bust ('Built like a brick shit-house') or legs anyway ('Hey, Legs!'), and he can find that somewhere else if he has to.

Thus sex privatization stereotypes women: it encourages men to see women as 'dolls' differentiated only by superficial attributes – not of the same species as themselves – and it blinds women to their sexploitation as a class, keeping them from uniting against it, thus effectively segregating the two classes. A side-effect is the converse: if women are differentiated only by superficial physical attributes, men appear more individual and irreplaceable than they really are.

Women, because social recognition is granted only for a *false* individuality, are kept from developing the tough individuality that would enable breaking through such a ruse. If one's existence in its generality is the only thing acknowledged, why go to the trouble to develop real character? It is much less hassle to 'light up the room with a smile' – until that day when the 'chick' graduates to 'old bag', to find that her smile is no longer 'inimitable'.

(3) *The beauty ideal.* Every society has promoted a certain ideal of beauty over all others. What that ideal is is unimportant, for any ideal leaves the majority out; ideals, by definition, are modelled on *rare* qualities. For example, in America, the present fashion vogue of French models, or the erotic ideal Voluptuous Blonde are modelled on qualities rare indeed: few Americans

are of French birth, most don't look French and never will (and besides they eat too much); voluptuous brunettes can bleach their hair (as did Marilyn Monroe, the sex queen herself), but blondes can't develop curves at will – and most of them, being Anglo-Saxon, simply aren't built like that. If and when, by artificial methods, the majority can squeeze into the ideal, the ideal changes. If it were attainable, what good would it be?

For the exclusivity of the beauty ideal serves a clear political function. Someone – most women – will be left out. And left scrambling, because as we have seen, women have been allowed to achieve individuality only through their appearance – looks being defined as 'good' not out of love for the bearer, but because of her more or less successful approximation to an external standard. This image, defined by men (and currently by homosexual men, often misogynists of the worst order), becomes the ideal. What happens? Women everywhere rush to squeeze into the glass slipper, forcing and mutilating their bodies with diets and beauty programmes, clothes and makeup, anything to become the punk prince's dream girl. But they have no choice. If they don't the penalties are enormous: their social legitimacy is at stake.

Thus women become more and more look-alike. But at the same time they are expected to express their individuality through their physical appearance. Thus they are kept coming and going, at one and the same time trying to express their similarity and their uniqueness. The demands of Sex Privatization contradict the demands of the Beauty Ideal, causing the severe feminine neurosis about personal appearance.

But this conflict itself has an important political function. When women begin to look more and more alike, distinguished only by the degree to which they differ from a paper ideal, they can be more easily stereotyped as a class: they look alike, they think alike, and even worse, they are so stupid they believe they are not alike.

*

These are some of the major components of the cultural apparatus, romanticism, which, with the weakening of 'natural' limitations on women, keep sex oppression going strong. The political use of romanticism over the centuries became increasingly complex. Operating subtly or blatantly, on every cultural level, romanticism is now – in this time of greatest threat to the male power role – amplified by new techniques of communication so all-pervasive that men get entangled in their own line. How does this amplification work?

With the cultural portrayal of the smallest details of existence (e.g., deodorizing one's underarms), the distance between one's experience and one's perceptions of it becomes enlarged by a vast interpretive network; if our direct experience contradicts its interpretation by this ubiquitous cultural network, the experience must be denied. This process, of course, does not apply only to women. The pervasion of image has so deeply altered our very relationships to ourselves that even men have become objects – if never *erotic* objects. Images become extensions of oneself; it gets hard to distinguish the real person from his latest image, if indeed the Person Underneath hasn't evaporated altogether. Arnie, the kid who sat in back of you in the sixth grade, picking his nose and cracking jokes, the one who had a crook in his left shoulder, is lost under successive layers of adopted images: the High School Comedian, the Campus Rebel, James Bond, the Salem Springtime Lover, and so on, each image hitting new highs of sophistication until the person himself doesn't know who he is. Moreover, he deals with others through this image-extension (Boy-Image meets Girl-Image and consummates Image-Romance). Even if a woman could get beneath this intricate image façade – and it would take months, even years, of a painful, almost therapeutic relationship – she would be met not with gratitude that she had (painfully) loved the man for his real self, but with shocked repulsion and terror that she had found him out. What he wants instead is the Pepsi-Cola Girl, to smile pleasantly to his Johnny Walker Red in front of a ski-lodge fire.

But, while this reification affects both men and women alike, in the case of women it is profoundly complicated by the forms of sexploitation I have described. Woman is not only an Image, she is the Image of Sex Appeal. The sterotyping of women expands: now there is no longer the excuse of ignorance. Every woman is constantly and explicitly informed on how to 'improve' what nature gave her, where to buy the products to do it with, and how to count the calories she should never have eaten – indeed, the 'ugly' woman is now so nearly extinct even she is fast becoming 'exotic'. The competition becomes frantic, because everyone is now plugged into the same circuit. The current beauty ideal becomes all-pervasive ('Blondes have more fun . . .').

And eroticism becomes erotomania. Stimulated to the limit, it has reached an epidemic level unequalled in history. From every magazine cover, film screen, TV tube, subway sign, jump breasts, legs, shoulders, thighs. Men walk about in a state of constant sexual excitement. Even with the best of intentions, it is difficult to focus on anything else. This bombardment of the senses, in turn, escalates sexual provocation still further: ordinary means of arousal have lost all effect. Clothing becomes more provocative: hemlines climb, bras are shed. See-through materials become ordinary. But in all this barrage of erotic stimuli, men themselves are seldom portrayed as erotic objects. Women's eroticism, as well as men's, becomes increasingly directed towards women.

One of the internal contradictions of this highly effective propaganda system is to expose to men as well as women the stereotyping process women undergo. Though the idea was to better acquaint women with their feminine role, men who turn on the TV are also treated to the latest in tummy-control, false eyelashes, and floor waxes (Does she . . . or doesn't she?). Such a crosscurrent of sexual tease and exposé would be enough to make any man hate women, if he didn't already.

Thus the extension of romanticism through modern media enormously magnified its effects. If before culture maintained male supremacy through Eroticism, Sex Privatization, and the Beauty Ideal, these cultural processes are now almost too effectively carried out: the media are guilty of 'overkill'. The regeneration of the women's movement at this moment in history may be due to a backfiring, an internal contradiction of our modern cultural indoctrination system. For in its amplification of sex indoctrination, the media have unconsciously exposed the degradation of 'femininity'.

146

In conclusion, I want to add a note about the special difficulties of attacking the sex class system through its means of cultural indoctrination. Sex objects *are* beautiful. An attack on them can be confused with an attack on beauty itself. Feminists need not get so pious in their efforts that they feel they must flatly deny the beauty of the face on the cover of *Vogue*. For this is not the point. The real question is: is the face beautiful in a *human* way – does it allow for growth and flux and decay, does it express negative as well as positive emotions, does it fall apart without artificial props – or does it falsely imitate the very different beauty of an *inanimate* object, like wood trying to be metal?

To attack eroticism creates similar problems. Eroticism is *exciting*. No one wants to get rid of it. Life would be a drab and routine affair without at least that spark. That's just the point. Why has all joy and excitement been concentrated, driven into one narrow, difficult-to-find alley of human experience, and all the rest laid waste? When we demand the elimination of eroticism, we mean not the elimination of sexual joy and excitement but its rediffusion over – there's plenty to go around, it increases with use – the spectrum of our lives.

8 (Male) Culture

Representation of the world, like the world itself, is the work of men; they describe it from their own point of view, which they confuse with absolute truth.

Simone de Beauvoir

The relation of women to culture has been indirect. We have discussed how the present psychical organization of the two sexes dictates that most women spend their emotional energy on men, whereas men 'sublimate' theirs into work. In this way women's love becomes raw fuel for the cultural machine. (Not to mention the Great Ideas born rather more directly from early-morning boudoir discussions.)

In addition to providing its emotional support, women had another important indirect relation to culture: they inspired it. The Muse is female. Men of culture were emotionally warped by the sublimation process; they converted life to art, thus could not live it. But women, and those men who were excluded from culture, remained in direct contact with their experience – fit subject matter.

That women were intrinsic in the very content of culture is borne out by an example from the history of art: men are erotically stimulated by the opposite sex; painting was male; the nude became a *female* nude. Where the art of the male nude reached high levels, either in the work of an individual artist, e.g., Michelangelo, or in a whole artistic period, such as that of classical Greece, men were homosexual.

The subject matter of art, when there is any, is today even more largely inspired by women. Imagine the elimination of women characters from popular films and novels, even from the work of 'highbrow' directors – Antonioni, Bergman, or Godard;

there wouldn't be much left. For in the last few centuries, particularly in popular culture – perhaps related to the problematic position of women in society – women have been the main subject of art. In fact, in scanning blurbs of even one month's cultural production, one might believe that women were all anyone ever thought about.

But what about the women who have contributed directly to culture? There aren't many. And in those cases where individual women have participated in male culture, they have had to do so on male terms. And it shows. Because they have had to compete *as men*, in a male game – while still being pressured to prove themselves in their old female roles, a role at odds with their self-appointed ambitions – it is not surprising that they are seldom as skilled as men at the game of culture.

And it is not just a question of being as competent, it is also a question of being *authentic*. We have seen in the context of love how modern women have imitated male psychology, confusing it with health, and have thereby ended up even worse off than men themselves: they were not even being true to homegrown sicknesses. And there are even more complex layers to this question of authenticity: women have no means of coming to an understanding of what their experience *is*, or even that it is different from male experience. The tool for representing, for objectifying one's experience in order to deal with it, culture, is so saturated with male bias that women almost never have a chance to see themselves culturally through their own eyes. So that finally, signals from their direct experience that conflict with the prevailing (male) culture are denied and repressed.

Thus because cultural dicta are set by men, presenting only the male view – and now in a super-barrage – women are kept from achieving an authentic picture of their reality. Why do women, for example, get aroused by a pornography of female bodies? In their ordinary experience of female nudity, say in a gym locker room, the sight of other nude females might be interesting (though probably only in so far as they rate by male sexual standards), but not directly erotic. Cultural distortion of sexuality explains also how female sexuality gets twisted into narcissism: women make love to themselves vicariously through the man, rather than directly making love to him. At times this cultural barrage of man/subject, woman/object desensitizes women to male forms to such a degree that they are orgasmically affected.[1]

There are other examples of the distorting effects on female vision of an exclusively male culture. Let us go back to the history of figurative painting once again: we have seen how in the tradition of the nude, male heterosexual inclinations came to emphasize the female rather than the male as the more aesthetic and pleasing form. Such a predilection for either one over the other, of course, is based on a sexuality which is in itself artificial, culturally created. But at least one might then expect the opposite bias to prevail in the view of women painters still involved in the tradition of the nude. This is not the case. In any art school in the country one sees classrooms full of girls working diligently from the female model, accepting that the male model is somehow less aesthetic, at best perhaps novel, and certainly never questioning why the male model wears a jock strap when the female model wouldn't dream of appearing in so much as a G-string.

Again, looking at the work of well-known women painters associated with the Impressionist School of the nineteenth century, Berthe Morisot and Mary Cassatt, one wonders at their obsessive preoccupation with traditionally female subject matter: women, children, female nudes, interiors, etc. This is partially explained by political conditions of that period: women painters were lucky to be allowed to paint anything at all, let alone male models. And yet it is more than that. These women, for all their superb draughtsmanship and compositional skill, remained minor painters because they had 'lifted' a set of traditions and a view of the world that was inauthentic for them. They worked within the limits of what had been defined as female by a *male* tradition: they saw women through male eyes, painted a male's

1. Female inability to focus on sexual imagery has been found to be a major cause of female frigidity. Masters and Johnson, Albert Ellis, and others have stressed the importance of 'sexual focusing' in teaching frigid women to achieve orgasm. Hilda O'Hare in *International Journal of Sexology* correctly attributes this problem to the absence in our society of a female counterpart for the countless stimulants of the male sexual urge.

idea of female. And they carried it to an extreme, for they were attempting to outdo men at their own game; they had fallen for a (lovely) line. And thus the falseness that corrupts their work, making it 'feminine', i.e. sentimental, light.

It would take a denial of all cultural tradition for women to produce even a true 'female' art. For a woman who participates in (male) culture must achieve and be rated by standards of a tradition she had no part in making – and certainly there is no room in that tradition for a female view, even if she *could* discover what it was. In those cases where a woman, tired of losing at a male game, has attempted to participate in culture *in a female way*, she has been put down and misunderstood, named by the (male) cultural establishment 'Lady Artist', i.e. trivial, inferior. And even where it must be (grudgingly) admitted she is 'good', it is fashionable – a cheap way to indicate one's own 'seriousness' and refinement of taste – to insinuate that she is good but irrelevant.

Perhaps it is true that a presentation of only the female side of things – which tends to be one long protest and complaint rather than the portrayal of a full and substantive existence – is limited. But an equally relevant question, one much less frequently asked, is: Is it any more limited than the prevailing male view of things, which – when not taken as absolute truth – is at least seen as 'serious', relevant, and important? Is Mary McCarthy in *The Group* really so much worse a writer than Norman Mailer in *The American Dream*? Or is she perhaps describing a reality that men, the controllers and critics of the Cultural Establishment, can't tune in on?

That men and women are tuned to a different cultural wavelength, that in fact there exists a wholly different reality for men and women, is apparent in our crudest cultural form – comic books. From my own experience: When I was little my brother had literally a room-size collection of comic books. But though I was a greedy reader, this vast comic book library interested me not in the least. My literary taste was completely different from his. He preferred 'heavies' like War Comics (Aak–Aak–Aak!) and Superman; and for relief, 'funnies' like Bugs Bunny, Tweetie and Sylvester, Tom and Jerry, and all the stuttering pigs who took forever to get a rather obvious message out. Though these 'funnies' grated on my more aesthetic sensibilities, I would read them in a pinch. But had I had an allowance as big, and as little parental supervision, I might have indulged in a 'heavy' library of Love Comics (LARGE TEAR. On Tod, don't tell Sue about us, she'd die), an occasional *True Confessions*, and for 'light' relief, Archie and Veronica. Or the occasional more imaginative variations of boys' comics, like Plasticman (Superman with a rubber arm that could reach around blocks) or Uncle Scrooge McDuck editions of Donald Duck; I loved the selfish extravagance of his bathing in money. (Many women – deprived of Self – have confessed the same girlhood passion.) Even more likely, I would not have invested in comic books at all. Fairy tales, much less realistic, were a better trip.

My brother thought girls' taste was 'drippy', and I thought he was a crude slob. Who was right? We both were; but he won (he owned the library).

This division continues to operate at higher cultural levels. I had to force myself to read Mailer, Heller, Donleavy, and others for the same reasons that I couldn't stand my brother's library: to me they seemed only complex versions of (respectively) Superman, Aak–Aak–Aak, and the Adventures of Bugs Bunny. But though the 'male' library continued to repel me, in the process of developing 'good taste' (male taste), I also lost my love for the 'female' library, indeed I developed an abhorrence; and I would – I'm ashamed to admit it – far sooner have been caught dead with Hemingway than with Virginia Woolf in my hands.

In order to illustrate this cultural dichotomy in more objective terms, we don't need to attack the more obvious paper tigers (all senses implied) who consciously present a 'male' reality – viz. Hemingway, Jones, Mailer, Farrell, Algren, and the rest. The new Virility School in twentieth-century literature is in itself a direct response, indeed a male cultural backlash, to the growing threat to male supremacy – Virility, Inc., a bunch of culturally deprived 'tough guys', punching away to save their manhood. And though they get more credit, these artists write about the 'male' experience no more perceptively than Doris Lessing,

Sylvia Plath, Anaïs Nin have written about the female experience. In fact they are guilty of a mystification of their experience that makes their writing phony.

Instead, we will examine a bias more insidious (because less obvious) in male writers who honestly attempt to describe the whole spectrum of male/female experience – Bellow, Malamud, Updike, Roth, etc. – but who fail because, often without realizing it, they have described this whole from a limited (male) angle.

Let's look briefly at a story by Herbert Gold, not a 'male' writer in either style or subject matter. He writes about what concerns women, that is, relationships, preferably male/female; marriages; divorces; affairs. In this story, 'What's Become of Your Creature?', he describes the affair of a harassed young college professor with his blonde, Bohemianish student.

The picture we get of Lenka Kuwaila from the male character's view is only sensual, if sensitive on those terms. The story begins:

A girl. A gay, pretty, and sullen girl, with full marks for both sweetness and cruelty. When he looked in her desk for cigarettes, there was a silken pile of panties folded like flowers, dizzying him with the joy of springtime. When she put on a pair of them, suddenly filling out the tiny pair of petals of cloth in two paired buds, it was as if the sun had forced a flower into delicate Easter bloom. Oh, he needed her, loved her, and so for honour to them both, let us tell the truth, as straight as truth comes.

But the truth that we get 'straight as truth comes' is only his view of the truth:

There is a time in the life of every man when he can do anything. It was this time in the life of Frank Curtiss. Despair with his wife had given up to deep gratification with a beautiful girl; he even did better at home; matters cooled and calmed; his work went well; he hardly needed sleep and did not suffer his usual rose fever during the spring he knew Lenka. No sniffles, no pink eyes. Expanded breathing, sharp sight. Of the occasional headache of fatigue and excess he was cured by the touch of her hand, her welcome when he came smiling, showing teeth, through her window.

But her truth must have been an altogether different one, a truth of which there is no trace in the story until one day (out of the blue) Lenka writes his wife a long letter. The failing marriage that had been improving steadily since Frank began his affair with Lenka is destroyed for good:

Lenka left New York without seeing him after his anguished phone call to her: 'Why? Why? Why did you have to do it that way, Lenka? Can't you see how it destroys everything between us, even the past?'
'I don't care about memories. What's over means nothing. Over. You didn't want to do more than crawl through my window a couple of times a week –'
'But to write to her like that – what meant – how –'
'You cared more about a cold bitch than you cared for me. Just because you had a child.'
'Why, why?'
She hung up on him.
He stood shrugging at the telephone. Women were hanging up on him all over the world. He was disconnected.

Feeling betrayed and tricked, Frank bewilderedly nurses his wounds; throughout the rest of the story one feels his puzzlement: he does not understand what led her to do it, he does not 'understand women'. Finally he lets it rest by granting her 'full marks for cruelty' as well as sweetness.

But Lenka's 'cruelty' is the direct result of his inability to see her as more than 'a girl' (gay, pretty, *or* sullen), as, instead, perhaps, a complex human being with a self-interest not identical with his. However, due to Gold's authentic recounting of incident and dialogue, a sensitive (probably female) reader might read between the lines: Lenka was the one betrayed. Here is Frank a few years later in Manhattan:

He found a girl to join him in biting into an apple, sucking the sweet juice of it at dawn, finally kissing in good friendship and turning on their sides to sleep . . . He felt free . . . He threw away his bottle of aspirins. His married vision of himself as a heavy, shaggy, weary buffalo, head low and muzzle hurt, gave way to another image – he was lean, his posture was good, he was an agile bucko. When his former wife remarried, his last vestige of guilt disappeared. Free, free. He played badminton twice a week with a French girl who pronounced it 'Badd-ming-tonn'.

A gay bachelor now, Frank impulsively calls Lenka up one day:

But after he told her how long he had been in New York, she said that she was not interested in seeing him.

'I held a grudge, you can understand that,' he said. 'I still think you were very wrong, but I'm grateful anyway. It worked out for the best.'

'And it's over,' she said.

Later he runs into her to find her wasted on junk, whoring for a black musician:

She may have invented a foolish lie [in order to invite him up to her room], but she recognized the glare of contempt on his face, and in her life of now a quarter of a century, she had learned only one way to answer the judgement of men. She slid against him, on her face a mixture of coyness and dread, a flirtatious half-smile, a slinking catlike practiced leaning against him, and her eyes filled with tears as she shut them, tears balanced on her wetted lashes, slipping down her cheeks. 'Frank,' she said haltingly. 'I stopped remembering for a long time, I don't know, things were difficult, I thought you were too angry ... But I've been remembering ... That's why ... Forgive ...'

He put his arms around her, held her to him, but with more confusion than either amorousness or tenderness ...

Then he thought of the letters she had just now lied about, and suddenly, as she turned her head up wanting to be kissed, his most vivid fantasy was this one: *She was unclean.* His uncurbed dread ran towards a muddle – deceit, illness, secret pity, slime, and retribution. Not knowing what he feared, he thought only: filth, cunning, running filth, blotches, sores. Because he could not bear her sorrows, he thought: *Deceit and cunning and disease!*

He pulled away before their mouths touched; her nails clawed along his arm, shredding skin; he fled, hearing her sobs at the open door as he careened down the infected stairs and into the free air of the street.

Curtain: Frank caresses his newly pregnant wife, wondering whatever-happened-to-Lenka.

This is not a male story in subject, and it is not a 'male' story in style – there is enough description of emotion in it to shame any male writer. But it is still a 'male' story by virtue of its peculiar limitation of vision: it does not understand women. Lenka's sensuality and loveliness is as much of her as Frank is able to comprehend. Her motives for writing to his wife, her refusal to see him, her attempted seduction, described with such guilty loathing – these Frank can't deal with, just as in real life men can't deal with them ('*Because he could not bear her sorrows,* he thought: Deceit and cunning and disease!'). To know a woman beyond the level of her delightfulness is too much for him. Women are judged only in terms of himself, and what they can bring to him, whether beauty and joy or pain and sorrow. Whichever it is, he does not question it, not understanding that his own behaviour had been or could be a determining influence.

One can imagine an entirely different story of the same affair, even using the same information and dialogue, only this time written by Lenka. Her behaviour then might appear not irrational, but entirely understandable; instead, the male character would come out shallow. Perhaps, indeed, we might end up with more than just an opposite sexual bias. We might get as much as three quarters of the picture (i.e. Frank shallow *because* he is unable to live up to his emotions), since women in general, through long oppression, have learned to be hipper to male psychology than vice versa. But this has seldom happened in literature, for most Lenkas are sufficiently destroyed by their use and abuse never to write their own stories coherently.

Thus the difference between the 'male' approach to art and the 'female', is not, as some like to think, simply a difference of 'style' in treating the same subject matter (personal, subjective, emotional, descriptive vs. vigorous, spare, hardhitting, cool, objective) but the very subject matter itself. The sex role system divides human experience; men and women live in these different halves of reality; and culture reflects this.

Only a few artists have overcome this division in their work. And one wonders whether homosexuals are correct in their claim. But if not through physical expression, then in some other way the greatest artists became mentally androgynous. In the twentieth century, for example, writers of the stature of Proust, Joyce, Kafka did it either by physically identifying with the female (Proust), by imaginarily crossing the line at will (Joyce), or by retreating to an imaginary world rarely affected by the dichotomy (Kafka). But not only do most artists not overcome, they are not even *aware* of the existence of a cultural limitation based on sex – so much is the male reality accepted by both male and female as Reality.

And what about women artists? We have seen that it has only been in the last several centuries that women have been permitted to participate – and then only on an individual basis, and on male terms – in the making of culture. And even so their vision had become inauthentic: they were denied the use of the cultural mirror.

And there are many *negative* reasons that women have entered art: affluence always creates female dilettantism, e.g., the Victorian 'young lady' with her accomplishments, or the arts of the Japanese geisha – for, in addition to serving as a symbol of male luxury, women's increasing idleness under advancing industrialism presents a practical problem: female discontent has to be eased to keep it from igniting. Or women may be entering art as a refuge. Women today are still excluded from the vital power centres of human activity; and art is one of the last self-determining occupations left – often done in solitude. But in this sense women are like a petty bourgeoisie trying to open up shop in the age of corporate capitalism.

For the higher percentages of women in art lately may tell us more about the state of art than about the state of women. Are we to feel cheered that women have taken over in a capacity soon to be automated out? (Like 95 Percent Black at the Post Office, this is no sign of integration; on the contrary, undesirables are being shoved into the least desirable positions – Here, now get in and keep your mouth shut!) That art is no longer a vital centre that attracts the best men of our generation may also be a product of the male/female division, as I shall attempt to show in the next chapter. But the animation of women and homosexuals in the arts today may signify only the scurrying of rats near a dying body.[2]

But if it has not yet created great women artists, women's new literacy has certainly created a female audience. Just as male audiences have always demanded, and received, male art to reinforce their particular view of reality, so a female audience

2. However, women's presence in the arts and humanities is still viciously fought by the few males remaining, in proportion to the insecurity of their own position – particularly precarious in traditional, humanist schools, such as figurative painting.

demands a 'female' art to reinforce the female reality. Thus the birth of the crude feminine novel in the nineteenth century, leading to the love story of our own day, so ever-present in popular culture ('soap opera'); the women's magazine trade; *Valley of the Dolls*. These may be crude beginnings. Most of this art is as yet primitive, clumsy, poor. But occasionally the female reality is documented as clearly as the male reality has always been, as, for example, in the work of Anne Sexton.

Eventually, out of this ferment – perhaps very soon – we may see the emergence of an authentic female art. But the development of 'female' art is not to be viewed as reactionary, like its counterpart, the male School of Virility. Rather it is progressive: an exploration of the strictly female reality is a necessary step to correct the warp in a sexually biased culture. It is only after we have integrated the dark side of the moon into our world view that we can begin to talk seriously of universal culture.

*

Thus, all of culture has been to different degrees corrupted by sexual polarization. We can summarize the various forms this corruption takes in the following way:

(1) *Male protest art*. Art that self-consciously glorifies the male reality (as opposed to taking for granted that it constitutes reality itself) is only a recent development. I see it as a direct response to the threat to male supremacy contained in the first blurring of rigid sex roles. Such an art is reactionary by definition. To those men who feel that this art best expresses what they are living and feeling, I recommend a major overhaul of personality.

(2) *The Male Angle*. This art fails to achieve a comprehensive world view because it does not recognize that male reality is not Reality, but only one half of reality. Thus its portrayal of the opposite sex and its behaviour (half of humanity) is false: the artist himself does not understand female motives. Sometimes, as in the Herbert Gold story quoted, the women characters can still come through if the author has been faithful to at least the *how* – if not the *why* – of their behaviour.

A better-known example: the character of Catherine in

Truffaut's film *Jules and Jim* is drawn from real life. There are many such vamps and *femmes fatales* around, in reality nothing more than women who refuse to accept their powerlessness. To keep an illusion of equality and to gain an indirect power over men, Catherine must use 'mystery' (Sphinx), unpredictability (jumping in the Seine), and wiles (sleeping around with Mystery Men to keep Him dangling). When, in the end, as all women must, she loses even this illegitimate power, her pride will not admit defeat: she kills the man who had dared escape her, along with herself. But even here, in an accurately drawn art, the male bias comes out. The director goes along with the Mystery Woman mystique, does not probe to find out what's beneath it. Moreover, he doesn't want to know: he is using it as a source of eroticism. The picture we get of Catherine comes only through a veil.

(3) (*Individually cultivated*) *androgynous mentality*. Even when the sex limitations have been overcome by the individual artist, his art must reveal a reality made ugly by its cleavage. A brief example, again from film: though the Swedish directors have been notably free from personal sex prejudice – the women they portray are human first and female second – Liv Ullman's portrayal of Noble Wife faithfully accompanying her husband into his growing madness (Bergman's *Hour of the Wolf*) or loving him through his moral degeneration (Bergman's *Shame*) or Lena Nyman's confused sensitivity in Sjoman's *I Am Curious (Yellow)* are descriptions not of a liberated sexuality but of a still-unresolved conflict between the sexual and the human identity.

(4) *Female art*. This is a new development, not to be confused with 'male' art, even if, so far, it has been guilty of the same bias in reverse. For this may signify the beginnings of a new consciousness, rather than an ossification of the old. Within the next decade we may see its growth into a powerful new art – perhaps arising in conjunction with the feminist political movement or at its inspiration – that will, for the first time, authentically grapple with the reality that women live in.

We may also see a feminist Criticism, emphasizing, in order to correct, the various forms of sex bias now corrupting art.

159

However, in our third category, that art which is guilty only of reflecting the human price of a sex-divided reality, great care would have to be taken that criticism be directed, not at the artists for their (accurate) portrayal of the imperfect reality, but at the grotesqueness of that reality itself as revealed by the art.

Only a feminist revolution can eliminate entirely the sex schism causing these cultural distortions. Until then 'pure art' is a delusion – a delusion responsible both for the inauthentic art women have produced until now, as well as for the corruption of (male) culture at large. The incorporation of the neglected half of human experience – the female experience – into the body of culture, to create an all-encompassing culture, is only the first step, a precondition; but the schism of reality itself must be overthrown before there can be a true cultural revolution.

9   Dialectics of Cultural History

So far we have treated 'culture' as synonymous with 'arts and letters' or at its broadest, 'humanities'. This is a common enough confusion. But it is startling in this context. For we discover that, while only indirectly related to art, women have been entirely excluded from an equally important half of culture: science. If at least with the arts we could find enough material about the relationship of women to culture – whether indirectly as influence, stimulus, or subject matter, or even occasionally as direct participants – to fill at least a chapter, we can hardly find a relationship of women to science worthy of discussion. Perhaps in the broadest sense our statement that women are the emotional force behind all (male) culture holds true – but we are stretching the case to include modern science, where the empirical method specifically demands the exclusion of the scientist's personality from his research. Satisfaction of his emotional needs through a woman in his off hours may make him more stable, and thus steadier on the job, but this is far-fetched.

But if even the indirect relationship of women to science is debatable, that there is no direct one is certainly not. One would have to search to find even one woman who had contributed in a major way to scientific culture. Moreover, the situation of women in science is not improving. Even with the work of discovery shifted from the great comprehensive minds of the past to small pragmatic university research teams, there are remarkably few women scientists.[1]

1. I was struck by this at a recent women's liberation workshop scheduled by the science department of a top-level eastern university: of the fifty women present, only one or two were engaged in research, let alone high-level

This absence of women at all levels of the scientific disciplines is so commonplace as to lead many (otherwise intelligent) people to attribute it to some deficiency (logic?) in women themselves. Or to women's own predilections for the emotional and subjective over the practical and rational. But the question cannot be so easily dismissed. It is true that women in science are in foreign territory – but how has this situation evolved? Why are there disciplines or branches of inquiry that demand only a 'male' mind? Why would a woman, to qualify, have to develop an alien psychology? When and why was the female excluded from this type mind? How and why has science come to be defined as, and restricted to, the 'objective'?

I submit that not only were the arts and humanities corrupted by the sex duality, but that modern science has been determined by it. And moreover that *culture reflects this polarity in its very organization*. C. P. Snow was the first to note what had been becoming increasingly obvious: a deep fissure of culture – the liberal arts and the sciences had become incomprehensible to each other. Again, though the universal man of the Renaissance is widely lamented, specialization only increases. These are some of the modern symptoms of a long cultural disease based on the sex dualism. Let us examine the history of culture according to this hypothesis – that there is an underlying dialectic of sex.

I
THE TWO MODES OF CULTURAL HISTORY

For our analysis we shall define culture in the following way: *culture is the attempt by man to realize the conceivable in the possible*. Man's consciousness of himself within his environment distinguishes him from the lower animals, and turns him into the only animal capable of culture. This consciousness, his highest faculty, allows him to project mentally states of being that do not exist at the moment. Able to construct a past and future, he becomes a creature of time – a historian and a prophet. More than this, he can imagine objects and states of being that

research. The others were lab technicians, graduate assistants, high school science teachers, faculty wives, and the like.

have never existed and may never exist in the real world – he becomes a maker of art. Thus, for example, though the ancient Greeks did not know how to fly, still they could imagine it. The myth of Icarus was the formulation in fantasy of their conception of the state 'flying'.

But man was not only able to project the conceivable into fantasy. He also learned to impose it on reality: by accumulating knowledge, learning experience, about that reality and how to handle it, he could shape it to his liking. This accumulation of skills for controlling the environment, technology, is another means to reaching the same end, the realization of the conceivable in the possible. Thus, in our example, if, in the B.C. era, man could fly on the magic carpet of myth or fantasy, by the twentieth century, his technology, the accumulation of his practical skills, had made it possible for him to fly in actuality – he had invented the aeroplane. Another example: In the Biblical legend, the Jews, an agricultural people stranded for forty years in the desert, were provided by God with Manna, a miraculous substance that could be transformed at will into food of any colour, texture, or taste; modern food processing, especially with the 'green revolution', will probably soon create a totally artificial food production, perhaps with this chameleon attribute. Again, in ancient legend, man could imagine mixed species, e.g., the centaur or the unicorn, or hybrid births, like the birth of an animal from a human, or a virgin birth; the current biological revolution, with its increasing knowledge of the reproductive process, could now – if only the first crude stages – create these 'monstrosities' in reality. Brownies and elves, the Golem of medieval Jewish lore, Mary Shelley's monster in *Frankenstein*, were the imaginative constructions that preceded by several centuries the corresponding technological acumen. Many other fantastical constructions – ghosts, mental telepathy, Methuselah's age – remain to be realized by modern science.

These two different responses, the idealistic and the scientific, do not merely exist simultaneously: there is a dialogue between the two. The imaginative construction precedes the technological though often it does not develop until the technological knowhow is 'in the air'. For example, the art of science fiction developed, in the main, only a half-century in advance of, and now co-exists with, the scientific revolution that is transforming it into a reality – for example (an innocuous one), the moon flight. The phrases 'way out', 'far out', 'spaced', the observation 'it's like something out of science fiction' are common language. In the aesthetic response, because it always develops in advance, and is thus the product of another age, the same realization may take on a sensational or unrealistic cast, e.g., Frankenstein's monster, as opposed to, let us say, General Electric's CAM (Cybernetic Anthropomorphic Machines) Handyman. (An artist can never know in advance just how his vision might be articulated in reality.)

Culture then is the sum of, and the dynamic between, the two modes through which the mind attempts to transcend the limitations and contingencies of reality. These two types of cultural responses entail different methods to achieve the same end, the realization of the conceivable in the possible. In the first,[2] the individual denies the limitations of the given reality by escaping from it altogether, to define, create, his own possible. In the provinces of the imagination, objectified in some way – whether through the development of a visual image within some artificial boundary, say four square feet of canvas, through visual images projected through verbal symbols (poetry), with sound ordered into a sequence (music), or with verbal ideas ordered into a progression (theology, philosophy) – he creates an ideal world governed by his own artificially imposed order and harmony, a structure in which he consciously relates each part to the whole, a static (and therefore 'timeless') construction. The degree to which he abstracts his creation from reality is unimportant, for even when he most appears to imitate, he has created an illusion governed by its own – perhaps hidden – set of artificial laws. (Degas said that the artist had to lie in order to tell the truth.) This search for the ideal, realized by means of an artificial medium, we shall call the Aesthetic Mode.

2. The idealistic mode, corresponding roughly to the suprahistorical, non-materialist 'metaphysical' mode of thought against which Marx and Engels revolted.

In the second type of cultural response the contingencies of reality are overcome, not through the creation of an alternate reality, but through the mastery of reality's own workings: the laws of nature are exposed, then turned against it, to shape it in accordance with man's conception. If there is a poison, man assumes there is an antidote; if there is a disease, he searches for the cure: every fact of nature that is understood can be used to alter it. But to achieve the ideal through such a procedure takes much longer, and is infinitely more painful, especially in the early stages of knowledge. For the vast and intricate machine of nature must be entirely understood – and there are always fresh and unexpected layers of complexity – before it can be thoroughly controlled. Thus before any solution can be found to the deepest contingencies of the human condition, e.g., death, natural processes of growth and decay must be catalogued, smaller laws related to larger ones. This scientific method (also attempted by Marx and Engels in their materialist approach to history) is the attempt by man to master nature through the complete understanding of its mechanics. The coaxing of reality to conform with man's conceptual ideal, through the application of information extrapolated from itself, we shall call the Technological Mode.

We have defined culture as the sum of, and the dialectic between, the two different modes through which man can resolve the tension created by the flexibility of his mental faculties within the limitations of his given environment. The correspondence of these two different cultural modes with the two sexes respectively is unmistakable. We have noted how those few women directly creating culture have gravitated to disciplines within the Aesthetic Mode. There is a good reason for this: the aesthetic response corresponds with 'female' behaviour. The same terminology can be applied to either: subjective, intuitive, introverted, wishful, dreamy or fantastic, concerned with the subconscious (the *id*), emotional, even temperamental (hysterical). Correspondingly, the technological response is the masculine response: objective, logical, extroverted, realistic, concerned with the conscious mind (the ego), rational, mechanical, pragmatic and down-to-earth, stable. Thus the aesthetic is the cultural recreation of that half of the psychological spectrum that has been assigned to the female, whereas the technological response is the cultural magnification of the male half.

Just as we have assumed the biological division of the sexes for procreation to be the fundamental 'natural' duality from which grows all further division into classes, so we now assume the sex division to be the root of this basic cultural division as well. The interplay between these two cultural responses, the 'male' Technological Mode and the 'female' Aesthetic Mode, recreates at yet another level the dialectic of the sexes – as well as its superstructure, the caste, and the economic-class dialectic. And just as the merging of the divided sexual, racial, and economic classes is a precondition for sexual, racial, or economic revolution respectively, so the merging of the aesthetic with the technological culture is the precondition of a cultural revolution. And just as the revolutionary goal of the sexual, racial, and economic revolutions is, rather than a mere levelling of imbalances, of class, an elimination of class categories altogether, so the end result of a cultural revolution must be, not merely the integration of the two streams of culture, but the elimination of cultural categories altogether, the end of culture itself as we know it. But before we discuss this ultimate cultural revolution or even the state of cultural division in our own time, let us see how this third level of the sex dialectic – the interaction between the Technological and Aesthetic Modes – operated to determine the flow of cultural history.

*

At first technological knowledge accumulated slowly. Gradually man learned to control the crudest aspects of his environment – he discovered the tool, control of fire, the wheel, the melting of ore to make weapons and ploughs, even, eventually, the alphabet – but these discoveries were few and far between, because as yet he had no systematic way of initiating them. Eventually however, he had gathered enough practical knowledge to build whole systems, e.g., medicine or architecture, to create juridical, political, social, and economic institutions. Civilization developed from the primitive hunting horde into an

166

agricultural society, and finally, through progressive stages, into feudalism, capitalism, and the first attempts at socialism.

But in all this time, man's ability to picture an ideal world was far ahead of his ability to create one. The primary cultural forms of ancient civilizations – religion and its offshoots, mythology, legend, primitive art and magic, prophecy and history – were in the aesthetic mode: they imposed only an artificial, imaginary order on a universe still mysterious and chaotic. Even primitive scientific theories were only poetic metaphors for what would later be realized empirically. The science and philosophy and mathematics of classical antiquity, forerunners of modern science, by sheer imaginative prowess, operating in a vacuum independently of material laws, anticipated much of what was later proven: Democritus' atoms and Lucretius' 'substance' foreshadowed by thousands of years the discoveries of modern science. But they were realized only within the realm of the imaginary aesthetic mode.

In the Middle Ages the Judaeo-Christian heritage was assimilated with pagan culture, to produce medieval religious art and the metaphysics of Thomas Aquinas and the Scholastics. Though concurrently Arab science, an outgrowth of the Greek Alexandrian Period (third century B.C. to seventh century A.D.), was amassing considerable information in such areas as geography, astronomy, physiology, mathematics – a tabulation essential to the later empiricism – there was little dialogue. Western science, with its alchemy, its astrology, the 'humours' of medieval medicine, was still in a 'pseudo-scientific' stage, or, in our definition, still operating according to the aesthetic mode. This medieval aesthetic culture, composed of the Classical and Christian legacies, culminated in the Humanism of the Renaissance.

Until the Renaissance, then, culture occurred in the aesthetic mode because, prior to that time, technology had been so primitive, the body of scientific knowledge so far from complete. In terms of the sex dialectic, this long stage of cultural history corresponds with the matriarchal stage of civilization: the Female Principle – dark, mysterious, uncontrollable – reigned, elevated by man himself, still in awe of unfathomable Nature. Men of

167

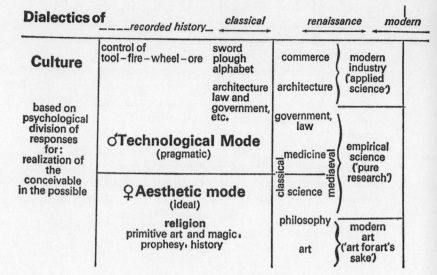

culture were its high priests of homage: until and through the Renaissance *all* men of culture were practitioners of the ideal aesthetic mode, thus, in a sense, artists. The Renaissance, the pinnacle of cultural humanism, was the golden age of the aesthetic (female) mode.

And also the beginning of its end. By the sixteenth century culture was undergoing a change as profound as the shift from matriarchy to patriarchy in terms of the sex dialectic, and corresponding to the decline of feudalism in the class dialectic. This was the first merging of the aesthetic culture with the technological, in the creation of modern (empirical) science.

In the Renaissance, Aristotelian Scholasticism had remained powerful though the first cracks in the dam were already apparent. But it was not until Francis Bacon, who first proposed to use science to 'extend more widely the limits of the power and the greatnesses of man', that the marriage of the modes was consummated. Bacon and Locke transformed philosophy, the attempt to understand life, from abstract speculation detached from the real world (metaphysics, ethics, theology, aesthetics,

168

Revolution	Transition	Ultimate Goal
Cultural Revolution scientific breakthrough, breakdown of cultural categories	Merging of Art and Reality	**Realization of the Conceivable in the Actual** disappearance of 'culture'

logic) to an uncovering of the *real* laws of nature, through proof and demonstration (empirical science).

In the empirical method propounded by Francis Bacon, insight and imagination had to be used only at the earliest stage of the inquiry. Tentative hypotheses would be formed by induction from the facts, and then consequences would be deduced logically and tested for consistency among themselves and for agreement with the primary facts and results of *ad hoc* experiments. The hypothesis would become an accepted theory only after all tests had been passed, and would remain, at least until proven wrong, a theory capable of predicting phenomena to a high degree of probability.

The empirical view held that by recording and tabulating all possible observations and experiments in this manner, the Natural Order would emerge automatically. Though at first the question 'why' was still asked as often as the question 'how', after information began to accumulate, each discovery building upon the last to complete the jigsaw, the speculative, the intuitive, and the imaginative gradually became less valuable. When once the initial foundations had been laid by men of the stature of Kepler, Galileo, and Newton, thinkers still in the inspired 'aesthetic' science tradition, hundreds of anonymous technicians could move to fill in the blanks, leading to, in our own time, the dawn of a golden age of science – to the technological mode what the Renaissance had been to the aesthetic mode.

II
THE TWO CULTURES TODAY

Now, in 1970, we are experiencing a major scientific breakthrough. The new physics, relativity, and the astrophysical theories of contemporary science had already been realized by the first part of this century. Now, in the latter part, we are arriving, with the help of the electron microscope and other new tools, at similar achievements in biology, biochemistry, and all the life sciences. Important discoveries are made yearly by small, scattered work teams all over the United States, and in other countries as well – of the magnitude of DNA in genetics, or of Urey and Miller's work in the early fifties on the origins of life. Full mastery of the reproductive process is in sight, and there has been significant advance in understanding the basic life and death process. The nature of ageing and growth, sleep and hibernation, the chemical functioning of the brain and the development of consciousness and memory are all beginning to be understood in their entirety. This acceleration promises to continue for another century, or however long it takes to achieve the goal of Empiricism: total understanding of the laws of nature.

This amazing accumulation of concrete knowledge in only a few hundred years is the product of philosophy's switch from the aesthetic to the technological mode. The combination of 'pure' science, science in the aesthetic mode, with pure technology, caused greater progress towards the goal of technology – the realization of the conceivable in the actual – than had been made in thousands of years of previous history.

Empiricism itself is only the means, a quicker and more effective technique, for achieving technology's ultimate cultural goal: the building of the ideal in the real world. One of its own basic dictates is that a certain amount of material must be collected and arranged into categories before any decisive comparison, analysis, or discovery can be made. In this light centuries of empirical science have been little more than the building of foundations for the breakthroughs of our own time and the future. The amassing of information and understanding of the laws and mechanical processes of nature ('pure research') is but a means to a larger end: total understanding of Nature in order, ultimately, to achieve transcendence.

In this view of the development and goals of cultural history, Engels's final goal, quoted above in the context of political revolution, is again worthy of quotation: 'The whole sphere of the conditions of life which environ man, and have hitherto ruled him, now comes under the dominion and control of man, who for the first time becomes the real conscious Lord of Nature.' Empirical science is to culture what the shift to patriarchy was to the sex dialectic, and what the bourgeois period is to the Marxian dialectic – a latter-day stage prior to revolution. Moreover, the three dialectics are integrally related to one another vertically as well as horizontally: The empirical science growing out of the bourgeoisie (the bourgeois period is in itself a stage of the patriarchal period) follows the humanism of the aristocracy (the Female Principle, the matriarchy) and with its development of the empirical method in order to amass real knowledge (development of modern industry in order to amass capital) eventually puts itself out of business. The body of scientific discovery (the new productive modes) must finally outgrow the empirical (capitalistic) mode of using them.

And just as the internal contradictions of capitalism must become increasingly apparent, so must the internal contradictions of empirical science – as in the development of pure knowledge to the point where it assumes a life of its own, e.g., the atomic bomb. As long as man is still engaged only in the means – the charting of the ways of nature, the gathering of 'pure' knowledge – to his final realization, mastery of nature, his knowledge, because it is not complete, is dangerous. So dangerous that many scientists are wondering whether they shouldn't put a lid on certain types of research. But this solution is hope-lessly inadequate. The machine of empiricism has its own momentum, and is, for such purposes, completely out of control. Could one actually decide what to discover or not discover? That is, by definition, antithetical to the whole empirical process that Bacon set in motion. Many of the most important discoveries have been practically laboratory accidents, with social implications barely realized by the scientists who stumbled into them. For example, as recently as five years ago Professor F. C. Steward of Cornell discovered a process called 'cloning': by placing a single carrot cell in a rotating nutrient he was able to grow a whole sheet of identical carrot cells, from which he eventually recreated the same carrot. The understanding of a similar process for more developed animal cells, were it to slip out – as did experiments with 'mind-expanding' drugs – could have some awesome implications. Or, again, imagine partheno-genesis, virgin birth, as practised by the greenfly, actually applied to human fertility.

Another internal contradiction in empirical science: the mechanistic, deterministic, 'soulless' scientific world-view, which is the result of the means to, rather than the (inherently noble and often forgotten) ultimate purpose of, Empiricism: the actualization of the ideal in reality.

The cost in humanity is particularly high to the scientist himself, who becomes little more than a cultural technician. For, ironically enough, to properly accumulate knowledge of the universe requires a mentality the very opposite of comprehensive and integrated. Though in the long run the efforts of the individual scientist could lead to domination of the environment in the interest of humanity, temporarily the empirical method demands that its practitioners themselves become 'objective', mechanistic, overprecise. The public image of the white-coated Dr Jekyll with no feelings for his subjects, mere guinea pigs, is not entirely false: there is no room for feelings in the scientist's work; he is forced to eliminate or isolate them in what amounts to an occupational hazard. At best he can resolve this problem by separating his professional from his personal self, by compart-mentalizing his emotion. Thus, though often well-versed in an academic way about the arts – the frequency of this, at any rate, is higher than of artists who are well-versed in science – the scientist is generally out of touch with his direct emotions and senses, or, at best, he is emotionally divided. His 'private' and 'public' life are out of whack; and because his personality is not well-integrated, he can be surprisingly conventional ('Dear, I discovered how to clone people at the lab today. Now we can go skiing at Aspen.') He feels no contradiction in living by convention, even in attending church, for he has never integrated the amazing material of modern science with his daily life. Often it takes the misuse of his discovery to alert him to that connection which he has long since lost in his own mind.

The catalogue of scientific vices is familiar: it duplicates, exaggerates, the catalogue of 'male' vices in general. This is to be expected: if the technological mode develops from the male principle then it follows that its practitioners would develop the warpings of the male personality in the extreme. But let us leave science for the moment, winding up for the ultimate cultural revolution, to see what meanwhile had been happening to the aesthetic culture proper.

With philosophy in the broadest classical sense – including 'pure' science – defecting, aesthetic culture became increasingly narrow and ingrown, reduced to the arts and humanities in the refined sense that we now know them. Art (hereafter referring to the 'liberal arts', especially arts and letters) had always been, in its very definition, a search for the ideal, removed from the real world. But in primitive days it had been the handmaiden of religion, articulating the common dream, objectifying 'other' worlds of the common fantasy, e.g., the art of the Egyptian tombs, to explain and excuse this one. Thus even though it was removed from the real world, it served an important social function: it satisfied artificially those wishes of society that couldn't yet be realized in reality. Though it was patronized and supported only by the aristocracy, the cultured elite, it was never as detached from life as it later became; for the society of those times was, for all practical purposes, synonymous with its ruling class, whether priesthood, monarchy, or nobility. The masses were never considered by 'society' to be a legitimate part of humanity, they were slaves, nothing more than human animals, drones, or serfs, without whose labour the small cultured elite could not have maintained itself.

The gradual squeezing out of the aristocracy by the new middle class, the bourgeoisie, signalled the erosion of aesthetic culture. We have seen that capitalism intensified the worst attributes of patriarchalism, how, for example, the nuclear family emerged from the large, loose family household of the past, to reinforce the weakening sex class system, oppressing women and children more intimately than ever before. The cultural mode favoured by this new, heavily patriarchal bourgeoisie was the 'male' technological mode – objective, realistic, factual, 'commonsense' – rather than the effeminate, otherworldly, 'romantic idealist' aesthetic mode. The bourgeoisie, searching for the ideal in the real, soon developed the empirical science that we have described. To the extent that they had any remaining use for aesthetic culture, it was only for 'realistic' art, as opposed to the 'idealistic' art of classical antiquity, or the abstract religious art of primitive or medieval times. For a time they went in for a literature that described reality – best exemplified by the nineteenth-century novel – and a decorative easel art: still lifes, portraits, family scenes, interiors. Public museums and libraries were built alongside the old salons and private galleries. But with its entrenchment as a secure, even primary, class, the bourgeoisie no longer needed to imitate aristocratic cultivation. More important, with the rapid development of their new science and technology, the little practical value they had for art was eclipsed. Take the scientific development of the camera: the bourgeoisie soon had little need for portrait painters; the little that painters or novelists had been able to do for them, the camera could do better.

'Modern' art was a desperate, but finally self-defeating, retaliation ('*épater le bourgeois*') for these injuries: the evaporation of its social function, the severance of the social umbilical cord, the dwindling of the old sources of patronage. The modern art tradition, associated primarily with Picasso and Cézanne, and including all the major schools of the twentieth century – cubism, constructivism, futurism, expressionism, surrealism,

174

abstract expressionism, and so on – is not an authentic expression of modernity as much as it is a reaction to the realism of the bourgeoisie. Post-impressionism deliberately renounced all reality-affirming conventions – indeed the process began with impressionism itself, which broke down the illusion into its formal values, swallowing reality whole and spitting it up again as art – to lead eventually to an art-for-art's-sake so pure, a negation of reality so complete as to make it ultimately meaningless, sterile, even absurd. (Cab drivers *are* philistine: they know a put-on when they see one.) The deliberate violating, deforming, fracturing of the image, called 'modern' art, was nothing more than a fifty-year idol smashing – eventually leading to our present cultural impasse.

In the twentieth century, its life blood drained, its social function nullified altogether, art is thrown back on whatever wealthy classes remain, those *nouveaux riches* – particularly in America, still suffering from a cultural inferiority complex – who still need to prove they have 'arrived' by evidencing a taste for culture. The sequestering of intellectuals in ivory tower universities, where, except for the sciences, they have little effect on the outside world, no matter how brilliant (and they aren't, because they no longer have the necessary feedback); the abstruse – often literally unintelligible – jargon of the social sciences; the cliquish literary quarterlies with their esoteric poetry; the posh 57th Street galleries and museums (it is no accident that they are right next door to Saks Fifth Avenue and Bonwit Teller) staffed and supplied by, for the most part, fawning rich-widows'-hairdresser types; and not least the vulturous critical establishment thriving on the remains of what was once a great and vital culture – all testify to the death of aesthetic humanism.

For in the centuries that Science climbed to new heights, Art decayed. Its forced inbreeding transformed it into a secret code. By definition escapist from reality, it now turned in upon itself to such degree that it gnawed away its own vitals. It became diseased – neurotically self-pitying, self-conscious, focused on the past (as opposed to the futurist orientation of the technological culture) and thus frozen into conventions and academies – orthodoxies of which 'avant-garde' is only the latest – pining for remembered glories, the Grand Old Days When Beauty Was In Flower; it became pessimistic and nihilistic, increasingly hostile to the society at large, the 'philistines'. And when the cocky young Science attempted to woo Art from its ivory tower – eventually garret – with false promises of the courting lover ('You can come down now, we're making the world a better place every day'), Art refused more vehemently than ever to deal with him, much less accept his corrupt gifts, retreating ever deeper into her daydreams – neoclassicism, romanticism, expressionism, surrealism, existentialism.

The individual artist or intellectual saw himself as either a member of an invisible élite, a 'highbrow', or as a down-and-outer, mingling with whoever was deemed the dregs of his society. In both cases, whether playing Aristocrat or Bohemian, he was on the margins of the society as a whole. The artist had become a freak. His increasing alienation from the world around him – the new world that science had created was, especially in its primitive stages, an incredible horror, only intensifying his need to escape to the ideal world of art – his lack of an audience, led to a mystique of 'genius'. Like an ascetic Saint Simeon on his pedestal, the Genius in the Garret was expected to create masterpieces in a vacuum. But his artery to the outside world had been severed. His task, increasingly impossible, often forced him literally into madness, or suicide.

Painted into a corner with nowhere else to go, the artist has got to begin to come to terms with the modern world. He is not too good at it: like an invalid shut away too long, he doesn't know anything about the world anymore, neither politics, nor science, nor even how to live or love. Until now, yes, even now, though less and less so, sublimation, that warping of personality, was commendable: it was the only (albeit indirect) way to achieve fulfilment. But the artistic process has – almost – outlived its usefulness. And its price is high.

The first attempts to confront the modern world have been for the most part misguided. The Bauhaus, a famous example, failed at its objective of replacing an irrelevant easel art (only a few optical illusions and designy chairs mark the grave), ending up with a hybrid, neither art nor science, and certainly not the

176

sum of the two. They failed because they didn't understand science on its own terms: to them, seeing in the old aesthetic way, it was simply a rich new subject matter to be digested whole into the traditional aesthetic system. It is as if one were to see a computer as only a beautifully ordered set of lights and sounds, missing completely the function itself. The scientific experiment is not only beautiful, an elegant structure, another piece of an abstract puzzle, something to be used in the next collage – but scientists, too, in their own way, see science as this abstraction divorced from life – it has a real intrinsic meaning of its own, similar to, but not the same as, the 'presence', the '*en-soi*', of modern painting. Many artists have made the mistake of thus trying to annex science, to incorporate it into their own artistic framework, rather than using it to expand that framework.

Is the current state of aesthetic culture all bleak? No, there have been some progressive developments in contemporary art. We have mentioned how the realistic tradition in painting died with the camera. This tradition had developed over centuries to a level of illusionism with the brush – examine a Bouguereau – that was the equal of, better than, the early photography, then considered only another graphic medium, like etching. The beginning of the new art of film and the realistic tradition of painting overlapped, peaked, in artists like Degas, who used a camera in his work. Then realistic art took a new course: either it became decadent, academic, divorced from any market and meaning, e.g., the nudes that linger on in art classes and second-rate galleries, or it was fractured into the expressionist or surrealist image, posing an alternate internal or fantastical reality. Meanwhile, however, the young art of film, based on a true synthesis of the aesthetic and technological modes (as Empiricism itself had been), carried on the vital realistic tradition. And just as with the marriage of the divided male and female principles, empirical science bore fruit; so did the medium of film. But, unlike other aesthetic media of the past, it broke down the very division between the artificial and the real, between culture and life itself, on which the aesthetic mode is based.

Other related developments: the exploration of artificial materials, e.g., plastics; the attempt to confront plastic culture itself (pop art); the breakdown of traditional categories of media (mixed media), and of the distinctions between art and reality itself (happenings, environments). But I find it difficult unreservedly to call these latter developments progressive: as yet they have produced largely puerile and meaningless works. The artist does not yet know what reality is, let alone how to affect it. Paper cups lined up on the street, pieces of paper thrown into an empty lot, no matter how many ponderous reviews they get in *Art News*, are a waste of time. If these clumsy attempts are at all hopeful, it is only in so far as they are signs of the breakdown of 'fine' art.

The merging of the aesthetic with the technological mode will gradually suffocate 'pure' high art altogether. The first breakdown of categories, the re-merging of art with a (technologized) reality, indicates that we are now in the transitional prerevolutionary period, in which the three separate cultural streams, technology ('applied science'), 'pure research', and 'pure' modern art, will melt together – along with the rigid sex categories they reflect.

The sex-based polarity of culture still causes many casualties. If even the 'pure' scientist, e.g., nuclear physicist (let alone the 'applied' scientist, e.g., engineer), suffers from too much 'male', becoming authoritarian, conventional, emotionally insensitive, narrowly unable to understand his own work within the scientific – let alone cultural or social – jigsaw, the artist, in terms of the sex division, has embodied all the imbalances and suffering of the female personality: temperamental, insecure, paranoid, defeatist, narrow. And the recent withholding of reinforcements from behind the front (the larger society) has exaggerated all this enormously; his overdeveloped 'id' has nothing left to balance it. Where the pure scientist is 'schiz', or worse, *ignorant* of emotional reality altogether, the pure artist *rejects* reality because of its lack of perfection, and, in modern centuries, for its ugliness.

And who suffers the most, the blind (scientist) or the lame (artist)? Culturally, we have had only the choice between one sex role or the other: either a social marginality leading to self-consciousness, introversion, defeatism, pessimism, oversensitivity, and lack of touch with reality, or a split 'professionalized' personality, emotional ignorance, the narrow views of the specialist.

THE ANTIKULTUR REVOLUTION

I have tried to show how the history of culture mirrors the sex dichotomy in its very organization and development. Culture develops not only out of the underlying economic dialectic, but also out of the deeper sex dialectic. Thus, there is not only a horizontal dynamic, but a vertical one as well: each of these three strata forms one more story of the dialectics of history based on the biological dualism. At present we have reached the final stages of Patriarchy, Capitalism (corporate capitalism), and of the Two Cultures at once. We shall soon have a triplicate set of preconditions for revolution, the absence of which is responsible for the failure of revolutions of the past.

The difference between what is almost possible and what exists is generating revolutionary forces.[3] We are nearing – I believe we shall have, perhaps within a century, if the snowball of empirical knowledge doesn't smash first of its own velocity – a cultural revolution, as well as a sexual and economic one. The cultural revolution, like the economic revolution, must be predicated on the elimination of the (sex) dualism at the origins not only of class, but also of cultural division.

What might this cultural revolution look like? Unlike 'cultural revolutions' of the past, it would not be merely a quantitative escalation, more and better culture, in the sense that the Renaissance was a high point of the aesthetic mode, or that the present technological breakthrough is the accumulation of centuries of practical knowledge about the real world. Great as they were, neither the aesthetic nor the technological culture, even at their respective peaks, ever achieved universality – either it was wholistic but divorced from the real world, or it achieved 'progress', at the price of cultural schizophrenia, and the falseness

3. Revolutionaries, by definition, are still visionaries of the aesthetic mode, the idealists of pragmatic politics.

SEX

CASTE
**EXTENDING TO
AGE AND RACE**

BASED ON
BIOLOGICAL DIVISION
INTO SEXES FOR:
REPRODUCTION
OF THE SPECIES

♀ **MATRIARCHY**

♂ **PATRIA**

VARIOUS FORMS OF SOCIAL ORGANIZATION THROUGHOUT HISTOR
ON THE BIOLOGICAL FAMILY UNIT—INCLUDING CLAI

CLASS

BASED ON
DIVISION OF LABOR
FOR:
PRODUCTION
OF
GOODS AND SERVICES

NOMADS

(ENGELS' "SAVAGERY")

ADAPTATION
TO
NATURE

TILLERS

(ENGELS' "BARBARISM")

INCREASING CONTROL
OF
NATURE

CIVIL

♀ ARISTOCRAC

♂ LOWER CLAS

CULTURE

BASED ON
PSYCHOLOGICAL DIVISION
OF RESPONSES FOR:
REALIZATION
OF THE CONCEIVABLE
IN THE POSSIBLE

**CONTROL
OF
TOOL . . . FIRE . . . WHEEL . . . ORE** } **SWORD** . . . **ALPHABET**
PLOW

**ARCHITECTURE
LAW AND GOVERNMENT, ETC.**

♂ **TECHNOLOGICAL MODE**
(PRAGMATIC)

♀ **AESTHETIC MODE**
(IDEAL)

———— **RELIGION** ————

PRIMITIVE ART AND MAGIC . . . PROPHESY . . . HISTORY

GOVT., LAW
& COMMERCE

ARCHITECTURE

MEDICINE

SCIENCE

PHILOSOPHY

ART

CLASSICAL   MEDIEVAL

RENAISSANCE → MODERN ↔

	REVOLUTION	TRANSITION	ULTIMATE GOAL
...RCHY ...LL BASED ...ACE, NATION, ETC.	**SEXUAL REVOLUTION** FEMINIST REVOLT (ALSO CHILDREN AND YOUTH, OPPRESSED RACES)	"SINGLE STANDARD" MONOGAMY DEVELOPMENT OF ARTIFICIAL REPRODUCTION MULTIPLE SOCIAL OPTIONS (INCLUDING THE REPRODUCTIVE "HOUSEHOLD") (EVENTUAL ELIMINATION OF CHILDHOOD, AGING AND DEATH)	**FULL SEXUAL FREEDOM** ALLOWING ATTAINMENT OF "HAPPINESS" DISAPPEARANCE OF CULTURAL SEX, AGE, AND RACE DISTINCTION AND OF THE PSYCHOLOGY OF POWER (INCLUDING "NEUROSIS," "SUBLIMATION," ETC.)
...ATION ELITE ...MIDDLE CLASS ...ORKING CLASS	**ECONOMIC REVOLUTION** PROLETARIAN REVOLT (INCLUDING THE THIRD WORLD AGAINST IMPERIALISM)	**SOCIALISM** DICTATORSHIP OF THE PROLETARIAT	**SELF-DETERMINATION** ("COMMUNISTIC ANARCHY") **AND PAN-WORLD LIVING** DISAPPEARANCE OF CLASS DISTINCTION AND OF THE STATE (NATIONALISM AND IMPERIALISM)
MODERN INDUSTRY ("APPLIED SCIENCE") EMPIRICAL SCIENCE ("PURE RESEARCH") MODERN ART ("ART FOR ART'S SAKE")	**CULTURAL REVOLUTION** SCIENTIFIC BREAKTHROUGH BREAKDOWN OF CULTURAL CATEGORIES	**MERGING OF ART AND REALITY**	**REALIZATION OF THE CONCEIVABLE IN THE ACTUAL** DISAPPEARANCE OF "CULTURE"

and dryness of 'objectivity.' What we shall have in the next cultural revolution is the reintegration of the Male (Technological Mode) with the Female (Aesthetic Mode), to create an androgynous culture surpassing the highs of either cultural stream, or even of the sum of their integrations. More than a marriage, rather an abolition of the cultural categories themselves, a mutual cancelation—a matter-antimatter explosion, ending with a poof! culture itself.

We shall not miss it. We shall no longer need it: by then humanity will have mastered nature totally, will have realized in *actuality* its dreams. With the full achievement of the conceivable in the actual, the surrogate of culture will no longer be necessary. The sublimation process, a detour to wish fulfillment, will give way to direct satisfaction in experience, as felt now only by children, or adults on drugs.* (Though normal adults 'play' to varying degrees, the example that illustrates more immediately to almost everyone the intense level of this future experience, ranking zero on a scale of accomplishment—'nothing to show for it'—but nevertheless somehow always worth everyone's while, is lovemaking.) Control and delay of 'id' satisfaction by the 'ego' will be unnecessary; the *id* can live free. Enjoyment will spring directly from being and acting itself, the process of experience, rather than from the quality of achievement. When the male Techonological Mode can at last produce in actuality what the female Aesthetic Mode had envisioned, we shall have eliminated the need for either.

* Recent attempts of the youth {hippie, drug} culture to return to this state of simplicity —even if one turns into a 'head' by artificial means of chemical stimulation—are bound to fail. People have developed layers of repression and defenses only because they *must* to live in our current real world. One now can achieve at best a (mannered and self-conscious) 'direct experience' only by 'dropping out,' ignoring the real world, for example, moving to Colorado (circa 1878) with people of like mind, and hoping hard they won't bother bombing out there. This is naïve—and reactionary, regressive, ahistorical, utopian, etc.—but above all, it is ineffective.

10   The Ultimate Revolution: Demands and Speculations

FEMINISM AND ECOLOGY

Empirical science left repercussions in its wake: the sharp acceleration of technology upset the natural order. But recent popular interest in ecology, the study of man's relationship to his environment, may, by 1970, have come too late. Certainly it is too late for conservationism, the attempt to *redress* natural balances. What is called for is a revolutionary ecological programme that would attempt to establish a *humane* artificial (man-made) balance in place of the natural one, thus also realizing the original goal of empirical science: human mastery of matter.

The best new currents in ecology and social planning agree with feminist aims. The way that these two social phenomena, feminism and revolutionary ecology, have emerged with such coincidence illustrates a historical truth: new theories and new movements do not develop in a vacuum, they arise to spearhead the necessary social solutions to contradictions in the environment. In this case, both movements have arisen in response to the same contradiction: animal life within a technology. In the case of feminism the problem is a moral one: the biological family unit has always oppressed women and children, but now, for the first time in history, technology has created real preconditions for overthrowing these oppressive 'natural' conditions, along with their cultural reinforcements. In the case of the new ecology, we find that *independent of any moral stance*, for pragmatic – survival – reasons alone, it has become necessary to free humanity from the tyranny of its biology. Humanity can no longer afford to remain in the transitional stage between simple animal existence and full control of nature. And we are much closer to a major evolutionary jump, indeed, to direction of our own evolution, than we are to a return to the animal kingdom through which we evolved. Thus in view of accelerating technology, a revolutionary ecological movement would have the same aim as the feminist movement: control of the new technology for humane purposes, the establishment of a new equilibrium between man and the artificial environment he is creating, to replace the destroyed 'natural' balance.

What are some of the concerns of ecology that are of direct interest to the feminist movement? I shall discuss briefly two issues of the new ecology that particularly pertain to the new feminism: reproduction and its control, including the population crisis and methods of fertility control; and cybernation, the full takeover by machines of increasingly complex functions, altering man's age-old relation to work and wages.

Previously I had taken copious notes, written whole drafts on the population explosion, quoting once again all sorts of frightening statistics about the rate of population growth. But on second thought, it seemed to me that I had heard it all before and so had everyone else. Perhaps for the purposes of this book, we would do better to discuss why these statistics are so consistently ignored. For, despite increasingly dire pronouncements from every expert in the field, few people are seriously worried. In fact, the *laissez faire* actually seems to grow in direct proportion to the urgency for immediate action.

The relation between the two situations is direct: inability to confront or deal with the problem creates a sham confidence, the extent of which is borne out by a recent Gallup poll (3 August, 1968) in which, to the question, 'What do you find to be the most pressing problem confronting the nation today?' less than 1 per cent of the national sample of adults questioned mentioned population. And yet at the very least, to quote population experts Lincoln H. Day and Alice Taylor Day, in their book *Too Many Americans*, 'To support an increase of another 180,000,000 (forty-four more years, at current rates) this country would have to undergo changes in the condition of life as radical as those that have occurred since Columbus.' This is the most conservative estimate. The majority of demographers, biologists, and ecologists are considerably more pessimistic. Books come out all the time on the subject, each with a new slant to the terrors of the population explosion (If we had reproduced at this rate since the time of Christ, by now we would have . . . If we continue at this rate, starvation will look like . . . by the year . . . So and so many rats congested in a room produce XYZ behaviour . . .), books with such titles as *Famine, 1975, The Population Bomb,* and so on. Scientists themselves are in a panic: a well-known biologist at Rockefeller University is reputed to have stopped speaking to his own daughter after the birth of her third child; his students multiply at their peril.

Yet the public remains convinced that science can solve the problem. One reason the man on the street believes so ardently that 'they' can handle it – in addition to the Witchdoctor Mystique that 'they' always seem to find an answer for everything – is that information filters down so slowly from above. For example, the public began to hear about the 'green revolution' only when scientists abandoned hope in it as anything but a desperate stopgap measure to delay worldwide famine for another generation; so rather than alarming, this information acted as a bromide.

The Miracle-of-Modern-Science is only one of a whole stockpile of arguments that, no matter how often they are disproven, keep bobbing up again. There is the Food Surplus argument, the Vast-Stretches-of-Unpopulated-Land argument, the Chinese Boogy-Woogy (population increases defence strength), and many more, varying in their sophistication with the social milieu of their propounders. It is useless to argue – so I won't do it here – for it is not at all a question of correct information, or logic. There is something else underlying all these arguments. What is it?

The chauvinism that develops in the family. We have discussed some of the components of this family psychology: the patriarchal mentality concerned with its sons only in so far as they are heir and ego extension, in the private bid for immortality (why worry about the larger social good just so long as *You And Yours* are 'happy'); Us-Against-Them chauvinism (blood is thicker); the division between the abstract and the concrete, the public and the private (what could be more abstract and public than a demographic statistic? what could be more private and concrete than one's own reproduction?); the privatization of the sex experience; the power psychology; and so on.

Leftists and revolutionaries, unfortunately, are no exception to this universal malpsychology generated by the family. They too indulge in Us-Against-Themism, though this time in reverse. If 'Us', the upper-class and highbrow intelligentsia, argues that 'We better not have a decrease in birth rates or the rabble and/ or the weakminded will take over', 'Them', the 'rabble' (lately known as the 'lunatic fringe'), counters with paranoia about being birth-controlled out of existence – 'Genocide!' This fear is well-founded. However, it is also responsible for a general failure of vision on the Left to see beneath the evil uses of birth control to a genuine ecological problem which no number of fancy arguments and bogey statistics can erase. It is true that capitalist imperialist governments are only too glad to dispense birth control devices to the Third World or to Blacks and the poor in the US (particularly welfare mothers, who are often made into guinea pigs for the latest experiments), while at home they think nothing of giving a man a ten-year jail sentence for dispensing Emko Foam to a young, white, unmarried coed; it is true that a redistribution of the world's wealth and resources would greatly ease the problem – even if it *could* happen tomorrow. But the problem would still remain, for it exists independently of traditional politics and economics, and thus could not be solved by traditional politics and economics alone. These political and economic complications are only *aggravations* of a genuine problem of ecology. Once again radicals have failed to think radically enough: capitalism is not the *only* enemy, redistribution of wealth and resources is not the *only* solution, attempts to control population are not *only* Third World Suppression in disguise.

But often there is a more serious error: results of the *misuse* of technology are very often attributed to the use of technology *per se*. (But do the black militants who advocate unchecked fertility for black women allow *themselves* to become burdened with heavy bellies and too many mouths to feed? One gathers that they find contraception of some help in maintaining their active preaching schedules.) As was demonstrated in the case of the development of atomic energy, radicals, rather than breast-beating about the immorality of scientific research, could be much more effective by concentrating their *full* energies on demands for control of scientific discoveries by and for the people. For, like atomic energy, fertility control, artificial repro-duction, cybernation, in themselves, are liberating – *unless* they are improperly used.

What are the new scientific developments in the control of this dangerously prolific reproduction? Already we have more and better contraception than ever before in history.[1] The old span-ner-in-the-works intervention against conception (diaphragms, condoms, foams, and jellies) was only the beginning. Soon we shall have a complete understanding of the entire reproductive process in all its complexity, including the subtle dynamics of hormones and their full effects on the nervous system. Present oral contraception is at only a primitive (faulty) stage, only one of many types of fertility control now under experiment. Arti-ficial insemination and artificial inovulation are already a reality. Choice of sex of the foetus, test-tube fertilization (when capaci-tation of sperm within the vagina is fully understood) are just around the corner. Several teams of scientists are working on the development of an artificial placenta. Even parthenogenesis – virgin birth – could be developed very soon.

Are people, even scientists themselves, culturally prepared for any of this? Decidedly not. A recent Harris poll, quoted in *Life* magazine, representing a broad sampling of Americans – includ-ing, for example, Iowa farmers – found a surprising number willing to consider the new methods. The hitch was that they would consider them only where they reinforced and furthered present values of family life and reproduction, e.g., to help a barren woman have her husband's child. Any question that

1. This chapter was written before the 'Pill Hearings', indeed before the mushrooming of the ecology movement itself. Such is the speed of modern communications – a book is outdated before it even makes it into galleys.

187

could be interpreted as a furthering of liberation *per se* was rejected flatly as unnatural. But note that it was not the 'test tube' baby itself that was thought unnatural (25 percent agreed off the bat that they themselves would use this method, let's say, in case the wife was barren), but the new value system, based on the elimination of male supremacy and the family.

It is clear by now that research in the area of reproduction is itself being impeded by cultural lag and sexual bias. The money allocated for specific kinds of research, the kinds of research done are only incidentally in the interests of women when at all. For example, work on the development of an artificial placenta still has to be excused on the grounds that it might save babies born prematurely. Thus, although it would be far easier technically to transfer an embryo than a nearly developed baby, all the money goes into the latter research. Or again, that women are excluded from science is directly responsible for the tabling of research on oral contraceptives for males. (Is it possible that women are thought to make better guinea pigs because they are considered by male scientists to be 'inferior'? Or is it only because male scientists worship male fertility?) There are great numbers of such examples.

Fears of new methods of reproduction are so widespread that as of the time of this writing, 1969, the subject, outside of scientific circles, is still taboo. Even many women in the women's liberation movement – perhaps especially in the women's liberation movement – are afraid to express any interest in it for fear of confirming the suspicion that they are 'unnatural', wasting a great deal of energy denying that they are anti-motherhood, pro-artificial reproduction, and so on. Let me then say it bluntly:

Pregnancy is barbaric. I do not believe, as many women are now saying, that the reason pregnancy is viewed as not beautiful is due strictly to cultural perversion. The child's first response, 'What's wrong with that Fat Lady?'; the husband's guilty waning of sexual desire; the woman's tears in front of the mirror at eight months – are all gut reactions, not to be dismissed as cultural habits. Pregnancy is the temporary deformation of the body of the individual for the sake of the species.

Moreover, childbirth *hurts*. And it isn't good for you. Three thousand years ago, women giving birth 'naturally' had no need to pretend that pregnancy was a real trip, some mystical orgasm (that far-away look). The Bible said it: pain and travail. The glamour was unnecessary: women had no choice. They didn't dare squawk. But at least they could scream as loudly as they wanted during their labour pains. And after it was over, even during it, they were admired in a limited way for their bravery; their valour was measured by how many children (sons) they could endure bringing into the world.

Today all this has been confused. The cult of natural childbirth itself tells us how far we've come from true oneness with nature. Natural childbirth is only one more part of the reactionary hippie-Rousseauean Return-to-Nature, and just as self-conscious. Perhaps a mystification of childbirth, true faith, makes it easier for the woman involved. Pseudo-yoga exercises, twenty pregnant women breathing deeply on the floor to the conductor's baton, may even help some women develop 'proper' attitudes (as in 'I didn't scream once'). The squirming husband at the bedside, like the empathy pains of certain tribesmen ('Just look what I go through with you, dear'), may make a woman feel less alone during her ordeal. But the fact remains: childbirth is at best necessary and tolerable. It is not fun.

(Like shitting a pumpkin, a friend of mine told me when I inquired about the Great-Experience-You're-Missing. What's-wrong-with-shitting-shitting-can-be-fun says the School of the Great Experience. It hurts, she says. What's-wrong-with-a-little-pain-as-long-as-it-doesn't-kill-you? answers the school. It is boring, she says. Pain-can-be-interesting-as-an-experience says the school. Isn't that a rather high price to pay for interesting experience? she says. But-look-you-get-a-reward, says the school: a-baby-all-your-own-to-fuck-up-as-you-please. Well, that's something, she says. But how do I know it will be male like you?)

Artificial reproduction is not inherently dehumanizing. At very least, development of the option should make possible an honest re-examination of the ancient value of motherhood. At the present time, for a woman to come out openly against motherhood on principle is physically dangerous. She can get away with it only if she adds that she is neurotic, abnormal, child-hating, and therefore 'unfit'. ('Perhaps later . . . when I'm better prepared.') This is hardly a free atmosphere of inquiry. At least until the taboo is lifted, until the decision not to have children or to have them by artificial means is as legitimate as traditional child-bearing, women are as good as forced into their female roles.

Another scientific development that we find difficult to absorb into our traditional value system is the new science of cybernetics: machines that may soon equal or surpass man in original thinking and problem-solving. While it may be argued, as with artificial reproduction, that such machines are barely past the speculative stage, remember that it was only five to ten years ago that experts in the field were predicting that five or six computers would satisfy permanently the needs of the whole country.

Cybernetics, like birth control, can be a double-edged sword. Like artificial reproduction, to envision it in the hands of the present powers is to envision a nightmare. We need not elaborate. Everyone is familiar with Technocracy, 1984: the increased alienation of the masses, the intensified rule of the élite (now perhaps cyberneticians), baby factories, computerized government (Big Brother), and so on. In the hands of the present establishment there is no doubt that the machine could be used – is being used – to intensify the apparatus of repression and to increase established power.

But again, as in the issue of population control, *misuse* of science has often obscured the value of science itself. In this case, though perhaps the response may not be quite so hysterical and evasive, we still often have the same unimaginative concentration on the evils of the machine itself, rather than a recognition of its revolutionary significance. Books and research abound on how to avoid Technocracy, 1984 (e.g., Alan Weston's *Privacy and Freedom*), but there is little thought about how to deal effectively with the qualitative changes in life style that cybernation will bring.

The two issues, population control and cybernetics, produce the same nervous superficial response because in both cases the underlying problem is one for which there is no precedent: qualitative change in humanity's basic relationships to both its production and its reproduction. We will need almost overnight, in order to deal with the profound effects of fertility control and cybernation, a new culture based on a radical redefinition of human relationships and leisure for the masses. To so radically redefine our relationship to production and reproduction requires the destruction at once of the class system as well as the family. We will be beyond arguments about who is 'bringing home the bacon' – no one will be bringing it home, because no one will be 'working'. Job discrimination would no longer have any basis in a society where machines do the work better than human beings of any size or skill could. Machines thus could act as the perfect equalizer, obliterating the class system based on exploitation of labour.

What might the immediate impact of cybernation be on the position of women? Briefly, we can predict the following: (1) While at first automation will continue to provide new service jobs for women, e.g., keypunch operator, computer programmer, etc., these positions are not likely to last long (precisely why women, the transient labour force *par excellence*, are sought for them). Eventually, such simple specialized control of machines will give way to a more widespread common knowledge of their control and, at the same time, at top levels, increased specialized knowledge of their newer, more complex functions by a new élite of engineers, cyberneticians. The kinds of jobs into which women have been welcomed, the lower rung of white-collar service jobs, will be phased out. At the same time, housework also will become more cybernated, reducing women's legitimate work functions even further. (2) Erosion of the status of the 'head of the household,' particularly in the working class, may shake up family life and traditional sex roles even more profoundly. (3) Massive unrest of the young, the poor, the unemployed will increase: as jobs become more difficult to obtain, and there is no cushioning of the cultural shock by education for leisure, revolutionary ferment is likely to become a staple. Thus, all in all, cybernation may aggravate the frustration that women already feel in their roles, pushing them into revolution.

A feminist revolution could be the decisive factor in establishing a new ecological balance: attention drawn to the population explosion, a shifting of emphasis from reproduction to contraception, and demands for the full development of artificial reproduction would provide an alternative to the oppressions of the biological family; cybernation, by changing man's relationship to work and wages, by transforming activity from 'work' to 'play' (activity done for its own sake), would allow for a total redefinition of the economy, including the family unit in its economic capacity. The double curse that man should till the soil by the sweat of his brow and that woman should bear in pain and travail would be lifted through technology to make humane living for the first time a possibility. The feminist movement has the essential mission of creating cultural acceptance of the new ecological balance necessary for the survival of the human race in the twentieth century.

REVOLUTIONARY DEMANDS

Women, biologically distinguished from men, are culturally distinguished from 'human'. Nature produced the fundamental inequality – half the human race must bear and rear the children of all of them – which was later consolidated, institutionalized, in the interests of men. Reproduction of the species cost women dearly, not only emotionally, psychologically, culturally but even in strictly material (physical) terms: before recent methods of contraception, continuous childbirth led to constant 'female trouble', early ageing, and death. Women were the slave class that maintained the species in order to free the other half for the business of the world – admittedly often its drudge aspects, but certainly all its creative aspects as well.

This natural division of labour was continued only at great cultural sacrifice: men and women developed only half of themselves. The division of the psyche into male and female to better reinforce the reproductive division was tragic: the hypertrophy in men of rationalism, aggressive drive, the atrophy of their emotional sensitivity, was a physical (war) as well as a cultural disaster. The emotionalism and passivity of women increased their suffering (we cannot speak of them in a symmetrical way, since they were victimized as a class by the division). Sexually men and women were channelled into a highly ordered – time, place, procedure, even dialogue – heterosexuality restricted to the genitals, rather than diffused over the entire physical being.

I submit, then, that the first demand for any alternative system must be:

(1) *The freeing of women from the tyranny of reproduction by every means possible, and the diffusion of the child-rearing role to the society as a whole, men as well as women.*

There are many degrees of this. Already we have a (hard-won) acceptance of 'family planning', if not contraception for its own sake. Proposals are imminent for day-care centres, perhaps even twenty-four-hour child-care centres staffed by men as well as women. But this, in my opinion, is timid if not entirely worthless as a transition. We're talking about *radical* change. And though indeed it cannot come all at once, radical goals must be kept in sight at all times. Day-care centres buy women off. They ease the immediate pressure without asking why that pressure is on *women*.

At the other extreme there are the more distant solutions based on the potentials of modern embryology, that is, artificial reproduction, possibilities still so frightening that they are seldom discussed seriously. We have seen that the fear is to some extent justified: in the hands of our current society and under the direction of current scientists (few of whom are female or even feminist), any attempted use of technology to 'free' anybody is suspect. But we are speculating about post-revolutionary systems, and for the purposes of our discussion we shall assume flexibility and good intentions in those working out the change.

To free women thus from their biology would be to threaten the *social* unit that is organized around biological reproduction and the subjection of women to their biological destiny, the

193

family. Our second demand also will come as a basic contradiction to the family, this time the family as an *economic* unit.

(2) *The political autonomy, based on economic independence, of both women and children.*

To achieve this goal would require revolutionary changes in our social and economic structure. That is why we must talk about, in addition to radically new forms of breeding, a cybernetic communism. For without advanced technology, even eliminating capitalism, we could withstand only a marginal integration of women into the labour force. Margaret Benston has pointed out the importance of distinguishing between the industrial economy based on commodity production, and the pre-industrial economy of the family, production for immediate use: because the work of women is not part of the modern economy, its function as the very basis of that economy is easily overlooked. Talk of drafting women *en masse* into the superstructure economy thus fails to deal with the tremendous amount of labour of the more traditional kind that – prior to full cybernation – still must be done. Who will do it?

Even paying the masses of women for doing this labour, could we swing it – multiply the 99.6 woman-hours per week (conservatively estimated by the Chase Manhattan Bank) by even a minimum hourly wage, times half the (previously slave) population, and you are calculating the overthrow of capitalism – would constitute only a reform in revolutionary feminist terms, for it does not begin to challenge the root division of labour and thus could never eradicate its disastrous psycho-cultural consequences.

As for the independence of children, that is really a pipe dream, realized as yet nowhere in the world. For, in the case of children, too, we are talking about more than a fair integration into the labour force; we are talking about the obsolescence of the labour force itself through cybernation, the radical restructuring of the economy to make 'work', i.e. compulsory labour, particularly alienated 'wage' labour, no longer necessary.

We have now attacked the family on a double front, challenging that around which it is organized: reproduction of the species by females and its outgrowth, the dependence of women

194

and children. To eliminate these would be enough to destroy the family, which breeds the psychology of power. However, we will break it down still further.

(3) *The complete integration of women and children into society.*

All institutions that segregate the sexes, or bar children from adult society, must be destroyed. (Down with school!)

And if male/female–adult/child cultural distinctions are destroyed, we will no longer need the sexual repression that maintains these unequal classes, uncovering for the first time natural sexual freedom. Thus we arrive at:

(4) *The sexual freedom of all women and children.* Now they can do whatever they wish to do sexually. There will no longer be any reason *not* to. Past reasons: full sexuality threatened the continuous reproduction necessary for human survival, and thus, through religion and other cultural institutions, sexuality had to be restricted to reproductive purposes, all non-reproductive sex pleasure considered deviation or worse: the sexual freedom of women would call into question the fatherhood of the child, thus threatening patrimony; child sexuality had to be repressed by means of the incest taboo because it was a threat to the precarious internal balance of the family. These sexual repressions increased proportionately to the degree of cultural exaggeration of the biological family.

But in our new society, humanity could finally revert to its natural polymorphous sexuality – all forms of sexuality would be allowed and indulged. The fully sexuate mind, realized in the past in only a few individuals (survivors), would become universal. Artificial cultural achievement would no longer be the only avenue to sexuate self-realization: one could now realize oneself fully, simply in the process of being and acting.

Three Failed Experiments

These structural imperatives must form the basis of any more specific radical feminist programme. But our revolutionary demands are likely to meet anything from mild balking ('utopian ... unrealistic ... farfetched ... too far in the future ...

impossible . . . so, the system stinks, but you haven't got anything better . . .') to hysteria ('inhuman . . . unnatural . . . sick . . . perverted . . . communistic . . . 1984 . . . what? creative motherhood destroyed for babies in glass tubes, monsters made by scientists?, etc.'). But we have seen that such defensive reactions on the contrary may signify how close we are hitting: revolutionary feminism is the only radical programme that immediately cracks through to the emotional strata underlying 'serious' politics, thus reintegrating the personal with the public, the subjective with the objective, the emotional with the rational – the female principle with the male.

What are some of the prime components of this resistance that is keeping people from experimenting with alternatives to the family, and where does it come from? We are all familiar with the details of Brave New World: cold collectives, with individualism abolished, sex reduced to a mechanical act, children become robots, Big Brother intruding into every aspect of private life, rows of babies fed by impersonal machines, eugenics manipulated by the state, genocide of cripples and retards for the sake of a super-race created by white-coated technicians, all emotion considered weakness, love destroyed, and so on. The family (which, despite its oppressiveness, is now the last refuge from the encroaching power of the state, a shelter that provides the little emotional warmth, privacy, and individual comfort now available) would be destroyed, letting this horror penetrate indoors.

Ironically, one reason for the continual recurrence of '1984' so frequently is that it grows directly out of, signifying an exaggeration of, the evils of our present male-supremacist culture. For example, many of its visual details are lifted directly from our orphanages and state-run institutions for children.[2] This is

2. Though it is true that children in orphanages do not get even the warmth and attention that parents give a child, with crippling results – tests have shown I Q's of children in institutions to be lower, emotional maladjustment higher, and even, as in the famous experiment with monkeys deprived of motherly care, sexual functioning to be crippled or destroyed – those who quote these statistics so triumphantly to discredit radical alternatives do not recognize that the orphanage is the antithesis of a radical alternative, that in fact it is *an outgrowth of what we are trying to correct.*
The orphanage is the underside of the family, just as prostitution is the

a vision of a society in which women have become like men, crippled in the identical way, thus destroying a delicate balance of interlocking dependencies.

However, we are suggesting the opposite: rather than the concentration of the female principle into a 'private' retreat, into which men can periodically duck for relief, we want to rediffuse it – for the first time truly creating society from the bottom up. Man's difficult triumph over Nature has made it possible to restore the truly natural: he could undo both his own and Eve's curse, to re-establish the earthly Garden of Eden. But in his long toil his imagination has been stifled: he fears rather the enlargement of his drudgery, the addition of Eve's curse to his own.

But there is a more concrete reason why this subliminal horror image operates to destroy serious consideration of feminism: the failure of past social experiments. Radical experiments, when they have solved problems at all, have created an entirely new – and not necessarily improved – set of problems in their place. Let us look briefly at some of these radical experiments to determine the causes of their failure – for I believe that in no case was

---

direct result of the institution of patriarchal marriage. In the same sense as prostitution complements marriage, the orphanage is the necessary complementary evil of a society in which the majority of children live under a system of patronage by genetic parents. In the one case, because women exist under patronage, unclaimed women pay a special price; in the other, because children are possessions of specific individuals rather than free members of the society, unclaimed children suffer.

Orphans are those unfortunate children who have no parents at all in a society that dictates that all children *must* have parents to survive. When all adults are monopolized by their genetic children, there is no one left to care about the unclaimed. However, if *no one* had exclusive relationships with children, then *everyone* would be free for *all* children. The natural interest in children would be diffused over all children rather than narrowly concentrated on one's own.

The evils of this orphanage system, the barracks-like existence, the impersonality, the anonymity, arise because these institutions are *dumping grounds* for the rejected in an exclusive family system; whereas we want to spread family emotions over the whole society. Thus child institutions and their consequences are at the furthest remove from revolutionary alternatives because they violate almost all of our essential postulates: the integration of children into the total society, and the granting of full economic and sexual freedoms.

197

the failure surprising given the original postulates of the experiment, within its particular social context. We can then use this information as another valuable negative guideline, teaching us what most to avoid in our own programme.

*

Of all the modern social experiments the most important failure was that of the Russian communes. (The failure of the Russian Revolution in general is a thorn in every radical's side; but its direct relation to the failure of the communes is seldom noted.) It led, ironically, to the assumption of a causal connection between the abolition of the family and the development of a totalitarian state. In this view, the later Russian reinstitution of the nuclear family system is seen as a last-ditch attempt to salvage humanist values – privacy, individualism, love, etc., by then rapidly disappearing.

But it is the reverse: *the failure of the Russian Revolution to achieve the classless society is traceable to its half-hearted attempts to eliminate the family and sexual repression.* This failure, in turn, was due to the limitations of a male-biased revolutionary analysis based on economic class alone, one that failed to take the family fully into account even in its function as an economic unit. By the same token, *all socialist revolutions to date have been or will be failures for precisely these reasons.* Any initial liberation under current socialism must always revert back to repression, because the family structure is the *source* of psychological, economic, and political oppression. Socialist attempts to soften the structure of power within the family by incorporating women into the labour force or army are only reformist. Thus it is no surprise that socialism as it is now constituted in the various parts of the world is not only no improvement on capitalism, but often worse.

This develops a major component of *1984*: the destruction of the family as the last refuge for intimacy, comfort, privacy, individualism, etc., and the complete encroachment of the superstructure economy into all aspects of life, the drafting of women into a *male* world, rather than the elimination of sex class distinction altogether. Because no provision has been made to re-establish the female element in the outside world, to incorporate the 'personal' into the 'public', because the female principle has been minimized or obliterated rather than diffused to humanize the larger society, the result is a horror.

Wilhelm Reich in *The Sexual Revolution* summarized the specific objective reasons for the failure of the Russian communes in the best analysis to date:

(1) Confusion of the leadership and evasion of the problem.

(2) The laborious task of reconstruction in general given the cultural backwardness of Old Russia, the war, and famine.

(3) Lack of theory. The Russian Revolution was the first of its kind. No attempt had been made to deal with emotional-sexual-familial problems in the formulation of basic revolutionary theory. (Or, in our terms, there had been a lack of 'consciousness raising' about female/child oppression and a lack of radical feminist analysis prior to the revolution itself.)

(4) The sex-negative psychological structure of the individual, created and reinforced throughout history by the family, hindered the individual's liberation from this very structure. As Reich puts it: 'It must be remembered that human beings have a tremendous fear of just that kind of life for which they long so much but which is at variance with their own structure.'

(5) The explosive concrete complexities of sexuality.

In the picture that Reich draws of the time, one senses the immense frustration of people trying to liberate themselves without having a well-thought-out ideology to guide them. In the end, that they attempted so much without adequate preparation made their failure even more extreme: *To destroy the balance of sexual polarization without entirely eliminating it was worse than nothing at all.*

*

Another experimental communal system, widely touted, is the kibbutz in Israel. Here, though, the failure is not extreme: the most common criticism is that children of the kibbutz lack individualism, that there is a 'groupiness' in their psychology that is the price of elimination of the family. ('And if *you* want to pay the price . . . well . . .') Here, though there are many studies of the effects of kibbutz life, I prefer to present my own experience.

The division of labour remains. In my short stay, I observed the following: an American registered nurse could not land a job in the infirmary – because all women were needed in the kitchen. A job in the sandal shop was given to a boy apprentice, rather than a woman skilled in leatherwork. Only foreign girls were so naive as to question why women aren't out in the fields, but instead confined to the laundry, the sewing room, or at best, the chicken house. (One woman explained to me that driving a tractor is apt to ruin a woman's complexion.)

Children identify strongly with their genetic parents (one hears over and over again the words *Ema Sheli*, *Abba Sheli*, '*My* mother, *My* father,' in the same tone as every child on every block in the US says, 'If you don't do it I'll tell my Dad', or 'My moma's gona beat your ass'). Family ties remain strong, even if their worst consequences have been avoided.

Above all, children are still segregated into their own special facilities and programmes: miniature animal farms, special mealtimes, etc. Schooling follows the European model, even if some of its worst aspects, such as 'grades', have been eliminated: the classroom continues, with its twenty-to-one ratio, adult approval still the final goal rather than learning for its own sake.

Sex role models are fostered, sexegration not eliminated (there are different bathrooms for male and female), and homo- or bi-sexuality so unheard of that when I brought it up several women walked out of the room in protest. All rumours to the contrary, the kibbutz is increasingly conservative sexually (if it is embarrassing for a single woman to ask for birth control pills, VD is a disgrace), and any alliance other than a long-term one with a socially approved partner is frowned upon. Sexuality on the kibbutz remains conventionally organized, little different from the sexuality of the larger society. The incest taboo with all its repressive consequences has simply been extended from the family to the peer group.

In fact the kibbutz is no radical experiment, but a limited communalism instituted to further specific agricultural aims. The kibbutz is nothing more than a community of farming

pioneers temporarily forced to sacrifice traditional social structures to better adjust to a peculiar set of national conditions. If
and when these conditions change, the kibbutz reverts to 'normal'. For example, women on the far left kibbutz at which I
stayed were concerned with demanding private kitchens in
addition to the communal one from which meals were served six
times a day. They were still cast in the role of Gracious Wife,
but had been denied the proper equipment to play the part.
Their interest in clothing, fashion, makeup, glamour, not easy
to indulge, resembled, indeed *was*, the longing of the farm girl
for the vices of the big city – the more as intense in fantasy as it
was difficult to achieve in practice. Or, going through the
residential section of the kibbutz in the early evening, I could
easily imagine that I was walking through a small town or a quiet
suburbia in the USA: the matchbox homes were cared for with
the attention to private property of any petit bourgeois, the
decoration of apartments just as devoted. (The reversion back to
property was explained to me as 'only realistic'. Formerly
kibbutzniks had shared even personal clothing, but soon got sick
of this.) Property is still the necessary extension of a deficient
self – because children are still property. The line of Little Ones
following Big Mama out of the House of Children looks like that
of any kindergarten anywhere. Children are still oppressed.

What is remarkable is that despite the lack of depth in the
kibbutz experiment it turned out as well as it did. The propor-
tionate results of even a weakening of the division of labour, the
nuclear family and the resulting of sex repression, property
mentality, etc., are spectacular. My impression was that the
children were healthier physically, mentally, and emotionally
than their counterparts in the American family structure; that
they were friendlier and more generous, with great curiosity
about the world outside; that their parents were not so nervous
and hassled, and thus were able to maintain better relationships
with them; and that their creativity and individuality were
encouraged as much as the community could afford.

*

Another limited but much-touted experiment which has produced disproportionately good results is A. S. Neill's Summerhill. In the famous book about his small experimental school in England, *Summerhill: A Radical Approach to Childrearing* (a book on the shelf of every self-respecting liberal, radical, Bohemian, and/or academic parent in the country), he describes the transition of normal children into 'free' self-regulating children. But Summerhill is no 'radical' approach to child-rearing – it is a liberal one. Neill, an educational innovation rather than a true revolutionary,[3] has set up a small retreat for those victims of our present system whose parents have the money and liberal views to send them there. Within this retreat children are spared the more harmful effects of the authoritarianism inherent in the family; equality is encouraged by those who govern the place, an obvious contradiction (Neill's vote counts as only one, though I imagine that in real crisis, the decision does not come up for vote. In any case, children always know who's boss, benevolent though he might be), and compulsory education is relaxed: children learn only when they want to. However, the structure of the class, if loosened, remains unchanged. Or, another example, though masturbation is not frowned on, sexual intercourse is definitely not encouraged (after all, Neill remembers, 'they' can close down the school). What's worse, sex roles have not begun to be eliminated,[4] something beyond the scope of such an

3. Neill says of himself: 'Although I write and say what I think of society, if I tried to reform society *by action*, society would kill me as a public danger. ... [I realize] that my primary job is not the reformation of society, but the bringing of happiness to some few children.'
4. Indeed, Neill and his wife Ena act as the role models, though for a rather extended family. Neill, baffled but nevertheless accepting comments on the recurrence of sex roles:

'On a good day you may not see the boy *gangsters* [?] of Summerhill. They are in far corners intent on their *deeds of derring-do*. But you will see the girls. They are in or near the house, and never far away from the *grown-ups*.

You will often find the Art Room full of girls painting and making things with fabrics. In the main, however, I think that the small boys are more creative; at least I never hear a boy say he is bored because he doesn't know what to do, whereas I sometimes hear girls say that.

Possibly I find the boys more creative than the girls because the school may be better equipped for boys than for girls. Girls of ten or over have little use for a workshop with iron and wood ... They have their art work,

experiment, since children are already psychosexually formed by the family by the time they come in, at five or over. In all respects then – psychologically, sexually, educationally – we have only a softening of some of the harshest aspects of the system.

Clearly the problem has not been attacked at the roots. Legally children are still under the jurisdiction of parents. (And kids can't mail away for the sort of parents who will send them to Summerhill.) Neill continually complains of parents, who can undo all his work in one vacation, or drag the child away the minute the worst effects of the victimization have disappeared. He is afraid of their power over him. After all, he is at their service: if they are not satisfied with the product, the shadowy 'they' will have the final say. Even when the parents are devoted followers of the Summerhill philosophy,[5] they are a nuisance with their constant visits and questions. Between the two, admiring visitors and dubious investigators (including a whole array of official ones), the children must get accustomed to living in a zoo, hardly much of an improvement on their usual status as 'precious' object.

And how could it be otherwise? Summerhill is an insulated refuge in which children are more – not less – segregated from adults, even from the ordinary life of the town. And the school owes its very existence to 'parents' and liberal donors. It is hardly a self-sufficient community with its own economy, and thus it is prone to become a year-round camp for disturbed

---

which includes pottery, cutting linoleum blocks and painting, and sewing work, but for some that is not enough . . .

The girls take a less active part in school meetings than the boys do, and I have no ready explanation for this fact.' (Italics mine)

5. If the isolated Summerhill school experiment works to a limited degree the Summerhill 'home' fails resoundingly. There is nothing as sad as the spectacle of parents trying to initiate their own private version of Summerhill into their family life, never realizing the deep contradiction between the nuclear family and true child freedom. I have been in homes in which mothers were reduced to begging children to stop hitting guests (me) – they didn't dare use the power that the child, at least, *knows* is there and, in fact, is provoking; there are other families where children are dragged off to family councils periodically; and so on. But nevertheless, despite all these progressive measures, children instinctively know – and act on this knowledge – that any real decisions will be controlled by the parents, *who hold the power.*

children, whose parents have been backed into liberalism as a last resort. Because children far outnumber the adults, and justify the project, their wishes and opinions are observed and 'respected' more than in most places in the world, but it is an artificial respect not based on a true integration into a real community.

And if, with only these superficial reforms, children illustrate remarkably improved behaviour, their aggression, repression, and hostility replaced by authentic courtesy, psychological breadth, and honesty, then think what we might expect under truly revolutionary conditions.

*

A detailed study of these and other social experiments from the radical feminist viewpoint would be a valuable contribution to feminist theory. We have been brief: we have discussed some of the more important modern social experiments primarily to show that they do not fulfil our four conditions for feminist revolution.

Let us summarize the causes of failure:

(1) The biological ties of women to reproduction (and thence child-rearing), leading to unequal division of labour, class based on sex, the psychology of power, and other evils, were never severed. The female role was extended rather than eliminated: some women were merely granted a new job to add to their old one. Thus although women may have been (partially) drafted into the superstructure male economy, usually only to fill a transient labour need, never has the female role been diffused throughout the larger society.

(2) In some cases, such as Summerhill, the experiment was dependent on the economy – and the good will — of a larger (and more repressive) community, and thus was parasitic, unsound at its foundations. However, in those communities with socialism at the origins of the experiment, this was not so much the problem. Children of the communes and the kibbutz feel as dependent on the community as a whole as they do on any specific person; often they even share in the productive work. Only in the division of labour are these experiments still (in economic terms) at fault, and that, we know, develops for other reasons.

(3) Continued segregation of children and a failure to do away with or at least radically restructure school. The methods of segregation have varied, ranging from the extreme of the barracks-like orphanage to the more liberal camp setting of a Summerhill, or the *Beit Yeladim* of the kibbutz. But though its destructive impact may have been cushioned, in no case has the concept of childhood itself been questioned, or the apparatus of childhood (the elementary school, special literature, 'toys', etc.) discarded altogether.

(4) Sexual repression continues, partly as the result of the failure to sever the umbilical-cord-tying special connection between women and children and partly because the pioneers were unable to overcome their own 'sex-negative' structures.[6]

I shall add a fifth cause of failure:

(5) There was no development of a feminist consciousness and analysis prior to the initiation of the experiment. The best example of this failing is our current American communal experiments, which merely extend the family structure to include a larger number of people. The division of labour remains, because woman's role in (child) bed or kitchen has not been questioned, nor male the role of provider. And since the mother/child symbiosis remains intact, it is no wonder that when the commune breaks up, all the 'godparents' disappear, as well as the genetic father himself, leaving the mother stuck – without even the protection of an ordinary marriage.

Thus never has there been a true instance of full membership of women and children in the larger society. The modern social experiment, like the matriarchal stage of human history, signifies only a relative loosening within the consolidation of male supremacy through history. It never altered the fundamental condition of sex oppression. Any benefits that accrued to women and children were *incidental* to other social objectives – which themselves were obstructed by the vast, unrecognized substratum of sex oppression. Because their ideology was not founded on the minimal feminist premises above, these experiments never

6. Wilhelm Reich discusses the Russian inability to handle the first signs of a free child sexuality: child sex was interpreted in Puritan terms as the sign of moral breakdown, rather than as the first stage of the reversion to a natural sexuality.

achieved even the more limited democratic goals their (male) theorists and leaders had predicted. However, their success within narrow spheres shows that the biological family unit is amenable to change. But we would have to discard it totally before we could hope to eliminate the oppression altogether.

*

However – to be fair – it is only recently, in the most technologically advanced countries, that genuine preconditions for feminist revolution have begun to exist. For the first time it is becoming possible to attack the family not only on moral grounds – in that it reinforces biologically-based sex class, promoting adult males (who are then divided further among themselves by race and class privilege) over females of all ages and male children – but also on functional grounds: it is no longer necessary or most effective as the basic social unit for reproduction/production. Cybernetics, in questioning not only man's relation to work but the value of work itself, will eventually strip the division of labour at the root of the family of any remaining practical value; and as for reproduction, we no longer need universal reproduction, even if the development of artificial reproduction does not soon place biological reproduction itself in question.

THE SLOW DEATH OF THE FAMILY

The increasing erosion of the functions of the family by modern technology should, by now, have caused some signs of its weakening. However, this is not clearly the case. Though the institution is archaic, artificial cultural reinforcements have been imported to bolster it: sentimental sermons, manuals of guidance, daily columns in newspapers and magazines, special courses, services, and institutions for professional couples, parents, and teachers, nostalgia, warnings to individuals who question or evade it, and finally, if the number of dropouts becomes a serious threat, a real backlash, including outright persecution of nonconformists. The last has not happened perhaps only because it is not yet necessary.

Marriage is in the same state as the Church: both are becoming functionally defunct, as their preachers go about heralding a revival, eagerly chalking up converts in the day of dread. And just as God has been pronounced dead quite often but has this sneaky way of resurrecting himself, so everyone debunks marriage, yet ends up married.[7]

What is keeping marriage so alive? I have pointed out some of the cultural bulwarks of marriage in the twentieth century. We have seen how the romantic tradition of nonmarital love, the hetairism that was the necessary adjunct to monogamic marriage, has been purposely confused with that most pragmatic of institutions, to render it more appealing – thus restraining people from experimenting with other social forms that could satisfy their emotional needs as well or better.

Under increasing pressure, with the pragmatic bases of the marriage institution blurred, sex roles relaxed to a degree that would have disgraced a Victorian. *He* had no crippling doubts about his role, nor about the function and value of marriage. To him it was simply an economic arrangement of some selfish benefit, one that would most easily satisfy his physical needs and reproduce his heirs. His wife, too, was clear about her duties and rewards: ownership of herself and of her full sexual, psychological, and housekeeping services for a lifetime, in return for long-term patronage and protection by a member of the ruling class, and – in her turn – limited control over the children until they reached a certain age. Today this contract based on divided roles has been so disguised by sentiment that it goes completely unrecognized by millions of newly-weds, and even by most older married couples.

But this blurring of the economic contract, and the resulting confusion of sex roles, has not significantly eased woman's oppression. In many cases it has put her in only a more vulnerable position. With the clear-cut arrangement of matches by parents all but abolished, a woman, still part of an underclass, must now, in order to gain the indispensable male patronage and protection, play a desperate game, hunting down bored males while yet appearing cool. And even once she is married, any

7. Ninety-five per cent of all American women still marry and 90 per cent bear children, most often more than two. Families with children in the median range (two to four) still predominate, no longer attributable to the postwar baby boom.

overlap of roles generally takes place on the wife's side, not on the husband's: the 'cherish and protect' clause is the first thing forgotten – while the wife has gained the privilege of going to work to 'help out', even of putting her husband through school. More than ever she shoulders the brunt of the marriage, not only emotionally, but now also in its more practical aspects. She has simply added his job to hers.

A second cultural prop to the outmoded institution is the privatization of the marriage experience: each partner enters marriage convinced that what happened to his parents, what happened to his friends can never happen to him. Though Wrecked Marriage has become a national hobby, a universal obsession – as witnessed by the booming business of guidebooks to marriage and divorce, the women's magazine industry, an affluent class of marriage counsellors and shrinks, whole repertoires of Ball-and-Chain jokes and gimmicks, and cultural products such as soap opera, the marriage-and-family genre on TV, e.g., *I Love Lucy* or *Father Knows Best*, films and plays like Cassavetes's *Faces* and Albee's *Who's Afraid of Virginia Woolf?* – still one encounters everywhere a defiant 'We're different' brand of optimism in which the one good (outwardly exemplary, anyway) marriage in the community is habitually cited to prove that *it* is possible.

Sex privatism is exposed in comments like, 'Well, I know I'd make a great mother.' It is useless to point out that *everyone* says that, that the very parents or friends now dismissed as 'bad' parents and 'poor' marital partners all began marriage and parenthood in exactly the same spirit. After all, does anyone *choose* to have a 'bad' marriage? Does anyone *choose* to be a 'bad' mother? And even if it were a question of 'good' vs. 'bad' marital partners or parents, there will always be as many of the latter as the former; under the present system of universal marriage and parenthood just as many spouses and children must pull a bad lot as a good one; in fact any classes of 'good' and 'bad' are bound to recreate themselves in identical proportion.[8] Thus the privatization process functions to keep people

8. But what does this dichotomy good/bad really mean? Perhaps after all, it is only a euphemistic *class* distinction: sensitive and open, as opposed to harassed and stultified. But even though a child born to educated or upper-

blaming themselves, rather than the institution, for its failure: though the institution consistently proves itself unsatisfactory, even rotten, the blinkers they wear allow them to believe that somehow their own case will be different.

Warnings can have no effect, because logic has nothing to do with why people get married. Everyone has eyes of his own, parents of his own. If she chooses to block all evidence, it is because she must. In a world out of control, the only institutions that grant the individual an *illusion* of control, that seem to offer any safety, shelter or warmth, are the 'private' institutions: religion, marriage/family, and, most recently, psychoanalytic therapy. But, as we have seen, the family is neither private nor a refuge, but is directly connected to – is even the cause of – the ills of the larger society which the individual is no longer able to confront.

But the cultural bulwarks we have just discussed – the confusion of romance with marriage, blurring its original functions and the sex roles necessary to maintain them; the illusions of control and refuge, sex privatism, all of which exploit the fears of the contemporary person living within an increasingly hostile environment – still are not the whole answer to why the institution of marriage continues to thrive. It would be facile to attribute the continuation of the family solely to reaction, but such negatives alone could never maintain the family as a vital institution. No, I am afraid we shall find, in measuring marriage against our four minimal feminist demands, that it fulfils (in its own miserable way) at least a portion of the requirements at least as well as or better than did most of the social experiments we have discussed.

(1) Freedom of women from the tyranny of reproduction and child-bearing is hardly fulfilled. However, women are often relieved of its worst strains by a servant class (that is, some slaves are given others as personal servants) – and in the modern marriage, by gynaecology, 'family planning', and the increasing

---

class parents is luckier in every respect, and is apt to receive a fair number of privileges by virtue of his class, name, and the property he is due to inherit, children are born equal among all classes – if indeed children born to the unfortunate do not outnumber the others – in this way reproducing in exact proportions the original inequality.

takeover, by the school, day-care centres, and the like, of the child-rearing function.

(2) Though financial *independence* of women and children is not generally granted, there is a substitute: physical *security*.

(3) Women and children, segregated from the larger society, are integrated within the family unit, the only place where this occurs. That the little interplay between men, women, and children is concentrated in one social unit makes that unit all the more difficult to renounce.

(4) Though the family is the source of sexual repression, it guarantees the conjugal couple a steady, if not satisfactory, sex supply, and provides the others with 'aim-inhibited' relationships, which are, in many cases, the only long-term relationships these individuals will ever have.

Thus there are practical assets of marriage to which people cling. It is not all a cultural sales job. On a scale of percentages, marriage – at least in its desperate liberalized version – would fare as well as most of the experimental alternatives thus far tried, which, as we have seen, also fulfilled some of the stipulations and not others, or only partially fulfilled all of them. And marriage has the added advantage of being a known quantity.

And yet marriage in its very definition will never be able to fulfil the needs of its participants, for it was organized around, and reinforces, a fundamentally oppressive biological condition that we only now have the skill to correct. As long as we have the institution we shall have the oppressive conditions built into it. We need to start talking about new alternatives that will satisfy the emotional and psychological needs that marriage, archaic as it is, still satisfies, but that will satisfy them better. But in any proposal we shall have to do at least one better than marriage on our feminist scale, or despite all warnings people will stay hooked – in the hope that just this once, just for them, marriage will come across.

ALTERNATIVES

The classic trap for any revolutionary is always, 'What's your alternative?' But even if you *could* provide the interrogator with a blueprint, this does not mean he would use it: in most cases he is not sincere in wanting to know. In fact this is a common offensive, a technique to deflect revolutionary anger and turn it against itself. Moreover, the oppressed have no job to convince all people. All *they* need know is that the present system is destroying them.

But though any specific direction must arise organically out of the revolutionary action itself, still I feel tempted here to make some 'dangerously utopian' concrete proposals – both in sympathy for my own pre-radical days when the Not-Responsible-For-Blueprint Line perplexed me, and also because I am aware of the political dangers in the peculiar failure of imagination concerning alternatives to the family. There are, as we have seen, several good reasons for this failure. First, there are no precedents in history for feminist revolution – there have been women revolutionaries, certainly, but they have been used by male revolutionaries, who seldom gave even lip service to equality for women, let alone to a radical feminist restructuring of society. Moreover, we haven't even a literary image of this future society; there is not even a *utopian* feminist literature yet in existence. Thirdly, the nature of the family unit is such that it penetrates the individual more deeply than any other social organization we have: it literally gets him 'where he lives'. I have shown how the family shapes his psyche to its structure – until ultimately, he imagines it absolute, talk of anything else striking him as perverted. Finally, most alternatives suggest a loss of even the little emotional warmth provided by the family, throwing him into a panic. The model that I shall now draw up is subject to the limitations of any plan laid out on paper by a solitary individual. Keep in mind that these are not meant as final answers, that in fact the reader could probably draw up another plan that would satisfy as well or better the four structural imperatives laid out above. The following proposals, then, will be sketchy, meant to stimulate thinking in fresh areas rather than to dictate the action.

*

What is the alternative to 1984 if we could have our demands acted on in time?

The most important characteristic to be maintained in any revolution is *flexibility*. I will propose, then, a programme of multiple options to exist simultaneously, interweaving with each other, some transitional, others far in the future. An individual may choose one 'life style' for one decade, and prefer another at another period.

(1) *Single professions.* A single life organized around the demands of a chosen profession, satisfying the individual's social and emotional needs through its own particular occupational structure, might be an appealing solution for many individuals, especially in the transitional period.

Single professions have practically vanished, despite the fact that the encouragement of reproduction is no longer a valid social concern. The old single roles, such as the celibate religious life, court roles – jester, musician, page, knight, and loyal squire – cowboys, sailors, firemen, cross-country truck drivers, detectives, pilots had a prestige all their own: there was no stigma attached to being professionally single. Unfortunately, these roles seldom were open to women. Most single female roles (such as spinster aunt, nun, or courtesan) were still defined by their sexual nature.

Many social scientists are now proposing as a solution to the population problem the encouragement of 'deviant life styles' that by definition imply nonfertility. Richard Meier suggests that glamorous single professions previously assigned only to men should now be opened to women as well, for example, 'astronaut'. He notes that where these occupations exist for women, e.g., stewardess, they are based on the sex appeal of a young woman, and thus can be only limited way stations on the way to a better job or marriage. And, he adds, 'so many limitations are imposed [on women's work outside the home] . . . that one suspects the existence of a culture-wide conspiracy which makes the occupational role sufficiently unpleasant that 90 per cent or more would choose homemaking as a superior alternative'. With the extension of whatever single roles still exist in our culture to include women, the creation of more such roles, and a programme of incentives to make these professions rewarding, we could, painlessly, reduce the number of people interested in parenthood at all.

(2) *'Living together.'* Practised at first only in Bohemian or intellectual circles and now increasingly in the population at

large – especially by metropolitan youth – 'living together' is becoming a common social practice. 'Living together' is the loose social form in which two or more partners, of whatever sex, enter a non-legal sex/companionate arrangement the duration of which varies with the internal dynamics of the relationship. Their contract is only with each other; society has no interest, since neither reproduction nor production – dependencies of one party on the other – is involved. This flexible non-form could be expanded to become the standard unit in which most people would live for most of their lives.

At first, in the transitional period, sexual relationships would probably be monogamous (single standard, female-style, this time around), even if the couple chose to live with others. We might even see the continuation of strictly non-sexual group living arrangements ('roommates'). However, after several generations of non-family living, our psychosexual structures may become altered so radically that the monogamous couple, or the 'aim-inhibited' relationship, would become obsolescent. We can only guess what might replace it – perhaps true 'group marriages', trans-sexual group marriages which also involved older children? We don't know.

The two options we have suggested so far – single professions and 'living together' – already exist, but only outside the mainstream of our society, or for brief periods in the life of the normal individual. We want to *broaden* these options to include many more people for longer periods of their lives, to transfer here instead all the cultural incentives now supporting marriage – making these alternatives, finally, as common and acceptable as marriage is today.

But what about children? Doesn't everyone want children some time in their lives? There is no denying that people now feel a genuine desire to have children. But we don't know how much of this is the product of an authentic liking for children, and how much is a displacement of other needs. We have seen that parental satisfaction is obtainable only through crippling the child: the attempted extension of ego through one's children – in the case of the man, the 'immortalizing' of name, property, class, and ethnic identification, and in the case of the woman, motherhood as the justification of her existence, the resulting attempt to live through the child, child-as-project – in the end damages or destroys either the child or the parent, or both when neither wins, as the case may be. Perhaps when we strip parenthood of these other functions, we will find a real instinct for parenthood even on the part of men, a simple physical desire to associate with the young. But then we have lost nothing, for a basic demand of our alternative system is some form of intimate interaction with children. If a parenthood instinct does in fact exist, it will be allowed to operate even more freely, having shed the practical burdens of parenthood that now make it such an anguished hell.

But what, on the other hand, if we find that there is no parenthood instinct after all? Perhaps all this time society has persuaded the individual to have children only by imposing on parenthood ego concerns that had no proper outlet. This may have been unavoidable in the past – but perhaps it's now time to start more directly satisfying those ego needs. As long as natural reproduction is still necessary, we can devise less destructive cultural inducements. But it is likely that, once the ego investments in parenthood are removed, artificial reproduction will be developed and widely accepted.

(3) *Households*. I shall now outline a system that I believe will satisfy any remaining needs for children after ego concerns are no longer part of our motivations. Suppose a person or a couple at some point in their lives desire to live around children in a family-size unit. While we will no longer have reproduction as the life goal of the normal individual – we have seen how single and group non-reproductive life styles could be enlarged to become satisfactory for many people for their whole lifetimes and for others, for good portions of their lifetime – certain people may still prefer community-style group living permanently, and other people may want to experience it at some time in their lives, especially during early childhood.

Thus at any given time a proportion of the population will want to live in reproductive social structures. Correspondingly, the society in general will still need reproduction, though reduced, if only to create a new generation.

The proportion of the population will be automatically a select group with a predictably higher rate of stability, because they will have had a freedom of choice now generally unavailable. Today those who do not marry and have children by a certain age are penalized: they find themselves alone, excluded, and miserable, on the margins of a society in which everyone else is compartmentalized into lifetime generational families, chauvinism and exclusiveness their chief characteristic. (Only in Manhattan is single living even tolerable, and that can be debated.) Most people are still forced into marriage by family pressure, the 'shotgun', economic considerations, and other reasons that have nothing to do with choice of life style. In our new reproductive unit, however, with the limited contract (see below), child-rearing so diffused as to be practically eliminated, economic considerations nonexistent, and all participating members having entered only on the basis of personal preference, 'unstable' reproductive social structures will have disappeared.

This unit I shall call a *household* rather than an extended family. The distinction is important: the word *family* implies biological reproduction and some degree of division of labour by sex, and thus the traditional dependencies and resulting power relations, extended over generations; though the size of the family – in this case, the larger numbers of the 'extended' family – may affect the strength of this hierarchy, it does not change its structural definition. 'Household', however, connotes only a large grouping of people living together for an unspecified time, and with no specified set of interpersonal relations.

How would a 'household' operate?

Limited Contract. If the household replaced marriage perhaps we would at first legalize it in the same way – if this is necessary at all. A group of ten or so consenting adults of varying ages[9] could apply for a licence as a group in much the same way as a young couple today applies for a marriage licence, perhaps even undergoing some form of ritual ceremony, and then might proceed in the same way to set up house. The household licence would, however, apply only for a given period, perhaps seven to ten years, or whatever was decided on as the minimal time in which children needed a stable structure in which to grow

9. An added advantage of the household is that it allows older people past their fertile years to share fully in parenthood when they so desire.

up – but probably a much shorter period than we now imagine. If at the end of this period the group decided to stay together, it could always get a renewal. However, no single individual would be contracted to stay after this period, and perhaps some members of the unit might transfer out, or new members come in. Or, the unit could disband altogether.

There are many advantages to short-term households, stable compositional units lasting for only about a decade: the end of family chauvinism, built up over generations, of prejudices passed down from one generation to the next, the inclusion of people of all ages in the child-rearing process, the integration of many age groups into one social unit, the breadth of personality that comes from exposure to many rather than to (the idiosyncrasies of) a few, and so on.

Children. A regulated percentage of each household – say one third – would be children. But whether, at first, genetic children created by couples within the household, or at some future time – after a few generations of household living had severed the special connection of adults with 'their' children – children were produced artificially, or adopted, would not matter: (minimal) responsibility for the early physical dependence of children would be evenly diffused among all members of the household.

But though it would still be structurally sound, we must be aware that as long as we use natural childbirth methods, the 'household' could never be a totally liberating social form. A mother who undergoes a nine-month pregnancy is likely to feel that the product of all that pain and discomfort 'belongs' to her ('To think of what I went through to have you!'). But we want to destroy this possessiveness along with its cultural reinforcements so that no one child will be *a priori* favoured over another, so that children will be loved for their own sake.

But what if there is an instinct for pregnancy? I doubt it. Once we have sloughed off cultural superstructures, we may uncover a sex instinct, the normal consequences of which *lead* to pregnancy. And perhaps there is also an instinct to care for the young once they arrive. But an instinct for pregnancy itself would be superfluous – could nature anticipate humanity's mastery of reproduction? And what if, once the false motivations for pregnancy had been shed, women no longer wanted to 'have' children at all? Might this not be a disaster, given that artificial reproduction is not yet perfected? But women have no special reproductive *obligation* to the species. If they are no longer willing, then artificial methods will have to be developed hurriedly, or, at the very least, satisfactory compensations – other than destructive ego investments – would have to be supplied to make it worth their while.

Adults and older children would take care of babies for as long as they needed it, but since there would be many adults and older children sharing the responsibility – as in the extended family – no one person would ever be involuntarily stuck with it.

Adult/child relationships would develop just as do the best relationships today: some adults might prefer certain children over others, just as some children might prefer certain adults over others – these might become lifelong attachments in which the individuals concerned mutually agreed to stay together, perhaps to form some kind of non-reproductive unit. Thus all relationships would be based on love alone, uncorrupted by dependencies and resulting class inequalities. Enduring relationships between people of widely divergent ages would become common.

Legal Rights and Transfers. With the weakening and severance of the blood ties, the power hierarchy of the family would break down. The legal structure – as long as it is still necessary – would reflect this democracy at the roots of our society. Women would be identical under the law with men. Children would no longer be 'minors', under the patronage of 'parents' – they would have full rights. Remaining physical inequalities could be legally compensated for: for example, if a child were beaten, perhaps he could report it to a special simplified 'household' court where he would be granted instant legal redress.

Another special right of children would be the right of immediate transfer: if the child for any reason did not like the household into which he had been born so arbitrarily, he would be helped to transfer out. An adult on the other hand – one who had lived one span in a household (seven to ten years) – might have to present his case to the court, which would then decide, as do divorce courts today, whether he had adequate grounds for breaking his contract. A certain number of transfers within the seven-year period might be necessary for the smooth functioning of the household, and would not be injurious to its stability as a unit so long as a core remained. (In fact, new people now and then might be a refreshing change.) However, the unit, for its own best economy, might have to place a ceiling on the number of transfers in or out, to avoid depletion, excessive growth, and/or friction.

Chores. As for housework: the larger family-sized group (twelve to fifteen people) would be more practical – the waste and repetition of the duplicate nuclear family unit would be avoided, e.g., as in shopping or cooking for three or four people, without the loss of intimacy of the larger communal experiment. In the interim, any housework would have to be rotated equitably; but eventually cybernation would take care of most domestic chores.

City Planning. City planning, architecture, furnishings, all would be altered to reflect the new social structure. The trend towards mass-produced housing would probably continue, but the housing might be designed and even built (perhaps out of prefabricated components) by the people living there to suit their own needs and tastes. Privacy could be built in: either through private rooms in every household, or with 'retreats' within the larger city to be shared by people of other households, or both. The whole might form a complex the size of a small town or a large campus. Perhaps campus is the clearer image: we could have small units of self-determined housing – prefabricated component parts set up or dismantled easily and quickly to suit the needs of the limited contract – as well as central permanent buildings to fill the needs of the community as a whole, i.e. perhaps the equivalent of a 'student union' for socializing, restaurants, a large computer bank, a modern communications centre, a computerized library and film centre, 'learning centres' devoted to various specialized interests, and whatever else might be necessary in a cybernetic community.

The Economy. The end of the family would require corresponding changes in the larger economy. Not only would reproduction be qualitatively different, so would production: just as we have had to purify the relation to children of all considerations of need we would first have to have, to be entirely successful in our goals, the socialism of a cybernetic economy, aiming

first to redistribute drudgery equitably, but eventually to eliminate it altogether. With the further development and wise use of
machines, people could be freed from toil, 'work' divorced from
wages and redefined: now adults as well as children could indulge
in serious 'play' as much as they wanted.

In the socialist transition, while we still had a money economy,
people might receive a guaranteed annual income from the state
to take care of basic physical needs. These incomes, if distributed equitably to men, women, and children, regardless of age,
work, prestige, birth, could in themselves equalize in one blow
the economic class system.

Activity. What would people do in this utopia? I don't think
that will present a problem. If we truly had abolished all unpleasant work, people would have the time and the energy to
develop healthy interests of their own. What is now found only
among the élite, the pursuit of specialized interests for their own
sake, would probably become the norm.

As for our educational institutions: the irrelevancy of the
school system practically guarantees its breakdown in the near
future. Perhaps we could replace it with non-compulsory
'learning centres,' which would combine both the minimally
necessary functions of our elementary educational institutions,
the teaching of rudimentary skills, with those of the higher, the
expansion of knowledge, including everyone of any age or level,
children and adults.

Yes, but what about basic skills? How, for example, could a
child with no formal sequential training enter an advanced
curriculum like architecture? But traditional book learning, the
memorizing of facts, which forms the most substantial portion of
the curriculum of our elementary schools, will be radically
altered under the impact of cybernetics – a qualitative difference,
to the apparatus of culture at least as significant a change as was
the printing press, even as important as the alphabet. McLuhan
pointed out the beginning of a reversal from literary to visual
means of absorbing knowledge. We can expect the escalation of
this and other effects with the further development of modern
media for the rapid transmittal of information. And the *amount*
of rote knowledge necessary either for children or adults will
itself be vastly reduced, for we shall have computer banks within

easy reach. After all, why store facts in one's head when computer banks could supply more comprehensive information instantaneously? (Already yesterday's children wondered why they must learn multiplication tables rather than the operation of an adding machine.) Whatever mental storing of basic facts is still necessary can be quickly accomplished through new mechanical methods, teaching machines, records and tapes, and so on, which, when they become readily available, would allow the abolition of compulsory schooling for basic skills. Like foreign students in the pursuit of a specialized profession, the child can pick up any necessary basic 'language' on the side, through these supplementary machine methods. But it is more likely that the fundamental skills and knowledge necessary will be the same for adults as for children: skill in operating new machines. Programming skills may become universally required, but rather than through years of nine-to-five memorizing, they could be absorbed instantly, only when required by a specific discipline.

As for 'career indecision': those people today whose initial 'hobby' has survived intact from childhood to become their adult 'profession' will most often tell you they developed it before the age of nine.[10] As long as specialized professions still existed, they could be changed as often as adults change majors or professions today. But if choice of profession had no superimposed motives, if they were based only on interest in the subject itself, switches in mid-course would probably be far fewer. Inability to develop strong interests is today mostly the result of the corruption of culture and its institutions.

Thus the new conception of work and education would resemble the medieval system of apprenticeship, people of all ages participating at all levels. As in academia today, the internal dynamics of the various disciplines would foster their own social organization, providing a means for meeting other people of like interests, and of sharing the intellectual and aesthetic pursuits now available only to a select few, the intelligentsia. The kind of social environment now found only in the best departments of the best colleges might become the life style of the masses,

10. If children today were given a realistic idea of the professions available – not just fireman/nurse – they might arrive at a special interest even sooner.

freed to develop their potential from the start: Whereas now only the lucky or persevering ones ever arrive at (usually only professing to) 'doing their thing', then everyone would have the opportunity to develop to his/her full potential.

Or not develop if she so chose – but this seems unlikely, since every child at first exhibits curiosity about people, things, the world in general and what makes it tick. It is only because unpleasant reality *dampens* his curiosity that the child learns to scale down his interests, thus becoming the average bland adult. But if we should remove these obstructions, then all people would develop as fully as only the greatest and wealthiest classes, and a few isolated 'geniuses', have been able to. Each individual would contribute to the society as a whole, not for wages or other incentives of prestige and power, but because the work he chose to do interested him in itself, and perhaps only incidentally because it had a social value for others (as healthily selfish as is only Art today). Work that had only social value and no personal value would have been eliminated by the machine.

*

Thus, in the larger context of a cybernetic communism, the establishment of the household as the alternative to the family for reproduction of children, combined with every imaginable life style for those who chose to live singly or in non-reproductive units, would resolve all the basic dilemmas that now arise from the family to obstruct human happiness. Let us go over our four minimal demands to see how our imaginary construction would fare.

(1) *The freeing of women from the tyranny of reproduction by every means possible, and the diffusion of child-rearing to the society as a whole, to men and other children as well as women.* This has been corrected. Child-*bearing* could be taken over by technology, and if this proved too much against our past tradition and psychic structure (as it certainly would at first) then adequate incentives and compensations would have to be developed – other than the ego rewards of possessing the child – to reward women for their special social contribution of pregnancy and childbirth. Most of child-*rearing*, as we have seen, has to do with the maintaining of power relations, forced internalization of

family values, and many other ego concerns that war with the happiness of the individual child. This repressive socialization process would now be unnecessary in a society in which the interests of the individual coincided with those of the larger society. Any child-rearing responsibility left would be diffused to include men and other children equally with women. In addition, new methods of instant communication would lessen the child's reliance on even this egalitarian primary unit.

(2) *The economic independence and self-determination of all.* Under a cybernetic communism, even during the socialist transition, work would be divorced from wages, the ownership of the means of production in the hands of all the people, and wealth distributed on the basis of need, independent of the social value of the individual's contribution to society. We would aim to eliminate the dependence of women and children on the labour of men, as well as all other types of labour exploitation. Each person could choose his life style freely, changing it to suit his tastes without seriously inconveniencing anyone else; no one would be bound into any social structure against his will, for each person would be totally self-governing as soon as she was physically able.

(3) *The complete integration of women and children into the larger society.* Fulfilled: the concept of childhood has been abolished, children having full political, economic, and sexual rights, their educational/work activities no different from those of adults. During the few years of their infancy we have replaced the psychologically destructive genetic 'parenthood' of one or two arbitrary adults with a diffusion of the responsibility for physical welfare over a larger number of people. The child would still form intimate love relationships, but instead of developing close ties with a decreed 'mother' and 'father', the child might now form those ties with people of his own choosing, of whatever age or sex. Thus all adult–child relationships will have been mutually chosen – equal, intimate relationships free of material dependencies. Correspondingly, though children would be fewer, they would not be monopolized, but would mingle freely throughout the society to the benefit of all, thus satisfying that legitimate curiosity about the young which is often called the reproductive 'instinct'.

(4) *Sexual freedom, love, etc.* So far we have not said much of love and sexual freedom because there is no reason for it to present a problem: there would be nothing obstructing it. With full liberty human relationships eventually would be redefined for the better. If a child does not know his own mother, or at least does not attach a special value to her over others, it is unlikely that he would choose her as his first love object, only to have to develop inhibitions on this love. It is possible that the child might form his first close physical relationships with people his own size out of sheer physical convenience, just as men and women, all else being equal, might prefer each other over those of the same sex for sheer physical fit. But if not, if he should choose to relate sexuality to adults, even if he should happen to pick his own genetic mother, there would be no *a priori* reasons for her to reject his sexual advances, because the incest taboo would have lost its function. The 'household', a transient social form, would not be subject to the dangers of inbreeding.

Thus, without the incest taboo, adults might return within a few generations to a more natural polymorphous sexuality, the concentration on genital sex and orgasmic pleasure giving way to total physical/emotional relationships that *included* that. Relations with children would include as much genital sex as the child was capable of – probably considerably more than we now believe – but because genital sex would no longer be the central focus of the relationship, lack of orgasm would not present a serious problem. Age-ist and homosexual sex taboos would disappear, as well as non-sexual friendship (Freud's 'aim-inhibited' love). All close relationships would include the physical, our concept of exclusive physical partnerships (monogamy) disappearing from our psychic structure, as well as the construct of a Lover Ideal. But how long it would take for these changes to occur, and in what forms they would appear, remains conjecture. The specifics need not concern us here. We need only set up the preconditions for a free sexuality: whatever forms it took would be assuredly an improvement on what we have now, 'natural' in the truest sense.

In the transitional phase, adult genital sex and the exclusiveness of couples within the household might have to be maintained in order for the unit to be able to function smoothly, with a minimum of internal tension caused by sexual frictions. It is unrealistic to impose theories of what *ought* to be on a psyche already fundamentally organized around specific emotional needs. And this is why individual attempts to eliminate sexual possessiveness are now always inauthentic. We would do much better to concentrate on overthrowing the institutions that have produced this psychical organization, making possible the eventual – if not in our lifetime – fundamental restructuring (or should I say destructuring?) of our psychosexuality.

Above, I have drawn up only a very rough plan in order to make the general direction of a feminist revolution more vivid: reproduction and production would both be, simultaneously, reorganized in a non-repressive way. The birth of children to a unit which disbanded or recomposed as soon as children were physically independent, one that was meant to serve immediate needs rather than to pass on power and privilege (the basis of patriarchy is the inheritance of property gained through labour) would eliminate the psychology of power, sexual repression, and cultural sublimation. Family chauvinism, class privilege based on birth, would wither away. The blood tie of the mother to the child would eventually be severed – if male jealousy of 'creative' childbirth actually exists, we shall soon have the means to create life independently of sex – so that pregnancy, now freely acknowledged as clumsy, inefficient, and painful, would be indulged in, if at all, only as a tongue-in-cheek archaism, just as already women today wear virginal white to their weddings. A cybernetic communism would abolish economic classes, and all forms of labour exploitation, by granting all people a livelihood based only on material needs. Eventually work (drudge jobs) would be eliminated in favour of (complex) play, activity done for its own sake, by adults as well as children. With the disappearance of motherhood, and the obstructing incest taboo, sexuality would be re-integrated, allowing love to flow unimpeded.